LIABLE TO FLOODS

LIABLE TO FLOODS

VILLAGE LANDSCAPE ON THE EDGE OF THE FENS
AD 450-1850

J. R. RAVENSDALE

Senior Lecturer in History, Homerton College, Cambridge

CAMBRIDGE UNIVERSITY PRESS

Published by the Syndics of the Cambridge University Press

Bentley House, 200 Euston Road, London NW1 2DB

American Branch: 32 East 57th Street, New York, N.Y.10022

© Cambridge University Press 1974

Library of Congress Catalogue Card Number: 73–80473

ISBN: 0 521 20285 X

First published 1974

Printed in Great Britain
at the University Printing House, Cambridge
(Brooke Crutchley, University Printer)

C C

CONTENTS

TO PAMELA

ILLUSTRATIONS

Acknowledgements for the illustrations

The author and publisher are grateful to the following for granting permission to reproduce illustrations: the Bodleian Library, Oxford, for Plates IV (a) and (b); Cambridge University Library for Plates III (a) and (b); Cambridgeshire and Isle of Ely County Council for Figs. 1 and 7; the Controller of H.M. Stationery Office for facsimilies of Crown-copyright records in the Cambridgeshire County Record Office – Figs. 1, 3 (a), 6 and 9; the Ely Diocesan Records Archivist and Cambridge University Library for Fig. 3 (b); the Great Ouse River Authority for Figs. 1, 4 and 8; the *Illustrated London News* for Plate II; the Master and Fellows of Corpus Christi College, Cambridge, for Fig. 1 (inset); the Master and Fellows of Queens' College, Cambridge, for Fig. 1 (inset); the Rector and Churchwardens of Landbeach for Fig. 12; the Trustees of the British Museum for Plate I.

ACKNOWLEDGEMENTS

I am most grateful to all those (far too numerous to mention here by name) who have helped me with access to documents, but my especial thanks are offered to the Master and Fellows of Corpus Christi College, Cambridge, and to those who took such a warm, encouraging interest in my work in the Parker Library, Professor Bruce Dickins, Dr R. I. Page, Mrs C. Hall, Mrs Rolfe and Mr Munns; to Mr and Mrs A. E. B. Owen who have constantly shown me the greatest kindness, and to their staff in the old Anderson Room; to Miss H. Peek, archivist to Cambridge University, who found more ways to help than I knew to ask; to the local historians, Mr Dennis Jeeps, Mr Francis Garrett, and Mr Mervyn Haird; and to my old friend, the Rev. Brian Dupré, rector of Landbeach.

I would also like to express special thanks to Professor Edward Miller for reading and commenting on an early draft of Chapter 3; to Drs Margaret and Peter Spufford, who always gave generously of their time even when there was no time to give; to Mrs Dorothy Owen and Mrs C. Hall for help with some of the knottier problems of transcription; and to Mrs E. Butt for help in producing the maps. The errors that remain are all my own.

Above all my thanks are due to Professor Alan Everitt and Dr Joan Thirsk, but for whose sympathetic encouragement this work would never have been finished, and to the generosity of the Syndics of the Cambridge University Press in making this publication possible, and to their staff for patience and kindness.

First and last my gratitude goes to that most understanding of scholarly critics, my wife, to whose memory this volume is dedicated.

Homerton College, Cambridge   J. R. RAVENSDALE
May 1973

ABBREVIATIONS

AgHR	*The Agricultural History Review.*
BM	The British Museum.
Cal. Pat.	*Calendar of Patent Rolls.*
CAS	The Cambridge Antiquarian Society.
CCCC	Corpus Christi College, Cambridge.
Common Rights	W. Cunningham, *The Common Rights of Cotten-ham, Stretham and Lode. Camden Miscellany* XII. Camden 3rd series, XVIII. 1910.
CPC	Cottenham Parish Chest.
CRO	Cambridgeshire County Record Office.
CSPD	*Calendar of State Papers Domestic.* (References to the originals rather than the Calendar are given under their PRO reference number, beginning SP.)
CUA	Cambridge University Archives, now in CUL.
CUL	Cambridge University Library.
CUL Queens'	The Crowland documents in the muniments of Queens' College, now deposited in CUL.
Draining	H. C. Darby, *The Draining of the Fens.* Cambridge, 1940. 2nd ed., 1956. Reprinted 1968.
ECA	F. M. Page, *The Estates of Crowland Abbey.* Cambridge, 1934.
EconHR	*The Economic History Review.*
EDR	The Ely Diocesan Registry.
EPNS	The English Place-name Society.
Landbeach	*A History of the Parish of Landbeach in the County of Cambridge.* CAS Quarto Publications, no. 6. Cambridge, 1861.
Liber Eliensis	E. O. Blake, (ed.), *Liber Eliensis.* Camden Society 3rd series, XCII. 1962.
LPC	Landbeach Parish Chest.
Notebook	A notebook in the possession of Mrs Leslie Norman of Cottenham, in which Jacob Sanderson wrote his memoirs.
PCAS	*Proceedings of the Cambridge Antiquarian Society.*
P & P	*Past and Present.*
PRO	The Public Record Office.

RCHM — Royal Commission on Historical Monuments, *An Inventory of Historical Monuments in the County of Cambridge: Volume One West Cambridgeshire*, 1968.

Rot. Hund. — *Rotuli Hundredorum*. Records Commission, 1812 and 1818.

Short Account — R. Masters, *A Short Account of the Parish of Waterbeach in the County of Cambridge and the Diocese of Ely, by a Late Vicar*. Cambridge, 1795.

TCHAS — *Transactions of the Cambridgeshire and Huntingdonshire Archaeological Society.*

TRHS — *Transactions of the Royal Historical Society.*

VCH — *The Victoria History of the Counties of England.*

Waterbeach — W. K. Clay, *A History of the Parish of Waterbeach in the County of Cambridge*. CAS Quarto Publications, no. 4. Cambridge, 1859.

WcD — A vellum-bound book of extracts in the Waterbeach Parish Chest bearing the title 'The Court Rolls of Waterbeach cum Denney'.

WPC — Waterbeach Parish Chest.

Wr. Pk. Ch. — The 'Wrest Park Chartulary' in the museum of the Gentlemen's Society, Spalding, Lincs.

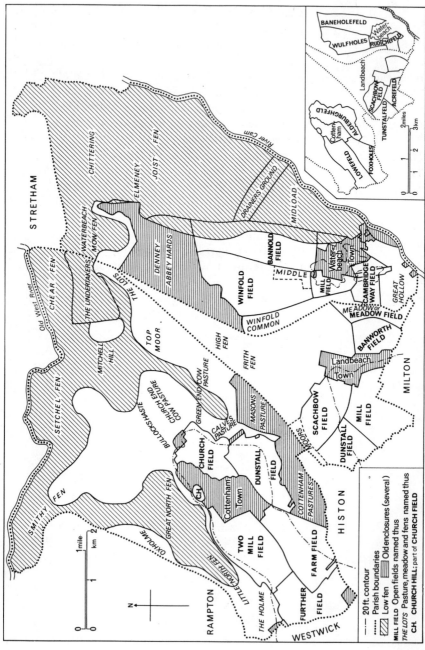

Fig. 1. The three villages and their parishes: several and commonable lands. (Based on the Ordnance Survey map of 1878. Other sources: CRO 152/P9; Q/RDc18 and 31; R59/31/40/1.) Inset: earlier open fields (sources: CUL Queens' Ad 34 1322; CCCC, XXXV, 2, 12th century).

INTRODUCTION

The area chosen for this study is on the southern margin of the fen, the fen first described by St Guthlac's Anglo-Saxon biographer:

There is in Britain a fen of immense size, which begins from the River Granta not far from the city which is named Grantchester. There are immense marshes, now a black pool of water, now foul running streams, and also many islands, and reeds, and hillocks, and thickets, and with manifold windings wide and long it continues to the North Sea.[1]

This fen can now only be found imprisoned and artificially maintained as a tiny remnant at Wicken; the rest of the landscape is tamed.

The general process of this change has long been set out in two vivid sketches by Professor H. C. Darby, but the detail and its particular effects on any community remain to be worked out.[2] Enough was known to suggest that social and economic evolution in this area and its consequences on the landscape were very complex, and many questions remained unanswered. The purpose of this study was to examine an area small enough for thorough investigation of the topography and documents, and wide enough for some effective comparisons. The fen margin, as distinct from the deep fen, offered a very delicate and sensitive indicator, since a change of a few inches in the water-table can result in invasion or retreat by the fen waters for miles.

It soon became clear that the quantity of documents was far too great for the whole area of North Cambridgeshire between the Ouse and the Cam to be included. Landbeach was particularly attractive as a centre because the pattern of the village, the housing and the earthworks, suggested that survivals of older landscapes were here available to an unusual degree in what was still a very small village, and these could be studied with the aid of a considerable quantity of relevant documents in the archives of Corpus Christi College, Cambridge, and in the parish chest. The College historian and rector of Landbeach, Robert Masters, had done sound antiquarian work at the end of the eighteenth century in collecting and copying. Some of this material had been published, written up by a later rector, W. K. Clay, in 1861.[3] More collection and arrangement had been done by a later

---

[1] C. W. Goodwin, *The Anglo-Saxon Life of St. Guthlac* (1848), p. 21. St Guthlac was the founder of Crowland Abbey in Lincolnshire, and the city of Grantchester is Cambridge; quoted by H. E. Hallam, *The New Lands of Elloe*, Department of English Local History, University of Leicester, Occasional Papers no. 6 (1954).

[2] *Draining* (reference is to the 1968 reprint throughout); *idem*, *The Medieval Fenland* (Cambridge, 1940).

[3] *Landbeach*.

rector, the Rev. Bryan Walker, but the greater part of the medieval documents had remained unread since Mathew Parker, as Master and rector, worked on them in the reign of Edward VI. His minute scholarly hand has left a trail of useful references in marginal notes and endorsements, and his paginations in red chalk testify to the quantity of detailed topographical work he managed to leave for us on the village as it was in his time.

Landbeach's western neighbour, Cottenham, again posed similar questions in the pattern of its village and the history of its fields. The documentation here, too, was considerable, but some aspects had been explored by that pioneer of English economic history, Archdeacon William Cunningham,[1] and much detailed work on the administration of the Manor of Crowlands in the Middle Ages was incorporated by Miss Page in her major study.[2] From the few specimen rolls published it was clear that there was a great deal of material awaiting exploitation for topographical purposes.

Landbeach's eastern neighbour takes us more deeply into the fen. Waterbeach offers immediately a great contrast in pattern, with discrete settlements of some considerable age, and the main village around a large straggling green. But if the documents are not in quite the same profusion as in the other two villages, they are far more plentiful than in most. As the study was designed to conclude with the landscape after the parliamentary enclosures, we were most fortunate in having the views of a small peasant who lived through this process preserved in both Waterbeach and Cottenham.[3] Robert Masters also collected historical materials for Waterbeach, publishing them privately (only twenty-five copies printed) in 1795.[4] Masters' son-in-law, Burroughes, added to these, and Clay later wrote them up for a fresh publication, but this work was very inferior to his work on Landbeach.[5]

Although good enclosure award maps exist for each of these villages, there are no strip maps available for either Landbeach or Waterbeach. Cottenham, however, has a remarkably detailed first draft map, and there are terriers of two estates to go with it. In addition there is, in the CRO an early nineteenth-century strip map for the Pratt estate.[6]

One aspect of the documentary information has proved particularly fortunate: the period richest in sources for purposes of comparison over the three villages has turned out to be the fourteenth century, which now seems to have been the most critical historical period for our fenmen to come to terms with the fen.

[1] *Common Rights.*   [2] *ECA.*
[3] J. Denson, *A Peasant's Voice to Landowners* (Cambridge, 1830); and Notebook.
[4] *Short Account.*   [5] *Waterbeach.*
[6] CRO 152/P9, 1842; CRO R/61/5/1.

2

The general point of departure for the study was that previous work had hinted that the peculiarities of the evolution of the Cambridgeshire landscape were due to its being agriculturally a region of transition between the 'Midlands System'[1] and the 'East Anglian System'.[2] In both the management of arable and of sheep, the complexities of Cambridgeshire were felt to be probably due in great part to the hybridisation of agricultural 'systems' from either side of the county. The view[3] which stressed instead the peculiarities of the northern fens had been neglected in the discussions of Cambridgeshire. But whatever causes were suggested, there remained something of a paradox in that the evidence of agrarian non-conformity pointed also to its going hand in hand with an archaic orthodoxy which delayed general enclosure until well into the nineteenth century.

[1] M. R. Postgate, 'The Open Fields of Cambridgeshire' (unpublished Ph.D. dissertation 1964, CUL).
[2] K. J. Allison, 'The Sheep-Corn Husbandry of Norfolk in the Sixteenth and Seventeenth Centuries', *AgHR* V (1957), 12, and Alan Simpson, 'The East Anglian Foldcourse: Some Queries', *AgHR* VI (1958), 86.
[3] N. Neilson (ed.), *A Terrier of Fleet, Lincolnshire, from a Manuscript in the British Museum*, British Academy Records of Social and Economic History of England and Wales (1920). Joan Thirsk, *Fenland Farming in the Sixteenth Century*, Department of English Local History, University of Leicester, Occasional Papers, no. 3 (1953).

THE SETTING

The three parishes under examination, Waterbeach, Landbeach and Cottenham, lie in the angle formed by the junction of the Old West River and the Cam (see Fig.1, p. xii). The Old West forms the northern boundary of Cottenham parish, except where the banking and straightening of the river at Queenholme[1] has left the boundary on the far side of the Washes on the north. The Cam forms much of the eastern boundary of Waterbeach. In the flat lands around the confluence, the rivers made their ways uncertainly before fen drainage: prolonged floods could end with shifted courses, and Stretham Mere and Harrimere[2] once marked old beds as silting took the junction northwards, downstream. On joining the Cam, the Old West dropped silt in the uncertain area of changing courses: 'a bed of gravel and sand, which the river of Ouse, at his meeting with Grant strongly casteth up, and the river of Grant, being the weaker stream feebly resisteth'.[3] Here, among the marshes, was an area of inter-common on both sides of the Cam, and from this the final division of parishes left a large portion of Stretham between the rivers, stretching from the south bank of the Old West to Chittering and the Waterbeach boundary.[4] From the end of Roman times, right through the great drainage schemes of the seventeenth century, until the nineteenth century, a large part of these parishes has been fen, subject to winter flooding, and more has been in danger from any extraordinary flood.

The margin between fen and upland has shifted in historical times according to changes in sea-level, climate, and the success or failure, vigour or neglect, of man's attempts at drainage. The twenty-foot contour (see Fig. 1, p. xii) marks off ground that seems to have been safe even from the great floods in the history of the area, and in general the critical height seems to have been rather below this, although sometimes flood-waters stand higher towards the Ouse than the Cam, any banks that hold making for relief towards the east. This was apparent again in the last general inundation of 1947.

Relief differentiates the nature of the three villages, and their situation in relation to the twenty-foot contour shows this very clearly. In Water-

---

[1] Queenholme, TL 430725.
[2] Stretham Mere, TL 525730; Harrimere, TL 535745.
[3] S. Wells, *The History of the Drainage of the Great Level of the Fens*, vol. II (1830), pp. 93–4.
[4] For the late inter-common see *Liber Eliensis*, p. 192.

beach, only the settled area stands above this level. Cottenham is built towards the end of a long spur of greensand and gravel reaching out into the fens. Around it once lay the arable of its open fields, whose outer boundary ran astonishingly close to the twenty-foot contour all the way. Between Cottenham and Rampton on the west there penetrates a long tongue of low ground, Little North Fen and The Holme, once Holmere.

On the eastern side of Cottenham there is a similar but smaller penetration of low ground between the villages along the line of the Beach Ditch. At the end of this, too, was a mere[1] ('Tossolmere', 'the mere' or 'Histon mere', in the field book and court rolls), in the region where Landbeach meets Histon near the Cottenham border.[2] Here, too, were the old moors of Histon, Landbeach and Cottenham, which were never ploughed up on the Cottenham side until after the parliamentary enclosure of the nineteenth century.

Landbeach village is settled along the line of the twenty-foot contour, again on a spur, but this one is shorter and more broad based. The village is not on the watershed, but low down on the eastern side, where the gault clay gives way to gravel. Both Landbeach and Cottenham are fen-edge villages, favoured by dry sites which combine the advantages of connection with the upland, with access to as much fen as possible.

The siting of Waterbeach village is different; in the wetter historical periods it was a true fen island, surrounded on all sides by land below the flood line, and cut off from the upland. If one adds the other parts of the parish settled at different times in the Middle Ages, Denney and Elmeney (as their names imply, also islands), we find medieval Waterbeach parish to have been a small fen archipelago. Its constituent islands were more isolated from each other than were the villages just to the north strung out along the Haddenham–Stretham ridge. Each of its elevated sites was a low deposit of gravel, just sufficient to give a drier surface than the surrounding fen. Causeways were necessary to join them.

Each of the three islands in Waterbeach provided a site for a monastery. Earthworks still remain even at the short-lived site of Elmeney; more complete earthworks at Waterbeach itself; and at Denney, as well as these, buildings from every period of use. These islands must have in one way been particularly suitable for early monasteries, in that they were then cut off from the world by the black waters of the fen. The eremitical tradition could fulfil itself in isolation in small communities: the hagiographer's description of St Guthlac's settlement at Crowland in the demon-tormented fens could well have been written of any of them.[3] The only other monastic site along this fen edge between the Ouse and the Cam was

[1] This mere was in the region of TL 455650.
[2] LPC, Field Book; CCCC, XXXV, 121–125, 170.
[3] See above, p. 1: H. T. Riley (ed.), *Ingulph's Chronicle of the Abbey of Croyland* (1854), pp. 8, 454.

at Swavesey, on a similar cramped fen island, again linked to the village of that time by a causeway only.

But the austerity imposed by such sites suited the zeal of the early reformed monasteries, rather than more sophisticated later Benedictine life, and it is significant that Swavesey later went to the Carthusians, and only the Poor Clares at Denney survived in our villages to the Dissolution. Elmeney is frankly described as an island in the charter of Robert, chamberlain of the Count of Brittany, in making the original grant to Ely. Some of the difficulties of life there, due to its topography, emerge clearly from the later charter of Aubrey Picot arranging for the transfer to Denney:

Having heard the frequent complaints of Reginald, monk, and of the brothers of Elmeney, namely that they are wont to be too much harassed in that isle by the waters and hindered in the service of God…let them transfer their house to the island which is called Denney namely in a higher place on account of the flood-waters, and to one more suitable to construct their church and buildings and to make gardens and orchards; from the island that is, as is said, unsuitable on account of the waters, to this more commodious island; the aforesaid island, namely Elmeney, still remaining to their use.[1]

The reason given for the transfer of the Poor Clares from Waterbeach to Denney in 1339 is similar. The date is one when we might well from other evidence expect the flooding to be near its worst:

the house of the Abbess and Minoresses of Waterbeche is situated in a place narrow, low and decayed, and otherwise inadequate for their residence.[2]

The RAF air photo taken in 1952 in time of flood, but not the worst of recent years, shows the earthworks of the abbey with the waters which filled The Hollow and The Little Hollow lapping against them.[3]

CHRONOLOGY OF THE WATER–TABLE

In this area the physical environment is subject to change, from variations in the water-table, the deposition of silt, and the formation or shrinkage of peat. There is evidence, often fragmentary, indirect, and inconclusive, which suggests three possible periods of a rising water-table in post-Roman times. The removal of the Benedictine cell from Elmeney to Denney because of the rising waters indicates a possible deterioration in the century after the Conquest; fourteenth-century documents are full of hints of still more serious and prolonged flooding; and the controversies

[1] *Liber Eliensis*, pp. 389–90, charter 141 (1133x1169); see Appendix B.
[2] *Cal. Pat.* Ed. III, vol. IV, 1338–40 (1898), p. 242, quoted in *Waterbeach*, p. 102; see Appendix B.
[3] RP: CPE/UK/1952 3095.

over drainage schemes in the early years of the seventeenth century may well indicate a third period of major deterioration.

It will be argued later that the deterioration in the fourteenth century and subsequent recovery played a dominant role in the evolution of the medieval open fields in Landbeach. But the source of much recent discussion of the water-table in this period, the 'Inquisitiones Nonarum', is singularly unhelpful for our three parishes.[1] Their representatives seem to have used what was virtually a common formula, blaming the shortfall in income on taxation, royal and ecclesiastical. Yet the neighbouring parish, Impington, reported 200 acres flooded, and the total area which suffered in this way in the county seems to have been very considerable. Perhaps flooding was by that time too much a normal seasonal expectation in our parishes to have been considered a plausible excuse.

There is further early fourteenth-century evidence from surveys of nearby manors. In 1325 Swavesey had floods over five acres of the glebes.[2] In the 1340 Survey of Swavesey three acres are again flooded, and the prior gets nothing for meadow in Fen Drayton because it is under water. In the 1358 Ely Survey of their manor of Willingham, fifteen acres of mowing meadow appear to be deteriorating because of repeated flooding, and thirty acres of fen meadow are then permanently under water.[3] This was not an entirely new problem there in the fourteenth century, but the situation appeared to be getting worse. The Ely Old Coucher Book in 1251 mentioned an extra four acres that could be mown, and beasts that could be pastured, only in time of drought. The earlier Survey of 1222 mentions thirteen arable acres which could not be ploughed, and which were in meadow and pasture because of too much rain.[4] By the thirteenth century cultivation would seem to have been pressing against the frontier with the fen. When the evidence is fragmentary and incidental, and its authors expect flooding as part of the order of things, it is difficult to assess the scale of the deterioration, but there cannot be much doubt that the early fourteenth century was a particularly difficult period on the fen edge from this cause.

The Court Roll of the Manor of Chamberlains in Landbeach for 1328 is unfortunately damaged towards the foot, but enough remains to suggest that this had been a peculiarly bad year.[5] Instead of the normal phrase for reporting damage due to stopped ditches, '*ad nocumentum vicinorum*' (with or without minor qualification), much more detail is given. Hugo le

[1] A. H. R. Baker, 'Evidence in the "Nonarum Inquisitiones" of Contracting Arable Lands in England During the Early Fourteenth Century', *EconHR* 2nd series, XIX (1966).

[2] BM Add. MS. 6164, p. 228; quoted by W. M. Palmer and C. E. Parsons, 'Swavesey Priory', *TCHAS*, I (1904).

[3] PRO E/143/9/2: cf. Chapter 3.

[4] BM Cotton Tiberius, B II, 118d.

[5] CCCC, XXXV, 121. It was also the year of a great sea flood.

Bray's ditch at Claystrate[1] (now Spalding's Lane) had overflowed, making a lake three perches by four. Another of his ditches next to the croft of the prior of Barnwell (Priors Close) had not been mended, 'through which the highway was submerged to the great injury of travellers' ('*per quod via regia submersa est ad magnum gravamen transseuntium*' [*sic*]).[2] If this is indeed Priors Close, as would appear, the ditch and road still being there in later years, then the trouble was occurring even in that part of the village most likely, because of the relief, to have escaped it. It may well have been due to excess rain and water-logging of the clay rendering the ditches inadequate. In the Survey of 1316 a new place-name emerges, 'le slo', the slough. It occurs in the Court Rolls in 1328 and 1338. The last appearance noted is in 1401–2. Stopped watercourses become one of the main concerns of the fourteenth-century Court Rolls in Landbeach, and this is so for both manors. There are, for example, fifteen reported at the Chamberlains Michaelmas Court of 1327, and fifteen more at Michaelmas 1375. Many intervening courts have still more.[3]

Topographical evidence from in and around this area is highly suggestive of a major rise in the water-table sometime in the Middle Ages, and some of it can be related to fourteenth-century documents. William Cole in his notes has preserved a record of a Tithe Dispute of 1315 from the now vanished Oldfield Register.[4] In this The Holme[5] in Cottenham appears as Holmere, and is the termination of the Oakington Brook. At this period The Holme had become a wet low fen, where it was reckoned normally as a hard, and from the spread of alluvium it would appear probable that this deterioration also caused the lower part of Oakington to be removed uphill; for the alluvium continues in a band on either side of the Oakington Brook, over the deserted ridge and furrow, croft and toft and house platforms, south of Water Lane. The name itself is suggestive, for it was obviously the main village street in the earlier Middle Ages. The clarity of some of the house platforms, where sub-divisions of buildings can be discerned, suggests that they were abandoned without time to rob the materials. Scarcely any more residential building took place on these deserted sites until the twentieth century. Several of the nearby manor houses have moved uphill: Westwick Hall, Crowlands at Cottenham, and Histon Manor: this general shift may well be associated with the same rise in the water-table.

The area of Landbeach immediately east and south of the cross-roads is low-lying and especially sensitive to such changes. In the Field Book of 1549 the first selion in Banworth's second furlong, next to the first tenement by the cross-roads, is noted as 'flud acre'. This appears as 'le

---

[1] See Fig. 10, p. 127.   [2] CCCC, XXXV, 121.

[3] CCCC, XXXV, 121, 2 Ed. III and 12 Ed. III; 124, 3 Hen. IV; 121, 1 Ed. III and 44 Ed. III.

[4] BM Add. MS. 5887, fol. 25f.

[5] TL 426670; for changes of site, see Fig. 2.

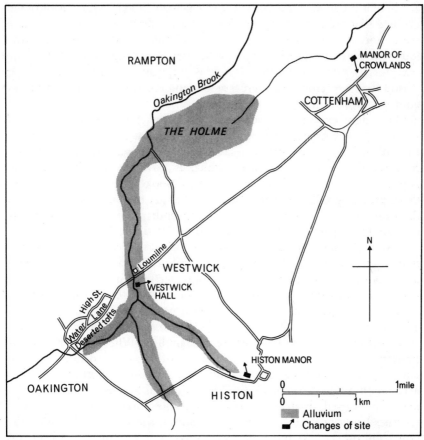

Fig. 2. Changes of site around Oakington: the uphill shift of both manor houses and peasant houses in this area seems to be associated with a great flood, especially of the Oakington Brook and its tributaries. Our only evidence of a flood on this scale is from the early fourteenth century.

Flodacre' in a Court Roll of 1362.[1] Matthew Parker's endorsement of the College copy of the Field Book dates it as a gift made by the lords of the village on 10 March 1313. Although there were Atte Flods in the Hundred Rolls the first mention of the tenement itself by name, 'le Flood', occurs in a Charter of 1317.

In 1404–5 there is reference to a tenement lying 'apud le Flood' which has no right of common.[2] There would appear to have been some building here on the lords' waste by this date; apparently the waters had receded somewhat.

[1] See Fig. 10, p. 127.
[2] LPC, Field Book; CCCC, XXXV, 121, 36 Ed. III, Court Roll; CCCC, XXXV, 19, Charter; CCCC, XXXV, 124, 6 Hen. IV, Brays Court Roll.

There is much less evidence on later changes. In 1518 a jury of old men claimed that the lode[1] was dug in the past for drainage, 'for at that time were more wetter and moist years than are now at this time'.[2] But the lode was there in 1325 already, and the very name suggests that drainage was not its principal purpose.[3] If it is impossible to refer this wetter period to any specific dates there is at least the survival of a folk memory of climatic improvement.

One might expect some reference to the general deterioration which seems to have been experienced towards the end of the sixteenth century, for which Shakespeare himself has provided much evidence. The nameless balke of the earlier field books, which is now the Waterbeach road, appears as 'Flood Lane'[4] in the Dukman Book's list of tenements, but this is probably as late as 1727. The great quantity of evidence dealing with drainage from the beginning of the seventeenth century is all from interested or hostile parties in the flurry of promotion of profit-seeking schemes.

In 1604 Richard Atkyns of Outwell surveyed the fens, and blamed any flooding in this area on defective drains, while at the same time he thought the banking and draining of Cottenham better than any other nearby fen town.[5] In the Survey of 1618, Cottenham and Landbeach fens are suffering from water shortage in summer time 'by reason of their banking and draining of them of late time...'[6] By Hayward's Survey of 1635–6 the situation appears to have worsened rapidly.[7] Wherever direct comparison of the area of a fen is possible at two of the survey dates, it is much enlarged in the later one. For instance, Joist Fen[8] in Waterbeach is 1,200 acres in 1618 and 2,200 in 1635. This could well be due to the failure to keep up normal drainage works during the anticipation of the new schemes being projected by Sir Miles Sandys, the Cromwell family, the Cutts and others.[9] As much was suggested in 1620 when a petition was made: 'the undertakers may now be compelled to perform their part, or else abandon the project, since, in the expectation of it, the drainage has been neglected for years'.[10] Atkyns had seen an engine, presumably a windmill in action, draining at Over in 1604.[11] There is the impression that a good deal of successful minor draining and embanking had taken place just before the documentation begins to become plentiful, but that its effects had been very short-lived. Probably provoked by wetter times, as so often in the fens where drainage produces peat shrinkage and so

[1] See Fig. 4, p. 20.
[2] CCCC, XXXV, 167; see also Dukman Book in LPC.
[3] Wr. Pk. Ch., fol. 248d. Lode in this area seems always to refer to a canal used for barge traffic.
[4] LPC; see Fig. 10, p. 127.   [5] BM Harleian 5011, and CUL, EDR A/1/8.
[6] BM Add. MS. 33466.   [7] Wells, History of the Drainage, vol. II, p. 177.
[8] See Fig. 6, p. 87.
[9] For examples see: BM Harleian 5011, fol. 14r.; Add. Ch. 33086; Add. MS. 33466, fol. 26.
[10] CSPD 1619–23, vol. CXVI, no. 113.
[11] BM Harleian 5011, fol. 41; cf. Draining, p. 114n.

subsidence and worse problems, successful local schemes soon created greater difficulties than ever. From this time on it is the state of the general drainage schemes and the increasing tasks that they have to cope with, which seem to determine the general condition of our area far more than any possible climatic changes.

Darby has shown the eighteenth century to be on the whole a period of deterioration for the South or Waterbeach level. The evidence cited suggests that each change at Denver Sluice (its building, blowing up, and rebuilding) made matters worse. He quotes Labelye to suggest that improvements, apparently so effective in 1743 (these may be attributed to the Act of 1740?), had been more than lost by 1745. Certainly the position after the mid-century seems worse than ever. Darby quotes a traveller in 1763[1] reporting that in Cottenham in winter the water was constantly above the inhabitants' ankles in their houses (an odd situation since there is a ten-foot fall on the main street from green to church). Cole's famous remark in 1769 when his estate was drowned for the third time in five years, 'Not being a water-rat, I left Waterbeach', is shown by Hills to have been occasioned by the blowing of the bank.[2] Hills suggests that a very considerable effort followed the Act of 1740: two mills were swiftly erected and a third followed by at least 1766.[3] The banks, on which the Bedford Level Corporation had spent very heavily in 1726–31, decayed very rapidly as they were used as haling-ways for the increasing barge traffic. The effort could not be sustained, and by 1795 mills were collapsing and banks washing away. The Act of 1797 which raised tolls on those using the banks, seems to have produced a dramatic improvement:[4] 500 acres of fen in Waterbeach reported by Masters[5] in 1794 were reduced to 100 by the time of Arthur Young's visit in 1805.[6] Enclosure was seen as a necessity in order to enable high enough taxes to be paid, so that adequate drainage works could be maintained. So it was a Drainage Act which enclosed Waterbeach and banned turf-cutting because of danger to the banks. A new mill was erected at Dowlode,[7] forming a double lift. But steam-engine drainage was already being canvassed. This was now the only way of turning all the fens from summer grounds only, into reasonably safe arable. Smithy Fen engine and Chear Fen[8] engine in Cottenham, began pumping in the same year as enclosure became effective there, and the fens were ploughed up. Even now very exceptional

---

[1] *Draining*, pp. 124ff.; p. 130 and 153n.
[2] R. L. Hills 'Drainage by Windmills in the Waterbeach Level', *PCAS* LVI–LVII (1963–4), 115–22; cf. his *Machines, Mills and Uncountable Costly Necessities* (Norwich, 1967); and *Waterbeach*, p. 18, quoting Warburton's *Life of Horace Walpole*, vol. II, pp. 371, 375 and 377.
[3] 14 Geo. II, Public, cap. 24.
[4] 37 Geo. III, cap. 88.   [5] *Short Account*.
[6] A. Young, *Annals of Agriculture*, vol. XLIII.
[7] Dowlode was in Stretham parish.
[8] See Fig. 1, p. xii.

conditions can overwhelm the whole system as in 1938 and 1947, but such floods are temporary, and the peat is slowly but surely being used up or blown away.

THE SETTLEMENT

Virtually all the villages of Cambridgeshire seem to have been established by the end of the Saxon period. In the few places where a later settlement may be suspected, conclusive proof exists only for Bar Hill, planted in the 1960s. But penetrating into the history of our villages beyond Domesday to their origins, is still hardly possible with much certainty.

Our three villages lie in an area which had been very intensively settled in Roman times for the production of corn, hides and wool[1] as military supplies. So intense was the settlement that it would have been impossible for the founders of later villages to pick good sites which had not previously been occupied by Romano-British farms. Their choice would have been further restricted by the rise in the water-table which began again in the fourth century. In any case, land which had once been cleared, even if it had reverted to scrub, would have been much easier to clear for the plough than virgin forest. Much later the Virginian colonists became established only after passing through a 'Starving Time': old sites might have enabled Saxon colonists to escape from this.

Pottery and coins from the Roman period have turned up in the soil in the centres of all our three villages as well as in the less disturbed soil of their fens. But identity of site does not prove continuity, even though the abandonment of a site never re-occupied, readily proves the opposite for that site. Some were not continuously occupied during the Roman period itself, while others were. In the third century, in face of fresh-water flooding the settled area shrank to far fewer centres, but expanded again sometimes by rebuilding old farms and sometimes finding new sites. Some of these were abandoned yet again before the end of Roman rule: others may have lasted longer. We know least of those under the later villages. When we can see clearly again, a landscape of small farmsteads has been replaced by a landscape of villages. Either a few surviving farms expanded into larger settlements, or the whole landscape was emptied and settled again with a new social and agricultural pattern.

Archaeological evidence suggests a very early penetration by Germanic peoples. Part of an early pagan cemetery was found at nearby Oakington; the cemetery at Girton College, with its mixture of Roman and Saxon ornaments is now interpreted as showing Teutonic settlement before the

[1] John Bromwich, 'Freshwater Flooding Along the Fen Margins South of the Isle of Ely in the Roman Period', in C. W. Phillips (ed.), Royal Geographical Society Research Series, no. 5, *The Fenland in Roman Times* (1970).

Roman authority was withdrawn; and the few poor Saxon huts which Lethbridge found on the bank of the Car Dyke at Waterbeach are taken as supporting this view.[1] The resettlement of the late Roman period can well have been directed by the government, and at this date is quite likely to have brought in men of Germanic stock. The archaeological hints suggest that the arrival of the first Saxons in the area was well before the traditional date of 449.

Place-name experts no longer make the absence of place-names ending in –*ingas* a proof that there was no early settlement,[2] but the minor place-names in our fens suggest recolonisation after a period of abandonment. In the name Car Dyke, which uses the adjective that describes the most densely overgrown fen, we can hardly fail to see a period of neglect before the Saxons named it. Aldeburh in Cottenham, which appears to have described one of the fen farm sites, again suggests a tumbled ruin. Other names, for places in which Romano-British sherds abound, suggest colonisation of waste. Smithy Fen, the smooth, improved, fen, is found gradually taking over from the wild Frith Fen. Reaney interprets Setchel as Sedge-haw, the sedge enclosure, Top More as Taeppa's Marsh, and Mitchell Hill as Micel-leah, the large clearing.[3] Collectively these names give the impression of the colonisation of an abandoned landscape where the works of man were in decay.

The possibilities seem to be that there was either a slow recolonisation of the abandoned areas near the fen from a few surviving centres, or the complete destruction of one social system and its settlement pattern, to be replaced later by one quite different. If the Roman re-occupation by the plantation of farms in the fourth century looks like a scheme directed by the government, the fewer but larger villages with their extensive fields look like the product of much slower but steady growth. Locally the balance of evidence probably still inclines to a break in continuity at some time in the fifth century after partial barbarisation, but the alternative is far from improbable. Further north in the fens Mrs Hallam has found what look to have been nucleated villages in the Roman period.[4] Some of these even had what appear to be fields ploughed in strips. If there were any such in our part of the Roman Fenland, we can be sure that they were those that were hidden under our present village centres, those that Mr

---

[1] T. C. Lethbridge, 'Anglo-Saxon Huts at Waterbeach', *PCAS* XXXIII (1931–2).

[2] J. M. Dodgson, 'The Significance of the Distribution of the English Place-Name in –*ingas*, –*inga*, in South-East England', *Medieval Archaeology* X (1966), 1–29; K. Cameron in K. C. Edwards (ed.), *Nottingham and its Region* (Nottingham, 1966), p. 214.

[3] P. H. Reaney, *The Place-names of Cambridgeshire and the Isle of Ely* (Cambridge, 1943), pp. 149–52. No early forms have been found for Mitchell Hill or Mitchellee, but topographically it would make very good sense as an –*eg* form: the largest of the islands in Cottenham's flooded fens would become a hill after drainage. Cf. Elmeney which became Elm Hill; Setchel, TL 470710; Smithy Fen, TL 455705; Top More, TL 482685; Mitchell Hill, TL 477698.

[4] In Phillips (ed.), *Fenland in Roman Times*.

Bromwich could not investigate. When we learn to date the local coarse pottery of sub-Roman and Dark Age types better it is possible that we may find a more definite answer to the question of continuity by studying areas of 'shrunken medieval villages'. As yet we must remain uncertain as to whom we may attribute the title of Founding Fathers of our villages.

By the time of the Domesday Survey all three of our villages, even Landbeach, the daughter of Waterbeach, seem to be well developed. Their population probably surpassed that of the former Roman farms in the area, but it was concentrated in fewer centres. It is now suggested that the Romano-British farms were much more pastoral and less arable in this area than was formerly thought. By the time that we can see clearly again, our villages, in spite of the pastoral riches that the fens conferred to them, all have a well-developed arable side to their economy. Perhaps it is in this change that we can find a glimpse of one of the forces transforming society and the landscape in the Dark Ages.

Our three villages appear in the Domesday as Coteham, Bece or Bech, and Utbech. The editor of the *Victoria County History for Cambridgeshire*[1] was unwilling to positively identify Utbech as Landbeach and Bece or Bech as Waterbeach, although the descent of the manors in later times demands this. The reason for doubt was that Inbeche appears in later Ely documents, where it refers to Landbeach, and Reaney treated it as opposite to Utbech, although these names were separated, in different texts, from different periods. Ekwall interprets the Inbeche of the Ely documents to mean Beche inland as distinct from Waterbeach. This is not the opposite of Utbech, Beach out of the water, but another way of saying the same thing; out of the water and inland can obviously be equivalents.[2]

The name Bech or Beche originally applied to both villages, Landbeach as well as Waterbeach, as it still can be in the local vernacular. The prefixes Land– and Water– seem to have been the natural way of distinguishing them if Landbeach had become a separate village in its own right as a result of floods, but again the earliest recorded use is early in the thirteenth century. This form of distinction has the vivid flavour of the vernacular contrasted with official attempts at designation in the Domesday Book and in the Ely records. The separation had certainly taken place before Domesday. The accepted meaning of Beche as 'shore' is very difficult to reconcile with Landbeach. Ekwall rejects the possibility of Bec, 'a brook' as a source on the grounds that the word so used is not found in this area.[3]

---

[1] *VCH Cambs.*, vol. I, pp. 367, 371, 396; 377, 395, 396, 398.

[2] Reaney, *Place-Names of Cambridgeshire*, p. 179; E. Ekwall, *A Concise Dictionary of English Place-names*, 4th ed. (Oxford, 1960), pp. 285, 501.

[3] Ekwall, *Dictionary*, pp. 285, 501; Reaney, *Place-names of Cambridgeshire* (p. 179), accepts stream or valley.

In fact the Oakington Brook in its earlier stages is known as the Beck Brook. Such a derivation was suggested for the name of the whole town of Beche in a Rental of 1459, and the brook in question was identified in this document in the heart of the old village.[1] But the Domesday term, Utbeche for Landbeach, where Waterbeach is simply Beche, again points to a secondary foundation, from the larger village.

The settlement pattern and place-names of this part of North Cambridgeshire encourage the view that the main villages in early times were the centres of arable cultivation, and that subsidiary centres developed out in the waste for the flocks and herds.[2] From these secondary settlements, villages grew. The name Westwick (western dairy-farm) would seem to hint that it was the place where some of the animals from Cottenham were pastured; although it was a hamlet in Oakington parish, its associations with Cottenham were such that the rector of the latter tried to claim the tithes in the fourteenth and seventeenth century;[3] and it was entered in the 'Nomina Villarum' as 'Cottenham cum Westwick'. The inhabitants of Cottenham had inter-common rights in Westwick, as did the inhabitants of Westwick in Cottenham. Rampton had similar rights in Willingham, as had Over. The name Rampton suggests that it, too, was a settlement originally for sheep, and the four-field system operating there on the eve of enclosure still depended on the manure of its extensive flock. Waterbeach, Thetford, and Stretham all inter-commoned in Stretham marsh, 'Thetford heyfen' in the angle between the two rivers, and the inter-commoning rights held in reverse in Bech Fen. The area between Cottenham and Landbeach, the old moors, was an inter-common until 1235. The lords of Milton had common rights in Banworth Meadow in Landbeach right up to enclosure. In the early phase of settlement the vast fens must have been like space itself, finite but unbounded. The size of the fens relative to the arable of the islands and peninsulas probably made division often unnecessary, while the difficulty of marking boundaries through land subject to winter flooding helped to maintain a very complex system of inter-commoning. Miss Neilson showed this operating in even greater complexity in the Fenland proper where parish boundaries were often not drawn until the thirteenth century or later.[4]

The parishes immediately south of the Old West River all have a share of fen contained in wedge-shaped boundaries. Waterbeach, Cottenham and Willingham all have the butt of the wedge against the river. The fens of Landbeach and Rampton are in the pointed end of wedges thrust in

---

[1] CCCC, XXXV, 150.
[2] M. M. Postan, *The Medieval Economy and Society* (1972), pp. 114–15 on filial villages. Publication came too late to make continual reference to this work, which provides much of the general setting for this local study.
[3] See above p. 8, and PRO E/134, 18 Car. I, Trin. 4.
[4] Neilson (ed.), *A Terrier of Fleet*.

between these bigger neighbours, but they fail to reach right through to the river. There is an artificial straightness about their boundaries here. From their appearance alone one would suspect a deliberate division in which the old-established villages managed to assert their prior claim and take the lion's share. The division between Cottenham and Landbeach took place only in 1235.[1]

Some of the furlong names in the old open field of Banworth in Landbeach reinforce the suggestion that Landbeach was a subsidiary village for sheep: Lamcot and Hammys occurred side by side, suggesting a shelter for lambs and an enclosed pasture.[2] Banworth is on a well-drained gravel that was responsible for the excellence of the later Sheepwalks in Landbeach. The settlement would have taken place on what had once been cleared Roman fields, just to the east of the gault clay and its probably denser forest. The conditions of the later Roman period and of the post-Roman rise in the water-table cannot have left much reliable dry ground suitable for sheep pasture any nearer to the settlement at Waterbeach than this. These conditions drove a Romano-Briton to remove his house in Bullocks Haste on to the bank of the Car Dyke, and it is significant that Lethbridge found his Saxon huts on the bank, too.[3] Indeed, flood conditions, if they occurred in the early years of the Saxons at Waterbeach, might well have been sufficient in themselves to send the sheep off to the higher gravels of Banworth in Landbeach, in the shelter at the edge of the forest. A flood that lasted might well turn such a temporary refuge into a permanent subsidiary settlement. Space for ploughland would still have been available in early Landbeach when Waterbeach arable was inundated, and open-field ploughing seems to have begun there on the higher ground above the village, the future Mill Field.[4]

The development of Denney may well have been due to similar purposes. It was to Chittering, beyond Denney, that the Waterbeach swineherd in Tudor times was still leading the village pigs in their daily search for mast and grazing. Although Denney became a subsidiary centre of population (and as the documentary evidence already cited suggests, it was flood-water that drove the monastery there), unlike Westwick, it never acquired its own open fields, and never became a separate parish. There was no great expanse of gault clay stretching away above it, inviting clearance for strong corn-growing land, as there was at Landbeach. Denney with its Low Grounds was more completely invested by the dark fen waters in wet times than Waterbeach itself. Most of its gault lay towards the river, under the fen.

[1] Wr. Pk. Ch., fol. 248d.   [2] LPC, Field Book; cf. CCCC, XXXV, 170.
[3] J. G. D. Clark, 'Report of the Excavations on the Cambridgeshire Car Dyke, 1947', *Antiquaries Journal* XXIX (1949), 145–63, Lethbridge, 'Anglo-Saxon Huts at Waterbeach', *PCAS* XXXIII, p. 133.
[4] See Fig. 8, p. 100, and Chapter 3, p. 101.

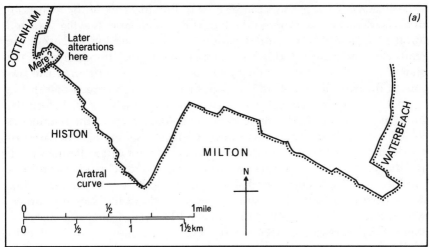

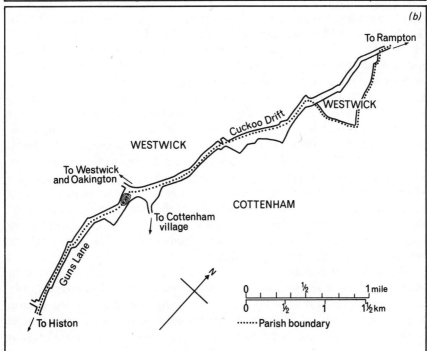

Fig. 3. Boundaries: (a) The old southern boundary of Landbeach parish seems to have been laid down where open-field ploughing halted (source: CRO Q/RDc18, 1813). (b) The boundary between Cottenham and Westwick seems to have been the ancient road to the Isle. Where the Westwick ploughs had crossed this by the early fourteenth century the parish boundary still follows their invasion of the Cottenham side (source: CUL Tithe Award Map for Westwick).

If the shape of the parishes can be used to find hints about the formation of the settlements, so, too, can the line of the boundaries (see Fig. 3 (a and b)). It is often argued that most parishes were defined by the end of the tenth century, tithes making such definition of great importance to the church. Where a parish boundary shows the characteristic irregular zig-zags of the ends of open-field furlongs, then it may be argued that this in itself shows that the plough had arrived there probably well before the Norman Conquest. In our three parishes the only parts of the boundaries which seem to come into this category are the southern boundaries of Landbeach which run out to the east and to the west of the Roman road. By the use of the enclosure award map and the field book, one can produce a plausible correspondence of the irregularities in the old boundaries (there was some later simplification of the south-western corner) with the ends of furlongs in Mill Field and Dunstall Field. The curves of some of the short sections seen exactly designed to follow a pair of edges of a selion to the north of them. In fact the old boundaries seem, for a great part of their length to be derived from the furrows of Landbeach ploughs. The abuttals of Mill Field are against the fields of Milton, Impington and Histon. Those of Dunstall are against Histon More, Bechmere and Tossol-mere, or simply The Mere. In the absence of any strip map one cannot develop the inference with much confidence that Dunstall Field in Land-beach had necessarily reached this boundary at a very early date, and in view of the lateness of the settling of the boundary with Cottenham, there is still less ground for dogmatic assurance. The old boundary line taken alone would have suggested that after the full establishment of Mill Field, the fields of Histon outflanked this during a pause in the expansion of Landbeach in this direction, but were soon checked by the development of Dunstall which outflanked them in their turn. There is no strip map of Histon to disprove this, but the revelation of the 'mere' lying between the fields of Landbeach and Histon in this sector (as is quite clear and certain from the field book), makes such an argument from the nature of the boundary line alone quite untenable.

The ending of the open fields of Cottenham against the boundary with Westwick reveals an even more tantalising picture which invites an even more hazardous argument. Here the line of the boundary, at first glance, follows for most of its length the kind of smooth sinuous pattern associated with clearance up to a forest path. However, the ends of the furlongs as shown by the strip map show that the Cottenham selions did not con-tinuously reach the road, but that alongside most of it there were left gores and irregular triangles of pasture, indicating clearly that the ploughs of Cottenham here came up against a frontier already defined. This road may well have been of very considerable antiquity at that time. Cole has preserved for us the evidence of a dispute of 1315 from the now lost

Crowlands Oldfield Register. In this it emerges quite clearly that some of the Westwick selions (and possibly some from Cottenham) actually crossed the road. The relic of this can still be seen in the deviation of the parish boundary from the road near Holme Meadow.[1] What this case does decisively show is that the ploughs of Cottenham had certainly reached their furthest possible limits in this direction by the early fourteenth century. Here, then, the colonisation begun by the early Saxon settlers was complete by that date. The invasion of the Cottenham side by the Westwick ploughs suggests that the expansion of arable under the population pressure of the previous centuries, may have produced more vigorous results in some of the secondary settlements which had more room in the first flush of expansion, than in the primary villages, which had neared their limits.

DRAINAGE AND WATERCOURSES

In 1618, in the middle of troubled times for the fenmen, the commissioners of sewers took another view of the state of the drainage. Edmonds reported:

The River of Ouse coming along by the Towns of Bedford, Huntingdon and St. Ives, and so passing down to his outfall at Lynn, is a goodly fair river throughout, but from below Ely downwards runneth with such a current that, as it is absolutely the best sewer of that country, so it is by the occasion of the great fall of waters thereinto, as well from the River of Grant out of Cambridgeshire as from the drains which run out of the Isle of Ely, much overcharged in winter and time of flood to the prejudice of the adjacent parts. For remedy whereof former times have provided some by sewers or slakers, and amongst other the West Water at Earith Bridge below St. Ives, to remove part of the overcharge of water and to ease the river where it is narrow and knare and the country apt to be overflown, and so to carry it through the Isle of Ely though otherwise to their prejudice...

But as he further reported, the West Water was silted up (in fact it was on its way to extinction) and running back into the Ouse instead of relieving it; the outfalls were clogging, and the whole position was deteriorating fast.[2]

The initial drainage from the uplands of the villages between the Ouse and the Cam is, for the most part, by short ditches running down the sides of the spurs, to the north-west or the south-east. These empty into the main drainage channels which flow with a slighter gradient, from south-west and south, to the north-east and north, at the bottom of the shallow valleys between the neighbouring parishes. Many of these main drainage channels are parish boundaries, and the aid given by the men of each

[1] BM Add. MS. 5887, fol. 25f., TL 424667; see also Fig. 3(b), p. 17.
[2] PRO SP 14/99, No. 52; quoted by Darby, *Draining*, p. 36.

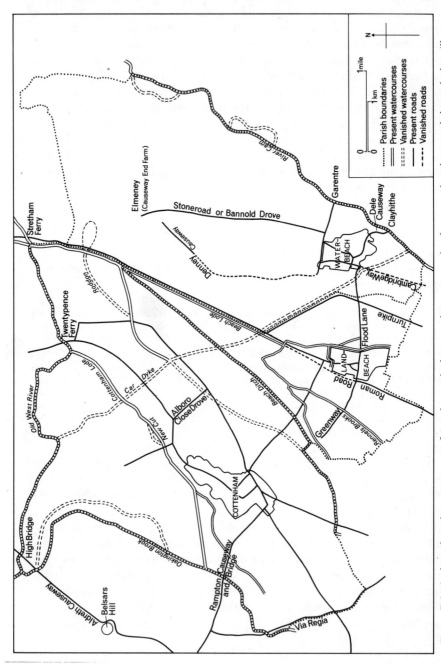

Fig. 4. Principal roads and watercourses: from the roads shown, a lesser network of ways and paths spread through the village centres, fields and to a lesser extent through the fens. (Based upon the Ordnance Survey map of 1878. Additional source: CRO R (ol.)(ol.))

parish by their ditching has aimed at getting the surface water to the boundary and on to the next parish as fast as possible.

The Cam itself, Beach Lode, Beach Ditch, and formerly the Oakington Brook, performed the double function of boundary and main drain. Part of the Roman Car Dyke, between Waterbeach and Landbeach had the same function, until Lode Ditch took over from it at Goose Hall. The old Cottenham Lode gave a similar outflow through the middle of Cottenham fens which lay remote from any boundary.[1]

The Isle of Ely sits obliquely athwart the lines of natural drainage, and so the upland waters from the parishes between the two rivers must pass through the Ouse at Earith or the Cam at Stretham. Now controlled by sluices at either end, the Old West can flow in either direction.[2] As well as water from Over, Willingham, Cottenham and Waterbeach, it takes the run-off from the southern slopes of the Isle on its northern bank. With its flat profile, the Ouse rises at an alarming rate in time of flood when the waters of the uplands of Bedfordshire pour in faster than the outflow can clear them. If the Old West and the Cam cannot then offer sufficient relief, the Ouse is likely to burst its banks and pour across the northern parts of the parishes which lie south of the Old West. If the banks of the Cam are in good repair at the time they are likely still to be easily holding when those of the Ouse burst. Although Waterbeach Fen has long been below the level of its immediate neighbour, the Cam, it has been in far greater danger of flooding from the Ouse.[3] On occasions the waters of the latter, after pouring in spate through the Old West, have forced their way up the Cam towards Cambridge,[4] reversing the outflow.

In this area, where the problems of drainage are so difficult, and the maintenance of adequate flow so delicate, throughout historical times men have both improvised and patched empirically, and also projected and attempted ambitious schemes. It is now scarcely possible with certainty to distinguish many of the waterways as natural or artificial. Gordon Fowler identified two portions of extinct watercourse in the area from an examination of the soils and levels. The first was the old course of the Oakington Brook before its waters were led off by the New Cut in Cottenham Lode (see Fig. 4, p. 20), at the Cottenham Enclosure. Its former course took a wide detour through North Fen.

He also noticed a roddon in the north-east corner of Cottenham parish, which swung round in a quadrant to the east and ended in the peaty soil of a former mere (see Fig. 5(b), p. 22). From the evidence of the map and from soil marks, this appears to have been the end of the former course of

[1] See Fig. 5(b), p. 22.
[2] *Draining*, p. 275, quoting Dugdale's *Diary* (1657), mentions the sasse, or sluice.
[3] BM Harleian 5011, Richard Atkyns' *Survey*, 1604.
[4] *Draining*, p. 124, quoting Badeslade.

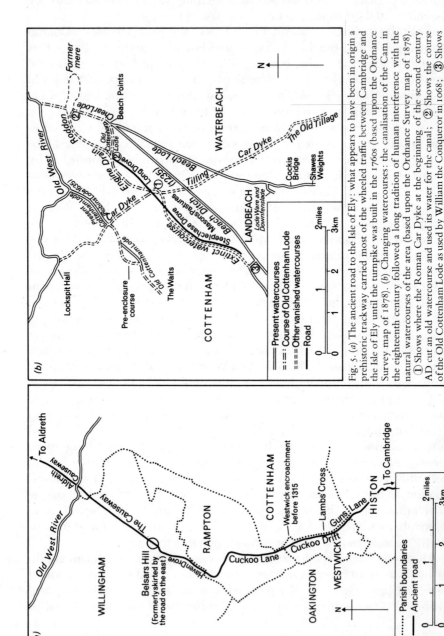

Fig. 5. (a) The ancient road to the Isle of Ely: what appears to have been in origin a prehistoric trackway carried most of the wheeled traffic between Cambridge and the Isle of Ely until the turnpike was built in the 1760s (based upon the Ordnance Survey map of 1878). (b) Changing watercourses: the canalisation of the Cam in the eighteenth century followed a long tradition of human interference with the natural watercourses of the area (based upon the Ordnance Survey map of 1878). ① Shows where the Roman Car Dyke at the beginning of the second century AD cut an old watercourse and used its water for the canal; ② Shows the course of the Old Cottenham Lode as used by William the Conqueror in 1068; ③ Shows the final diversion of the old watercourse into the Beach Ditch by the Enclosure Commissioners in the nineteenth century.

the ditch that runs along the boundary of Cottenham and Histon, the medieval Claidich. This ditch has now been diverted at right angles to join the Beach Ditch, but its former course appears to have continued straight along the line of modern field boundaries and the line of a field path, to cross the road from Landbeach to Cottenham a few yards to the west of the present Steeplechase Drove. Black soil marks indicate some of its meanders through the low ground alongside this drove northwards towards Long Drove. On the Fen Office map[1] and the first draft enclosure award map[2] there is a long thin tongue of wet fen through which this former watercourse flowed. It then seems to have followed the line of the sinuous section of the present Chear Fen Engine Drain, and so on to Gordon Fowler's roddon.

The first interference by man to this natural watercourse appears to have been the cutting of the Car Dyke at the beginning of the second century of our era. This passed through the gravel watershed near Mitchell Hill where this watershed came closest to the old watercourse.[3] The key to the design of the canal was probably the water supply from this natural watercourse to the highest central section of the Car Dyke.

Gordon Fowler showed that the Old West River from the Hermitage Sluice at Earith[4] to Lockspit Hall,[5] was for the most part the old Roman Car Dyke, but from Lockspit Hall to Stretham was the course which the flood-waters carved for themselves when the Roman engineering collapsed. The Car Dyke connecting the Rivers Ouse and Cam appears to have been cut to enable the produce of the rich fen edge, grain, hide or wool, to be transported by inland waterways to the northern garrisons at Lincoln and York. Its value as a drainage channel is extremely doubtful as it led water from the less dangerous Cam to the more dangerous Ouse. In the later years of Roman rule when it was reconstituted, it could conceivably have functioned to some extent as a catchwater drain. But cutting across the natural flow of drainage to the north and east, it would have left an inheritance of trouble for medieval man. The main medieval lodes and ditches of the area restore the natural direction of drainage, but only at the cost of cutting through the Car Dyke.

The very name, Car Dyke, is eloquent as to the condition in which the Saxons found it, one of complete neglect and decay. Car, as in car fen, means overgrown with rushes, reeds, shrubs and small trees. But some of the medieval names which still survive, Waterbeach Tillage, Landbeach Tilling, Rudiche (Rowditch), Eldelode, suggest that lengths of the canal

---

1   CRO R59/31/40/1.
2   CRO 152/P9.
3   TL 478688.
4   TL 395747.
5   TL 462713.

were still operative, between portages that replaced decayed locks. The Fen Office copy of Atkyn's map of 1604[1] shows a section of the Car Dyke serving as a stretch of the Old Cottenham Lode. But Grahame Clark's excavations showed that it had ceased to be a continuous canal shortly after AD 360.[2] The second cut through the now extinct water-course was the Old Cottenham Lode, which may have used a section of the natural stream as it used a section of the Car Dyke. Cottenham Lode was functioning when William the Conqueror besieged the Isle of Ely, for he used it as the assembly point for his invasion fleet before the assault:

Then indeed the king charged that boats everywhere with the sailors should hasten to his arrival at Cotingelade, to carry the pile of timber and stones collected there across to Alrehethe.[3]

The editor of the *Liber Eliensis* gives a comparative footnote from the *Gesta Herewardi*: 'And he ordered all the fishermen of the region to come to Cotingelade with their boats' ('*Et omnes piscatores provinciae cum naviculis ad Cotingelade adesse iussit*'). The name 'Cottenham Lode' as used in Hayward's Survey of 1635–6 clearly does not refer to the present watercourse of that name, but to the part of what is now Chear Lode between Beach Points[4] and the Old West. In a final concord of 1235 which authorises the digging of the Beach Ditch, this latter is to terminate in the middle of the angle between Beach Lode and Cottenham Lode, i.e. at Beach Points. There are repeated medieval references in the Court Book of Waterbeach to Cottenham Lode as the boundary between Waterbeach and Cottenham. There are frequent presentations of the Town of Cottenham for either failing to scour it, or for putting the scourings on the lady's soil, i.e. upon the Waterbeach bank. In 2 Hen. VI the homage testified 'that the town of Cottingham, by reason of their tenure and ancient custom, ought to scour the ditch called Cottingham Lode'. They also testified that the scourings had been put on the lady's soil by leave of the previous abbess. Further they declared that any beasts crossing the Lode should be impounded. Under 14 Ed. IV appears, 'That the town of Cottenham ought to make a certain ditch called Cottingham Lode, being within Chitteringe and Cottingham Fen, and have not done it. Therefore the town fined iij s. iiij d. and appointed to amend it by a day, sub pena xl s.'[5] It is thus quite clear that Hayward's usage is the old one, and that the eastern bank of this part of the old Cottenham Lode constituted the parish boundary; the ditch itself was included in Cottenham.

[1] CRO R59/31/40/1.
[2] Clark, 'Report of the Excavations'.
[3] *Liber Eliensis*, p. 185 and fn.; see Appendix B.
[4] TL 495698.
[5] WcD.

This is still the situation today at the only place where these parishes are contiguous, between Beach Points and the Old West River. The difference is that the ditch here is now called Chear Lode, the present Cottenham Lode entering the Old West River much further to the west.

There is little doubt on the other hand that that section of the present Cottenham Lode which comes closest to the village was part of the old watercourse of the same name. Behind the old rectory, immediately across the road from the Church, is a grove of trees called 'The Waits'.[1] Through this grove and the rectory garden runs a sunken path leading to what is now a dry pond. This pond and path were recognised some years ago by Dr Peter Eden as a turning point and cut for barges. It is common in the fen to find a stone church built on the first firm ground at the end of a lode. The Waits were the unloading point for large stones still when the Crowlands manor house was being rebuilt in the mid-fifteenth century, even though the house was some distance away, nearer the centre of the village.[2] The Waits were still the terminus of the Cottenham Lode for the stone-carrying barges. The earliest datable stone in the fabric of the church is re-used and of Norman workmanship. The lode cannot have been of Roman origin, since it would make no sense at all in the Roman scheme as it must have cut right across the Car Dyke, the main local artery of that system. It could conceivably be a product of the Dark Ages or the later Saxon and Danish periods, but what evidence there is suggests that it was yet another of the early Norman lodes cut to import stone, in this case Barnack from Northamptonshire, for church building.

If both ends of this earlier Cottenham Lode can be identified with reasonable precision, the rest of its course is a good deal less clear. Since air photographs have as yet failed to show more than the slightest hints of possible short sections the probability is that its path is involved with earlier or later landmarks. It is quite possible that the ditch running to the east just south of Alboro Close Drove (along the line of the older Alboro Close Drove of pre-enclosure times) represents a section of it. The more sinuous section of Chear Fen Engine Drain, itself part of the original now extinct stream, would most easily and logically have brought it towards the junction at Beach Points. Part of the Car Dyke itself might well also have been included as the easiest way to cross the watershed without extensive excavation, excavation that would have left visible traces today. The 1727 copy of William Hayward's map of the Fens of 1604 shows a section of the Car Dyke apparently so used.[3]

---

[1] TL 454688.

[2] CUL Queens', Ad 8, 33–4 Hen. VI: 'the carriage of great stones from ley Weightes...' The whole of this box of rolls does not appear to have been noticed by Miss Page, and would have almost closed her longest gap in the series of collectors' accounts.

[3] The section is TL 470700–478688. See Fig. 5(*b*), p. 22.

The complete extinction of this watercourse would have come with the diversion of its headwaters into the ditch between Histon and Cottenham, and so into the Beach Ditch. From the Draft Map for Cottenham, this would appear to have been the work of the enclosure commissioners.

Both Beach Ditch and Beach Lode are identified in the Final Concord of 1235 mentioned above.[1] This was an agreement between all the lords and freeholders of Cottenham and those of Landbeach to divide the inter-common area between them by a ditch and hedge ('*haya*'). This area at that time consisted of fen and pasture ('*marisco et pastura*'). The land alongside the Beach Ditch is still called Hay Lane,[2] and the remnants of the hedge are still there along its southern portion. This dates the creation of the Beach Ditch, but Beach Lode was already there since the ditch was to terminate in the middle of the angle between Cottenham Lode and Beach Lode.[3]

Beach Lode continues the first two sections of the Tillage, i.e. the Car Dyke; it gives direct access to the Old West via the old Cottenham Lode; and it forms part of the parish boundary between Waterbeach and Landbeach. It also has a southern extension in Landbeach parish, running conveniently down the eastern boundary of the village tofts, past old unloading places in front of the rectory great barn, and near the cross-roads, to join and continue Banworth Ditch. A westerly fork, Downfens-lade, around the Meadow Croft, ends in what, until very recently, was a large square pond, Lode Ware in Tudor times, and more recently, Town Pond.

Two sixteenth-century documents reveal a tradition of the digging of the lode, and identify some of the features. The first is from Dr Nobys' original 'Laying Out and Ditching of the Frith Fen':

That the old men, inhabitants of Landbeach, say and depose upon their conscience, that a certain ditch called Lode Ditch, lying between the High Fen and the ground of Denney, stretching from the south-west corner of Denney Closes, by the side of the said High Fen of Landbeach unto the north-east corner of Frith Fen, was never scoured nor made of duty, nor as no defence lawful for any cattle between ground and ground; but the inhabitants of Landbeach made the ditch at their own liberty and will to drain their common pasture from water falling and draining into Tilling, and so from Tilling to run forth into the Fens in the aforesaid ditch called Lode Ditch; for at that time were more wetter and moist years than are now at this present time.[4]

The court roll evidence, however, makes it appear that the lode did have to be made up of duty. At the Chamberlains Manor Court in 1359 the

---

[1] Wr. Pk. Ch., fol. 248d.

[2] TL 464 665–459 662.

[3] Beach Lode appears to be the lode referred to in the description of Cottenham Fens in the Hundred Rolls; *Rot. Hund.*, vol. II, p. 411.

[4] CCCC, XXXV, 167. Landbeach Tilling was the section of the Car Dyke which passed through Landbeach Fen.

Master of the College, Thomas de Eltislee, and three of the principal freeholders are presented for failing to clean 'the lode between the fen of this township and the fen of the township of Waterbeach' (' *le Loode inter mariscum ville et mariscum ville de Waterbech* ').[1] But this suggests that the duty did not fall on the villein tenants necessarily: it may only have been the lord and some of the freeholders with rights in it as a waterway who were responsible for its maintenance. This would not prevent the ditch being important to the village from the point of view of drainage as well, although the name 'Lode' itself suggests that the primary purpose of the ditch was to carry barges.

The original copies of the Field Book of 1549 carry a note on the ditches of Landbeach:

The ditch lying on the north quarter of the Frith Fen is called Landbeach Tilling, the said ditch lying between the Frith Fen and the High Fen, otherwise called the Common Fen.

Item, the ditch lying on the east quarter of Frith Fen reckoning from the Barrs otherwise called prynceall, towards Landbeach till ye come at Lode Ware over Down Fen Slade is called the Lode, and so forth to Madcroft the ditch is called the Lode or the Common Drain, and from thence it goeth to a place sometime called Cockis Bridge, and from thence to Shawes Weights. The said cocks bridge is nigh to the common plot that is at this present in the town's hand. Shawes Weight is as well lying on the backside of Thomas Ward's house betwixt the said house and his little grove.[2]

Clay could not believe the tradition that boats had come up the ditch and unloaded on the common, not believing that they could get so high. But although the old pond is largely filled in, the squareness of its northern bank clearly shows the remains of an old hithe. Thomas Ward's house and little grove place Shaw's Weights at the extreme southern end of Banworth Ditch. It may well have operated only during high spring water, as apparently did the abbot of Crowland's dock at Cottenham. Lode Ware may have been the summer port, and the only unloading point for heavy draught barges carrying stone.[3] All the building stone to be seen in the village is concentrated between the church and this point. Thus this may be yet another lode originally dug for building the first stone church in a parish. The water gate of the manor, the apron in front of the main door of the present rectory barn, would have been the handiest unloading place for both church and manor, but probably could only be reached by the narrowest barges of shallow draught. Thomas de Eltislee was presented for blocking the ditch here, at his own court in 1367.[4] After this the water gate fades from the records, and no manor house seems to be standing here.

[1] CCCC, XXXV, 121.
[2] CCCC, XXXV, 170, p. 130. See Fig. 4 and 5(b), pp. 20 and 22.
[3] *ECA*, pp. 438 and 443.
[4] CCCC, XXXV, 121, 41 Ed. III.

27

The major change in watercourses in the early modern period, the construction of the present Cottenham Lode, is less well attested and much less well documented than the abortive schemes of the same period. As has been shown, Atkyns' identification of the Cottenham Lode in 1604 clearly applies to the old course to join the Beach Ditch, but he also describes Robins Lode as the boundary between Setchel and Michelee. This is the course of the present Cottenham Lode. At some later date the subsidiary lode must have taken over the name as well as the function of its predecessor. It would certainly have offered advantages in being shorter with less difficulty of relief to contend with, and so easier for maintenance. At the parliamentary enclosure it was straightened and shortened further by the making of the New Cut.[1]

The early years of the seventeenth century saw a series of schemes for improving the drainage and navigation of the Ouse and the Old West. Sir Miles Sandys, who had considerable landed interests in both sides of the river in Willingham, Haddenham and Wilburton, was deeply involved both as a landlord and as a commissioner of sewers. The construction of Bathing Bank aroused violent controversy between Over and Willingham, since in so far as it protected the latter it increased the pressure higher up on the former.[2] Sir Miles went to the length of attempting to revive labour rents in order to put pressure on his Willingham tenants, but in the part of the area covered by this study all these attempts seem to have come to nothing in the end. Such improvement as there was seems to have come from the general draining further north and the patching of local works from time to time.

The problem the drainers had to contend with at the beginning of the seventeenth century is outlined in Atkyns' Survey of 1604.[3] In Waterbeach he reported of Midload:[4] 'This fen is embanked round about, and no sewer or ditch passeth through it, yet many years it is long drowned by reason that Ouse (over Joist Fen and Chittering) holdeth the water up.'
Of Joist Fen:

The South end...is used much for turbary. It may easily be defended from Granta but it is commonly drowned by Ouse overflowing Chittering...West of Midload Fen and a part of Joist Fen, there lie certain low grounds by the skirt of Beach Field, between the field and the fen, about 200 acres by estimation, which be often drowned, partly by the downfall for want of a sewer, and partly by water breaking in out of Joist Fen ditches at low places, even when Joist Fen itself is not overflown, which I think soon done.

If the north fens of Waterbeach were in this bad state, Cottenham Fens, which stood between Waterbeach and the source of the trouble (the Ouse

[1] See Fig. 4, p. 20.
[2] Wells, *History of the Drainage*, vol. II, p. 88.
[3] BM Harleian, 5011, fol. 23f.
[4] See Fig. 6, p. 87.

waters), were not much better: 'Cottenham Fens be all embanked, and good provision made to convey their water more than any other fen town hereabout hath, yet are these banks in many places defective insomuch as Chear Fen lieth oft and long drowned, and overfloweth into Chittering.' He found all the fens between Cottenham and Rampton as far as Aldreth Causeway, 'All pitifully drowned with very little water, and standeth long here, by reason of the high land...in Cottenham and the bank of Chear Fen and other fens, which lie between these fens next Rampton and their outfall.' One of the greatest sources of the trouble was a weir at Stretham, and 'a gravel[1] laid by Stretham men to cart their fodder out of Willow Fen, where the water runneth not above two feet deep, a great cause of drowning of these fens'.

For the next twenty years the solution for this area was looked for from scouring the rivers and removing all impediments, straightening their courses, and adding catchwater drains north and south of the Old West. By a Law of Sewers of 1608 Sir Miles Sandys and Sir Richard Cox were given power to perfect all the commissioners' works in Cambridgeshire and the Isle of Ely, including 'full liberty and authority for the cutting, digging down, pulling up, carrying away and clearly avoiding the great obstacles, annoyances, lets, impediments, encroachments and hindrances into and upon the River of Ouse and Grant'.[2]

Proposals scouted in this period involved three possible new cuts: one was simply to straighten the Old West by cutting off the bends north of Setchel Fen. Both better drainage and improved navigation were put forward as justification:[3]

Certain sudden crooks, turnings and windings of the river of Ouse, especially between the fenny grounds of Cottenham and Wilburton, being observed by his Majesty's Commissioners of Sewers in their personal view and survey of the said river...to be not only very dangerous unto navigators and watermen in times of storms and tempests, but also great and notorious hindrance to the fall and descent of the waters...

A new cut at least four feet deep and twenty feet wide was proposed, 'Beginning at the upper corner or crook of the said river, and extending from thence line straight to the lower corner or crook thereof, containing in length about eight furlongs, and at or near a place called Twentypence Water...' This scheme was made on 30 May 1618 at a Session of Sewers at Wisbech. Its scope was increased later in the year at a General Session of Sewers at Peterborough on 20 August:

[1] The term 'a gravel' is applied to an underwater path of small stones, often artificial, to create a ford or towpath.
[2] BM Add. Ch. 33806.
[3] BM Add. Ch. 33107 and Add. MS. 33466 fol. 26. See Plate I for the sketch plans on the back of the report which appear to have been made during the discussions.

The channel of the River of Ouse, between the manor of Cottenham in the county of Cambridge and Wilburton in the Isle of Ely being utterly insufficient to convey the winter waters which necessarily must have their fall by the same towards the sea, and thereby causing the said waters to swell and surround, as well the marshes belonging to the said towns, as the rich and fertile grounds lying near about the same...

A new sewer was to be 'tiked out and made at the costs and charges of the owners, farmers inhabitants and commoners of Cottenham...' It was to begin,

at the bridge in Audrey Causey being next southwards from the place where the Great Bridge lately stood, and to be carried through the fens and marshes belonging to the said town of Cottenham to fall into the said river of Ouse, Provided always that the said sewer be cut and made in all places throughout the track thereof full forty feet distant from the river of Ouse...

This seems to have been an attempt to provide a straight by-pass and catchwater drain along much of the south side of the Old West.[1] The other proposal, which is drawn out in the map in the Book of Sewers in the University Archives, showing 'Mare Gores' and the 'New Intended River', was designed for the same purposes along the whole of its length to the north.[2]

These schemes seem to have been initially opposed by the local inhabitants on various grounds: that the old drains were sufficient if the inhabitants of the Isle would clean theirs; that any expense was unnecessary, and that they had never before paid for works in the Isle; the towns south of the Old West were higher than the level in the Isle 'where the new Drain is begun, every sudden flood being usually fallen again into the said river before it be come to the place where the new river is begun...' Waterbeach folk were especially suspicious: 'And do therefore desire that such new inventions may be forborne, for fear of danger yet unknown that may happen thereby, than any good like to succeed.' Further, it was clear that if anyone benefited, the greatest beneficiary would be Sir Miles himself, the only commissioner with interests south of the Old West. They feared that the scheme was 'partially set for private men's good, and not public nor according to equity'.[3]

The map in the University Archives,[4] although accurate neither in scale nor direction, seems to refer to all the schemes for this area being discussed between 1608 and 1619, including Sir Miles Sandys' proposed New Cut through Bathing Bank in Willingham. It also shows an enclosure of a hundred acres of common for Sir Miles. Under such circum-

[1] CUA, Sewers, L. 80. See also Plate I.
[2] Cf. BM Add. MS. 33466, 'Mere Gore being an ancient sewer.'
[3] Cf. Edmonds in SP 14/99, no. 52.
[4] See jacket.

stances even a much milder people than the 'fen tigers' would have been suspicious and violent. Sir Miles changed his tactics from threats to blandishment, and in 1613 we find him offering to pay any charges levied upon Cottenham for the ditch below the Isle.[1]

But the opposition went on. In 1619 at a Session of Sewers at Peterborough it was reported, 'The commoners cry out not to have their commons taken away.'[2] In 1622 it was complained against the drainers, 'Their schemes are impracticable; fens were made fens and must ever continue such, and are useful in multiplying fowl and fish, producing turf, etc.... The people think the Undertakers will work by witchcraft, no persons of experience supposing their designs possible.'[3] In time the king became personally concerned: 'The King found that the multitude of the Commissioners preferred their little benefit before the general good, and did but perplex and hinder the work.'[4] His taking over the draining for his own good only made matters worse. The local popular champion did better: 'It was commonly reported by the commoners in the Ely Fens and the Fens adjoining, that Mr Cromwell of Ely, had undertaken, they paying him a groat for every cow they had upon the common, to hold the drainers in suit of law for five years, and that in the meantime they should enjoy every part of their common.'[5]

The power of the University, backing those interested in navigation on the Cam, defeated the drainers of this period (1618–35). In the University Book of Sewers there are complaints that the New Cut at Stretham would drain the Ouse (i.e. the Old West) in summer, taking away its waters and those of the Grant too fast.[6] The Vice-Chancellor is found in 1618–19 putting the claims of navigation against the demand for removing gravels, since they help to keep enough water for the Cam to remain navigable in summer. Barges were supplying sea-coal, wood and sedge, from Lynn, Ely and the Fens. The colleges had changed to sea-coal because of the high price and scarcity of charcoal: 'so as most colleges are driven to use sea-coal provision for their meat, as well roast as boiled, which in former times they were not wont'.[7]

If navigation be taken away (which is feared) the university cannot subsist and this point being heard before King James it was made a matter of state, and that no sufficient security could be given on this thing. Whereupon it was ordered that no new cuts or drains should be made upon the rivers of Grant or Ouse without the express consent of the Vice-Chancellor.[8]

[1] BM Harleian 5011, 14r.
[2] CSPD 1619, no. 104.
[3] CSPD 1622, vol. CXXVIII, no. 105.
[4] CSPD 1631, vol. CLXXXVII, no. 76.
[5] CSPD 1631–33, vol. CCXXX, no. 51; quoted in Draining, p. 56.
[6] CUA, Sewers, L 80. 1. 1618.
[7] CUA, Sewers, L 80.3; cf. Wells History of the Drainage, vol. II, p. 92, 1618.
[8] CUA, Sewers, L 77–77d. Undated, but probably 1618–19.

This seems to have been enough to stop all new drainage in our area, and to concentrate attention further north for a century. Only after the success and decay of the Great Drainage, did new schemes begin to be made for our three parishes in the mid-eighteenth century. The function of the watercourses as drains, had, for the time, given way to the needs of navigation.

COMMUNICATIONS – WATERWAYS

Water was not only a problem: it was also the great means of communication in the area for most traffic from early medieval times until well into the nineteenth century. In earlier days the Romans had their main supply-artery by water in the shape of the Car Dyke, and waterways appear to have been in full operation in early Norman times. Only the coming of the railways killed them.

The great monastic houses of the Fens had their own systems of communications by water, and without this, and the access which it provided to markets, the 'federated grain factories, producing largely for cash'[1] in the days of medieval high farming would have scarcely been possible on the same scale. It is not without significance that three of the fairs with the greatest international importance were on the main barge-ways of the Fens: Sturbridge, St Ives, and Boston.

The Ely Old Coucher Book shows villein carrying services by water from Willingham to Cambridge, Earith, Aldreth, Somersham, St Ives, Doddington, Ditton and Ely.[2] In the exceptionally detailed entry in the Hundred Rolls for Longstanton, Henry de Cheney's villeins are carrying the lord's corn for sale at Cambridge and the market town newly planted by the de la Zouches at Swavesey. In 1316 in Landbeach the villeins of Agnes de Bray are required to provide a rowing service for both passengers and freight to Ely, Wisbech, or elsewhere. Transport is required for the lord, lady, their children, servants, their bailiff and their attorney. Corn and other necessities must be fetched or carried.[3]

This water-traffic, on some of the feeder canals at least, seems to have been seasonal. In the demesne leases for Oakington and Cottenham by the abbot of Crowland in 1430, the malt rent has to be delivered on the Feast of the Purification to the abbot's barges (*naviculae*=narrow barges of the Fens?) at Cottenham. The delivery must be made 'in sufficient time while there was plenty of water' ('*tempore competanter dum aqua habunderaverit fieri poterit*'). There is a penalty clause so that if delivery were late 'so that the Abbot's own transport should be upset and delayed by the falling of

[1] M. M. Postan, 'The Chronology of Labour Services', *TRHS* 4th series, XX (1937).
[2] CUL, EDR, Liber R; BM Cotton Claudius, CXI; Gonville and Caius College, MS. no. 485/489.
[3] CCCC, XXXV, 146.

the water in part or in whole...' ('*ita quod Cariagium ipsius abbatis per decrementum aque perturbatur et aretro fuerit in parte vel in toto*') then the tenant would have to be responsible for the whole carriage right to Crowland at his own cost.[1]

The little information that we have about this traffic in the early Middle Ages comes from lists of villein duties, but it is probable that professional watermen were also operating: a charter of 1352 mentions an Isabelle le Maryner who had lived up against the great bank in Waterbeach. Perhaps even then there was some equality of opportunity for women among the bargees.[2] The forinsec tenants in Chesterton from Landbeach and Water-beach mentioned in the Hundred Rolls of 1278–9 look as if they were taking commercial advantage of the river. Their little holdings in Ditton being convenient to their homes by water. A few years earlier, the carrying services to Fen Ditton in the Ely Old Coucher, suggest that the abbot may have been using his manor there, near the great Sturbridge Fair, as a depot.

Navigational hazards could come from other uses of the rivers. The Commission of Sewers 1616–17 ordered the cleaning of the Old West to its former bottom and the removal of 'all wares, damms, driftways, passages, gravells, clamps, slakes, cradgings, hills, houses, encroachments, and all other letts and impediments hindering the fall of the waters within all the aforesaid limits of Ouse'.[3] One of the gravels in question had been put by the men of Stretham to enable them to get to their inter-common grounds south of the river. But if too large an obstruction would impede navigation, complete clearance might be even worse: Sir Clement Edmonds reported in 1618

the said river of Ouse from Huntingdon to the High Bridge at Ely was generally foul and overgrown with woods [sic], stopt with weirs, and against Ely (as in other parts) made shallow by gravel and fords (which they call hards) and in reason ought to be removed from the opening of the river and readier passage of the water in time of floods: yet it was generally acknowledged that the removing of these impediments, especially near about Ely, would take away all navigation and passage by boats in summer time, to the great prejudice of the University and Towne of Cambridge...[4]

The fenmen had adjusted their way of life so well to their environment that no change at all could be made without upsetting some cherished arrangements. Atkyns in the same year is reporting complaints from places that lay up-river from Willingham, that the embanking of this parish was depriving them of the relief which they previously had when the flood-waters had poured across Willingham lands.

[1] *ECA*, p. 443.   [2] CCCC, XXXV, 41.
[3] Wells, *History of the Drainage*, vol. II, pp. 50–1.
[4] Edmonds' Report of 1618 in Wells, *History of the Drainage*, vol. II, p. 62.

Between Clayhive and Cambridge there be certain sand beds and shallows in the river, which if they be removed the passage would be the worse, by means the water which is limited by the going or not going of the mill, would, when the mill stands, fall so fast away as there would not be left any store sufficient for navigation; so as the defect is in the want of water from Cambridge; which though these gravels hold up what they can, except the mills go, none but small boats can pass: and sith the water of Cambridge River cannot any way be increased by adding of more, men must fashion their vessels to the water, and not the water to every vessel.[1]

For a moment in one short stretch of the Cam, then, navigation was dependent on the drainage to supply the water, and not its rival.

The barge traffic drawn by horses wading in the Cam along the Backs was not quite extinguished in the early years of this century. But the effectual death blow had been dealt long before when the railways opened. R. L. Hills, in *Machines, Mills and Uncountable Costly Necessities*,[2] has a graph which shows a dramatic rise in the tolls immediately after the Eau Brink Cut was made, and an even more dramatic fall to well below the original levels after the railways were built. Swavesey is an eloquent visual monument to the change: the old docks were cut off, and decayed; the new dock across the railway line became a deserted reed bed. The speed of the railways opened a vast market in London and the Midlands to the perishable produce of the Fens. Here barge traffic could not possibly compete. Thus the old commercial arteries of the Fens became little more than drainage channels, often neglected and silted up in their connections to the villages.

COMMUNICATIONS – ROADWAYS

If the waterways were a great asset to the fens and to the fen edge, they were never the only means of communication. The old way from Cambridge to the Isle of Ely can still be traced, and where it passes through our area under discussion here, can still, for the most part, be walked by the hardy. Guns Lane from Histon forms half of the boundary between Cottenham and Westwick. Now narrowed down to a parallel-sided bridleway, and almost impenetrably over-grown, it was once the great medieval Via Regia of North Cambridgeshire.[3] It ran along a drift-way past Cottenham fields, and continued across the road from Westwick to Cottenham along the way now called Cuckoo Drift, to Rampton. Here it is now a green bridleway passable except for the last section into Rampton, where it turns into a nettle-grown path, much encroached upon. From Rampton it runs as another greenway, Haven Drove, to Belsars Hill and Aldreth Causeway, and so, by Aldreth High Bridge, into the Isle. The

[1] Atkyns' Report of 1618 in *ibid.*, p. 87.
[2] P. 63.
[3] Fig. 4, p. 20.

dating of this track still awaits more expert study: it may well prove to be prehistoric: chance finds suggest an intense concentration of Neolithic and Bronze Age settlement along the lower reaches of the Cam, and such a route would link this area to the other trackways on the bluff of Castle Hill above Cambridge. The junction would be where the only known Iron Age settlement of any size in this area has been discovered.

Belsars Hill is even more mysterious than the track itself. In form it is a simple round earthwork fort with a single ditch and rampart. Selions, showing a clear, medieval aratral curve run inside its banks, putting its origin back at least to the early medieval period. If it was once a simple Iron Age ring fort, subsequent modification must have closed the entrance. The Iron Age ring fort at Arbury, south of Histon, may well have guarded the other end of the same route. The map in the Book of Sewers in the University Archives associates Belsars Hill fort with William the Conqueror[1] as do Atkyns and Dugdale. This would seem to have been the local tradition before antiquaries of the eighteenth century introduced Belisarius by fanciful derivation from the name. The name, Bellassise,[2] in its old form as it appears in the Hundred Rolls, seems very like a bad joke of Norman French soldiers who suffered duty there. Even if it was in part an older structure, the probabilities are that it was used by the Normans. It is one of the possible identifications for the Conqueror's castle of Alrehethe.

The relative importance of this route is shown by the fact that it normally had a bridge in early medieval times when the other navigable river crossings in the area, except those at Cambridge itself, had only ferries. In fact it had a long causeway and a series of small bridges as well as the High Bridge itself to cross Willingham Fens and the Old West River. In 1278–9 the bridge had been broken for some sixteen years and a substitute ferry was running:

They say that the causeway and bridge of ALDERHETHE is the king's highway and it was broken and collapsed sixteen years ago now and it ought to be repaired by the Bishop of Ely and by his tenants and that the crossing there was made by boat and a man crossing with a horse paid a halfpenny for his passage and a man without a horse a farthing.

They said that the causeway and bridge were then repaired anew by the bishop.[3]

The other river crossings, Twentypence, Stretham Ferry, and Clayhithe,[4] were without bridges. One might have expected Stretham Ferry to have had some importance as the river crossing of the old Roman road

[1] CUA, Sewers, L 80. See jacket.
[2] Reaney, *Place-names of Cambridgeshire*, p. 174.
[3] *Rot. Hund.*, vol. II, p. 453; Appendix B.
[4] Twentypence, TL 480711; Stretham Ferry, TL 502722; Clayhithe, TL 503643. See Fig. 4, p. 20.

from Cambridge to Ely, but much of this road north of the village of Landbeach was probably under water in medieval times as it was in the eighteenth century. The Cam was the preferred highway.

Communication between the villages was of lesser importance than communication between the fields and the houses and yards at the centres of the villages. The inter-village roads seem to have been best when inter-common rights necessitated regular passage. This affected the routes between Oakington, Cottenham and Westwick, and Cottenham and Rampton. The former had a timber bridge, and the other a causeway as well as a bridge.[1] The centralisation of the Crowlands Cambridgeshire courts at Oakington, and the administrative economy represented, for example, by the employment of the vicar of Oakington as buyer of building materials for both Cottenham and Oakington at the Cambridge fairs, made the Westwick connection of especial importance. The repair of the bridge there figures prominently in the Crowlands accounts for Oakington.[2]

Where the surveys for enclosure make it clear, gravelled surfaced roads appear in this area to have been confined to the village centres and to those ways which led from them to the middle of the fields only. From then on there appears little to distinguish most of the main roads out of the villages from the web of greenways, balks, doles or droves so characteristic of open-field agriculture. The main road from Landbeach to Waterbeach appears simply in the field books as an unnamed 'balke'.

Waterbeach, owing to its fenny nature, was again different in needing special causeways between its various parts. There was a short causeway from the village to Clayhithe, the Dele Causeway, and one of the longer ones to Denney and Elmeney is still in use, and at its end the farm is still called Causeway End. In the vernacular the causeway's name is 'stunrud', the stone road.

Few schemes of road improvement before enclosure in the area are documented. An exception is the Cambridge-Ely Turnpike Act of 1763.[3] By this time carriages had become the sign of pretension to gentility, and the river journey from Cambridge to Ely seemed rather unfitting to the dignity of the bishop and his fellows. The route chosen took the 'right-hand' way from Milton through Landbeach, ignoring the village centre and the Roman road, until it took up the line of the latter at Goose Hall. Before it crossed the Landbeach–Waterbeach road, it followed an old field path through Banworth Meadow in Landbeach. This had never been a right of way, and the field books jealously record it as

[1] See Fig. 4, p. 20.
[2] CUL Queens', Cd 26a, Cd 63.
[3] 3 Geo. III, cap. 36: cf. 5 Geo. III, cap. 79. The preamble to the second Act shows that flooding was still rendering the road impassable.

'path by permission' ('*semita ex permissione*'). Thus the route was longer than it would have been through the centre of Landbeach. It brought undesirable traffic and possible thieves to the least-guarded extremes of Landbeach commons. To both insult and injury were added demands on the parishioners to maintain the road by parish labour.

When Masters' legal battle against parish labour appeared to have been successful, another Act was passed, into which a clause was inserted without the knowledge of the interested party in Landbeach, and the parishioners found themselves faced with a doubled demand for parish labour as well as tolls when they were going about their traditional ways in the fen.[1]

At the enclosure of Landbeach the commissioners intended to improve the Roman road from the Impington–Milton highway into a carriage road, but this was never carried out. In 1854 Worts' Trustees, as lords of the Manor of Brays, called a public meeting and floated an appeal to carry out such improvement by voluntary contributions from interested parties. Only the rector of Landbeach, John Tinkler, joined them, contributing £60. The trustees gave something over £500, and the road was improved only from Cockfen Lane end to the farmhouses. The rest of the road, the Mereway, still remains an over-grown green track, passable when not too wet.

The Parliamentary Enclosures of the three parishes were occasions for considerable straightening and improvement of internal parish roads.[2] Difficulties were greatest in Cottenham Fens where the extent of the ground to be divided up meant that considerable stretches of new per-manent road had to be made on peaty foundations. Jacob Sanderson remembered the difficulties:

For the first few years the roads were in a bad state. In the second spring we were set with only a plough in the cart with two horses; could not turn round; slid the plough to Top Moor; had to draw the cart backwards to the Poplar Tree; from that to the Engine Drain. Put 1300 loads of gravel besides bushes and straw.[3]

Enclosure and the metalling of the roads meant a concentration on fewer and better. Much of the Roman road in Landbeach, and the old Cambridge Way from Waterbeach to Milton, were ploughed up, while the improved turnpike carried the traffic of both of them.

[1] LPC, Collectanea.
[2] Landbeach: 47 Geo. III, sess. 2, cap. 55, 1807: Waterbeach; 53 Geo. III, cap. 107, 1813: Cottenham: 5 Vic. sess. 2, cap. 3, 1842. The Awards are dated 1813, 1818, and 1847 respectively.
[3] Notebook.

COMMUNICATIONS – THE RAILWAY

The Great Eastern Railway line, which opened in 1845, put Waterbeach directly in touch with the London market.[1] When Clay wrote in 1859 he recorded that a hundred gallons of milk went daily to London. But the smaller market gardens relied much more on the local market at Cambridge. Local carriers collected (and still do) garden produce, no matter how small the quantities, left out for them by the producer, and in due course returned the payment. This scheme, simplicity itself for the grower, has enabled small-scale garden production to continue as a practical commercial proposition through all the farming depressions since Clay's time.

The fruit growers of the three parishes found a local market of increasing importance to them after 1870, when the Chivers family began to make jam in a barn in Histon. The growth of the firm meant there was always a market of last resort, but it was not the place to expect high prices as small growers competed with professional buyers in fixing the prices of very perishable goods. The railway connections to London and the Midland industrial areas offered a more profitable opportunity, and around 1900 a scheme was afoot to connect Cottenham to the railway at Oakington by a single-track light railway. If carried out this would have made a great difference to the appearance of the village, as the track was planned to run right down the main street, negotiating corners by crossing over the full width of the road and back. The motor-car soon made this scheme unnecessary; it demanded metalling which drove the mud from the village streets; and brought the intrusive dormitory estates from Cambridge, which are slowly engulfing the old villages.

[1] *VCH Cambs.*, vol. II, p. 132.

FEN, MEADOW AND PASTURE

In the Fens, vegetation, like drainage, was very much the resultant of human effort and human neglect on the natural environment. Unfortunately the medieval documents give us no very precise idea as to the amount and kind of the tree cover in any part of the area, but hints and fragments only. Examination of vegetable remains and pollen analysis have shown that the old car fen developed a cover of buckthorns, guelder rose, sallow and dwarf willow in the mixed sedge, just as at Wicken today, and that it also contained in abundance alders which have been mysteriously reluctant to re-establish themselves at Wicken.[1] Alders appear from time to time in the documents for our area; early in the fifteenth century there is a grant in Landbeach of a cottage with three acres of land and an alder ground.[2] By this time timber was precious. With further neglect of the fen, birch, oak and ash colonise. On the fen islands the larger trees would find life easier. Elmeney is interpreted by Reaney as 'Elm Island'.[3] The Ministers' Accounts of 37 Hen. VIII mention at Denney:

...the great Grovette on the Backside of the Orchard there and the little Grovette behind the Kiln house there with all large Oakes, Ashes and Elms or Witch Elms upon the premises or any part thereof growing and being beyond the growth of twenty years.[4]

Nearly all the references to trees in the court rolls are concerned with conservation, presentation for cutting trees down without licence being quite common from the fourteenth century.[5] This may of course reflect an improvement in building standards rather than a change in vegetation. Very early in the court Book of Waterbeach cum Denney (22 Ed. III) a close of two acres of marsh is granted 'Excepting all trees thereon growing or which should grow, saving the lop of the said trees for hedgbote.' Much later, 7 Eliz., there is a ban on the sale of wood out of Chittering. In 1610, one of the charges against John Yaxley, steward of the Manor of Water-

---

[1] The National Trust, *A Guide to Wicken Fen* (Cambridge, 1950).
[2] CCCC, XXXV, 123, 2 Hen. IV.
[3] TL 503695. The name survives as Elm Hill, a small field on Causeway End Farm.
[4] Cf. CUL, EDR, A 14/1. WPC, *Masters vs. Standley*. One is tempted to read Denney as 'Oak Island' in contrast to Elmeney.
[5] E.g. CCCC, XXXV, 121, 2 Ed. III, felling and selling five trees out of a bondage tenement; felling and carrying off, 'two ashes, two willows, and two plums' ('*duos ffraxinos, duos salices at duos prunarios*'), CCCC, XXXV, 126, 22 Hen. VI, felling of two trees called 'Wyches'; such entries are numerous in all the series of court rolls for this area.

beach cum Denney, then in royal hands again, was misappropriation and felling of timber:

Mr. Yaxley hath already and without licence caused all the wood as well timber as other with green upon one copyhold close of his within the said manor to be felled down and that he hath bargained with those that bought it of him, to root it all up, whereof some part is digged up already, and the rest they make account shall be.[1]

Most of the recorded plantings of trees, except in recent times, are of willows on the banks by the rivers and ditches. Their main purpose was to hold the peaty soil together more securely against the strain of flood-waters. The loppings could provide incidental income and were subject to tithe. In 1430 Master Adam's lease laid it down that he should wall, defend and surround the garden of the manor at his own expense with the lopps and underwood of the willows and other trees growing in the same garden.[2] In 1549 Richard Kirby was accused of appropriating a row of willows in Landbeach, set and planted by the town to defray expenses from the profits of lopping. Henry Clifford concerned with the tithe of lopping has left a note in the Parish Field Book of Landbeach:

Item; at my riding into Waterbeach with Dowse I found willows planted on the great Eye Bank in number xiij these are young and small trees. 1587.
  Item; on the Stone Rude bank there were some great and other smaller in number xxvij.
  Item; on the little Eye bank there were finde great willows estimated xix score in number.

Scripsi 1587 novembris 14
Henry Clifford.[3]

While there are many scattered references to the illegal felling of trees, a few to plantings on banks and around manorial enclosures, and a few identifications of the kind of tree, there is little direct documentary evidence of forest clearance.[4] A charter from the mid-twelfth century refers to 'a bovate of land within the boundaries of Landbeach, the one which is called "*Terra de busco*"' ('*unam bovatam terre in terratoris de Landbec Illam scilicet que appelatur "terra de busco"*').[5] This might well refer to forest clearance: it might instead be an attempt to translate 'Frith Fen'.

Field archaeology points strongly to a phase of forest clearance in making the first three open fields. Romano-British finds, which appear in profusion on the gravels of Landbeach and the fens of the area, are very scarce indeed on the gault. Thus the soils where we would expect the

---

[1] PRO SP 14/57/43.　　　　　　　　　[2] CCCC, XXXV, 110.
[3] CCCC, XXXV, 194. LPC, Field Book.
[4] E.g. *Common Rights*, pp. 206–7, the lords and tenants in Cottenham 'may plant and set any kind of Wood or Willows, Osiers, Sallows, or other Wood upon that part or parts of the banks or ditches to him or them limited', and may take from it.
[5] CCCC, XXXV, 12.

40

heaviest vegetation to be, appear to have been left alone in the Roman period, and the work of tackling them passed to successors. One has the impression that the first settlers chose sites where a Roman farm had left an area where quick, easy breaking in of the land was possible, and from this, later generations slowly moved out into the less tractable but rewarding clays of the forest. The charters of Landbeach suggest that a good deal of this was still fairly recent in the twelfth century in that village. The only other hint we have near this area comes from Dry Drayton. Here there is a twelfth-century record of the division of lands in field and meadow which had long been out of cultivation.[1] It is difficult to see in this other than an early halt to assarting and abandonment of assarted lands, but not of reversion to forest. One would very much like to know whether this was due to demographic change, or to the disturbances of the conquest, and whether nearby villages suffered a similar cycle.[2]

There must be some time-lag between the creation of the fields and their appearance in charters, especially when the number of these is few for the period. The extensive development of the ploughland of Landbeach as shown in Domesday would indicate very vigorous forest clearance there before the late eleventh century. Probably the conjunction of population pressure that called for assarting, and the floods that would have struck Waterbeach arable long before they drove the monks from Elmeney to Denney, produced an intensity of colonisation in Landbeach of which we have no direct record.

THE GRASSLANDS

The making of the landscape in the grasslands of these villages was a continuous process through most of the Middle Ages. With the rise of the water-table in the late Roman period almost all of what were to be the medieval grasslands would have begun to revert to car fen. The areas of future grass least affected would have been Winfold Common in Water-beach, Banworth Meadow in Landbeach, and Bullocks Haste and the Cow Pastures in Cottenham. But none of these was immune to flooding, and in none of them were there Roman farms which lasted continuously right to the end.[3]

If we take the popular definition of the fens, and divide them into the two normal classes, the peat fen, and the silt fen near the sea, then we are dealing with only the former in this area, and are excluding not merely the pastures just mentioned, but also areas like Frith Fen in Landbeach which

[1] ECA, p. 162.
[2] Cf. VCH Cambs., II, p. 53.
[3] Bromwich, 'Freshwater Flooding Along the Fen Margins', in Phillips (ed.), The Fenland in Roman Times, p. 125.

were clearly fen to the fenmen of the past. There is a description of the
Fens by an anonymous 'Fenman' in the Book of Sewers in the Cambridge
University Archives. This is part of an argument for drainage, written,
according to the internal evidence, not earlier than 1618–19:

The Fennes are lowe groundes drowned and overflowne with the abundance of waters
falling from the Hilles towards the Staye and they be of three sortes & well above XXtie
miles square.

    1. as are nearest to the Hilles & in the best parte, soonest drowned, and soonest drayned,
& the best soyle receyving, refreshing, & as it were manured by the overfloweing Water
from the Hilles & higher meadowes.

    2. The second are meere Fennes whose soil is commonly mare & being further from
the head Rivers do yield Turfe & Haffes which swimmeth.[1]

    3. I may alsoe accompte for the third kinde marishes next to the sea for they are the
lowest but by the floweing of the Sea & the Silte left uppon them they are now heightened
and Sandye, of these some are imbanked and some not imbanked.

There are marshes next the Sea and Marish Fennes, and in the Fennes of each kinde
imbancked and not imbancked, & those which be saved from drowning with banckes doe
make the other fennes (not imbancked) both to be the deeper groundes, and longer to
remain soe then otherwayes they would bee.[2]

The pastures listed above, and other areas like the Holme Meadow in
Cottenham, or the nearby Great Mare in Longstanton, would have been
united to the fen in the wettest periods in the Middle Ages, but in spite of
their names they were never inundated long enough to form substantial
peat soil. How much peat was formed in such marginal fen areas as these,
or the old moors of Histon, Landbeach and Cottenham, we do not know.
They were 'soonest drained', but in this area the natural geology had not
given them 'the best soil'.

It was not possible to use only land immune to flooding for permanent
pasture. Even the arable might be submerged in part: it might even in part
revert to fen for a time, and become, for agricultural purposes, an area of
hazard. But the normal risks of agriculture, under medieval conditions
were always present in far greater measure than today.[3] Changes in the
water-table could mean that the only hope of recovery lay in immediate
greater expense in draining and banking at the very time when the income
from which these costs should be borne was reduced:

And because in times past many wet years happened together and the inhabitants being
then very poor, for that in those times their benefit and advantage out of the fens was very
small and some years nothing at all, by reason of the great abundance of the moisture that

---

[1] Haffes or hassocks are small tufted mounds of grass or reed which flourish on the surface of a bog and
make it so treacherous.

[2] CUA, Sewers, L. 80. I am grateful to the University Archivist and to Mrs C. Hall for permission to
use the latter's transcript.

[3] ECA, p. 241 for flooded arable; CCCC, XXXV, 145 for reversion – see Chapter 2 above; ECA,
p. 372 shows a fair selection of risks – see Chapter 2.

then happened, for in one moist summer and a hard winter following they lost more by death and drowning of the cattle than they gained by the fens in three years. The said inhabitants for their more ease and mitigation of charges (which they were evil able to endure) and because that every poor person that had part in the fens was not able presently at every beck and rage of water to disburse money towards the repair of the banks bridges ditches and drains, which at that time were most chargeable to maintain and notwith-standing must of necessity be done...[1]

If the arable was relatively rarely affected, except in Waterbeach, the fenland frontier ebbed and flowed, the areas of the different kinds of use of the fen changed, and progress and improvement could not be hoped for as a steady forward march. But cumulative change in the land use there was, from the days when the car fen offered little but hunting, fowling and fishing, to clearing and mowing, first for coarse fen vegetation, then for the lushest hay and richest summer pasture, to ploughland for oats and then for wheat, and then more and more for intensive market gardening. At every change some profited, but some were displaced, losing their livelihoods.

When Hayward made his great Survey of the fens in 1635, he estimated the extent of the fens in this area as:

Cottenham	2,296½ acres
Cottenham and Rampton	550 acres
Waterbeach	3,374 acres
Total	6,220½ acres

Atkyns, in 1604, had noted of Landbeach: 'They have little fen ground but between the town and Deney be good sheepcourses, only by Chare-fenn side they have a long sponge of marsh ground, on the face thereof it is somewhat marish, but underneath gravel.'[2]

Hayward's Survey, then, is likely to have underestimated the extent of the fens in this area. Both these surveys were made at one of the wetter periods.

At the enclosure of Cottenham in the 1840s, apart from old enclosures (i.e. the village crofts and little more than the pastures taken out of the commons in the sixteenth century) and the Adventurers' lands, the grasslands are classified in two groups, as shown in table 1 (see p. 44).

At 1,576 acres, and 11 poles, the open fields of Cottenham were scarcely larger than the mow fens, and very much smaller than the feeding commons. The old enclosures, and this includes the very extensive tofts attached to most of the houses and the empty closes used as home paddocks, added up to 913 acres, 2 rods, and 33 poles, thus making

[1] CRO 65 T 1 & 2, Transcript of the Royal Survey of Over, Aug. 17 Eliz.
[2] Wells, *History of the Drainage*, vol. II, p. 177, for Hayward's Survey; BM Harleian 5011 for Atkyns; cf. CUL, EDR A/1/8.

a grand total of 7,037 acres, 2 rods, and 23 poles. Thus grass was then dominant in the landscape and agriculture of Cottenham. Most of this area represented centuries of reclamation or improvement of fen, and on the eve of the parliamentary enclosure most of it was still used jointly by the holders of the 169 common rights.[1]

TABLE I. *The old grasslands of Cottenham*

	Acres	Rods	Poles			
1 Mow fens						
Smithy Fen	1,169	0	30			
The Lotts	271	1	20			
The Holme (Meadow)	125	1	2	1,565	3	12
2 Feeding commons						
Setchell from bridge						
to drain	276	3	28			
Setchell further side						
of drain	202	0	24			
Chare Fen and Mitchell						
Hill	899	2	8			
Green End Cow Pasture	466	2	2			
Church End Cow Pasture	266	1	37			
Bullocks Harste	90	0	17			
Great North Fen	453	2	35			
Little North Fen	266	0	32			
Ditto (Mr Linton's						
Sheepwalk)	56	2	14			
Rampton Bank	3	3	26	2,982	0	23

With the Hundred Rolls we get some topographical detail; the bounds of Cottenham Fens are given:

the fen COTEHAM begins at CLAYBREGE and extends up to the great bridge of HALDERHETH and from the said bridge by the great bank [river?] up to CHAR' and from the CHAR' extends up to TYLLINGE'.[2]

The great bridge at Halderheth is clearly Aldreth High Bridge, which is reported as having collapsed sixteen years before. The great bank from there would take us along the Old West on the south side to Chear Fen (le CHAR'). The TYLLINGE, the Old Tillage or Landbeach Tilling, is the Car Dyke. This entry shows that the great stretch of the fens of Cottenham was the most impressive topographical feature of the area in the thirteenth century: their extent was the same on the eve of enclosure, but by then centuries of feeding would have smoothed the turf of the hards

---

[1] Cottenham Award, CRO Q/RDc66.
[2] *Rot. Hund.*, vol. II, p. 410; Appendix B.

and reduced their coarse grasses, while centuries of turf-digging would have turned Chear Fen, the Delphs, to a lake or bog.

The wet fen, if left to itself, soon develops a thick cover. To the grasses and peat, reeds, sedges and flags, it adds shrubs and trees, in car fen.[1] This 'primeval' fen is improved by drainage and mowing, or where it is dry enough in summer, simply by mowing and feeding. Once the scrubby growth of bushes and small trees is cleared, control of the intervals between mowing determines which crop develops at the expense of the others, reeds, sedge, flags, or grass. The reverse process also happens: if water prevents the mowing, the vegetation moves back again towards car. A passage in the Survey of Willingham in 1356 illustrates this:

And there are there 15 acres of mowing meadow which are worth 15s., price per acre 12d., and no more because the said meadow lies under water, and for the greater part is mixed with flags. And there are there 30 acres of 'Fennmadwe' which are nothing worth by the year, in that they always lie under water and no profit can be got from them.[2]

Place-names enable us to see a little of the later stages of 'improvement' at work in the medieval Fens. In all three parishes a Frith Fen is mentioned more than once in the earlier court and account rolls. In Cottenham it appears in one of our earliest rolls,[3] and before disappearing, becomes more frequent in the first half of the fourteenth century: '3 rods in the Frith Fen in the First Cast' ('*iij rodas in le Frithfen in primo cast*'): 'one acre in the Frith Fen lying in the Threerodcast' ('*una acra in le Frithfen iacens in le Threrodcast*').[4] These two entries would seem to identify it with Smithy Fen, or part of it.[5] Reaney quotes Atkyns' Survey: 'The Isles of Norney and Thorney have certain low grounds called Fryths on the skirts of the highland belonging to them…on which they gather winter fodder', and says that this common fenland term must mean brushwood or undergrowth.[6] Only in Landbeach among our three villages, does a fen so named survive into the modern period. Since the Frith Fen in Cottenham was being mown in the thirteenth century the process was fairly recent, and the mentions in the fourteenth century, mean that the battle against the rising water-table was not wholly lost. The alternative name Smithe or Smithy, meaning smooth, in obvious contrast to Frith, represents success in clearance.[7] One enclosure in Denney Low Grounds appears as Charles Frith[8] (Ceorl's Frith?), which becomes romanticised

---

[1] See above, p. 39.
[2] PRO E/143/9/2.
[3] CUL Queens', Cd 5, 1282–3 (Page) or 1281–2 (Aston).
[4] *Ibid.*, Dd 1, 1346, and Ad 26, 1348.
[5] See Fig. 1, p. xii.
[6] Reaney, *Place-names of Cambridgeshire*, p. 180.
[7] *Ibid.*, p. 152. Cf. 'The Smeeth' near Wisbech.
[8] See Fig. 6, p. 87.

into Chalice Fruit (Challis Fruit). Similarly we saw that Reaney interprets 'Mitchell Hill' as deriving from 'micel-leah', meaning 'large clearing', again recalling the development from the untouched fen.[1]

The division between mow fens and feeding commons in Cottenham was not a simple by-product of the improvement of the fens and drainage. For the mow fens, winter flooding is a decided asset, giving much heavier hay and a lusher aftermath. The richness of the summer pastures was probably Cottenham's most precious natural resource up until the middle of the nineteenth century. But the North Fens could be wet, too, and Setchel as wet as any; Chear Fen probably the worst of all. Jacob Sanderson, who remembered the land before enclosure, said that Chear Fen had been used for digging turf for fuel and that the greater part of it had become a bog.[2] He remembered the first man to cross it on a horse. Setchel was a wild-fowling area where the fenmen moved about in boats. It would seem that as the dominance of cattle increased in the village, and as the older Fenland occupations were squeezed out with the improvement of the car fen, those fens still too wet for regular mowing, became feeding commons. What had long been one of their subsidiary functions became their only one. It took steam drainage, which came in 1846, to make them more than summer lands except in favoured parts. Here the local topo- graphy helped them to take their new role; each fen had parts that were above the reach of normal winter floods, islands of refuge, enabling cattle to be risked for pasture there. These fens were part of the 'hards', whereas those areas which were 'summer grounds' only, were called 'low fens' in the local terminology. Thus Smithy Fen contained both low fen and hards.

Any theoretical scheme of the development of assarting and improve- ment of the fen, then, has to take into account minute variations in local topography. On the edge of the fens two or three feet difference in altitude can make all the difference in the type of fen and its use. So, too, can the micro-geology; both Setchel and Chear fens are on gravel. The relief, geology, and distance from the village in Cottenham of different parts of the fen, enabled the ordermakers and fen reeves to develop highly specialised sub-divisions as they produced orders to solve immediate practical problems that arose from time to time.

In that part of Waterbeach known as The Hollow,[3] an area still sensitive to changes in the water-table, the various uses for land on the fen

[1] But see p. 13 for a different possible meaning for this name.
[2] This fen appears on the seventeenth-century maps as a main feature of the parish: e.g. Bedford Level Collection in CRO, R. 59.31.40.1., 'A Generall Plotte and Discription of the Fennes...compassed by Mr. Wm. Hayward, Anno 1604...An exact copy from the original, by Mr. Tayler Smyth, Anno Dom. 1727.' In the series of printed maps issued by Hondius and J. Blaeu in that century it appears as a heart-shaped area called 'The Delphs'. See VCH Hunts., vol. III (1936), pp. 291ff., 'Maps of the Fenland'.
[3] See Fig. 6, p. 87.

edge existed side by side, and almost certainly competed. Arable never finally won, and would probably never have had a place there had not the shortage of reliably dry ground in Waterbeach forced the people to be prepared to gamble on floods as other farmers gamble on weather. It was never possible to classify The Hollow in the way Cottenham lands were all classified as mow fens or feeding grounds.[1]

In the Court Book of Waterbeach cum Denney, from 1332 to 1354 there are nine entries relating to The Hollow which specify the kind of land. Of these one is meadow, one mare, and the rest marsh (Latin *mariscum*, meaning fen). There was also one reference to 'land' ('*terre*'): this may well have been arable. In 1354 an inquest was held to decide that an acre of arable in The Hollow was not parcel of the fen. In the same year were mentioned two arable plots there, each of 3 acres 1½ rods, and both were counted in the demesne. Mentions of meadow, fen and land come frequently in subsequent years, with meadow the most frequent. In 1371 there was a change; we find an entry relating to Rushfen del Holough. In the next year we find both Lugfen and Rushfenne in The Hollow. In 1414 we find Rusholough and Lugholough. These names occur with great frequency from then on. In this reign the only variation is several mentions of Ferne, or Fur, or Further, Hollow. In 1547 there is an Osier Holt in The Little Hollow. In 1609 an additional name begins to crop up, Reed Hollow, and there are also references to Fodderfennes in Hollow. Here most possible uses for land existed side by side, and the holdings seem to have been mostly very small plots, in severalty as demesne land, reclaimed from the lord's waste.

In discussing Frith Fen in Landbeach Reaney quotes from the 1621 Book of Sewers, D, to illustrate the different uses of fen: 'Fen grounds…of several natures. That is to say some mowing grounds some feeding grounds some used for digging the necessary firing for the Inhabitants there as flags hassocks and turves and a great part whereon there groweth reed and sedge.'[2] All such uses and more were made of the common fens in our villages until the final enclosure, and the fens were so extensive that it was from them that both lord and peasant frequently found a surplus for sale, either of the produce, or of the use of a limited area.

---

[1] Cf. PRO Requests 2, 21/17 'also the gate of twenty of his own proper bullocks in Cottenham Fens from May Day to Michaelmas *if the said fens should be dry so long*'.

[2] Reaney, *Place-names of Cambridgeshire*, p. 179.

FISHING AND FOWLING

Fowling and fishing were probably of greater importance early on, although fowling retained some of its possibilities right up to the nineteenth century. Fishing figures prominently in the Domesday entries for the area: the two manors in Waterbeach respectively provided 450 eels and 1000 eels and 12*d.* from the tribute of fish. This was from very small manors, with 3 villeins and 13 bordars, and 8 bordars and 6 cottars respectively. The second manor was only worth 20*s.* altogether. In Cottenham the Manor of Crowlands provided 500 eels and 12*d.* from the tribute of fish, and Roger's manor 150 eels. In Landbeach no produce from fishing is mentioned. The relative importance of wet fen is clearly reflected by these figures. Waterbeach was the only true fen island of the three.

Unlike Domesday, the Hundred Rolls account for fishing, not in numbers of eels and values of fish, but in numbers of fisheries and their rentable values. The abbot of Crowland had one in Cottenham worth 40*s.* Robert de Lisle, who, like the abbot, kept five hides of meadow, pasture and fen in demesne, had one worth 36*s.* The fishery of the Manor of Burdeleys was worth only 4*s.*, as was that of Pelhams. Some Waterbeach fisheries were named. The Templars held Mareware for 1 mark, and Garentre,[1] worth 18*s.* Dyonisia de Munchensey (Waterbeach proper as distinct from Denney) had a 40*s.* fishery. In Landbeach there is no mention of fishery or fen.

There is an inquiry into the Crowlands fisheries in Cottenham in the Court Roll for 1391 printed by Miss Page.[2] The abbot had half of two meres called Fyltyngmere and Lokmondmere, except that the Burdeleys tenants had each of them for nine nights: he also had half of a certain fishery called Brodelode and Newlode.[3] The above were worked by Robert Cadman who was ordered to show on what terms. This uncertainty might be due to the custom of normally letting fisheries in Cottenham on very long-term leases. He also had half a fish weir on the high bank a furlong west of Charcote, and called of old, Almyngeweresen. This had been swept away by a great flood, and so brought in no rent to the lord. Order was therefore given to re-build it by the next court. At the next court seven men, including one from Histon were presented for fishing in Cottenham commons where they had no common. There must have been a common right of fishing outside the several fisheries. Four

---

[1] Garentre (later corrupted to Garden Tree) was on the boundary of Midload, on the site of the later toll-house and lock; TL 508658. For the Domesday I have used the text in *VCH Cambs.*, vol. I, p. 359f., for the Hundred Rolls, the Record Commission's vol. II, pp. 453–6 and 409–11.

[2] *ECA*, p. 416.

[3] These fisheries cannot be located with precision, but their general location is discussed below.

years later an ordinance was made forbidding non-commoners to fish without a licence. If this was enforced it would have detracted from the ability of the fens to support poor and landless men. These were comparatively lawless times, and the measure represents one of the last efforts to re-assert detailed seigneurial control in Cottenham. At the St James Court in 1413 there were twenty presentments for illegal fishing.

In January 1326 the lord's several fishery was let for 21s. until Michaelmas. This was in a time of vacancy, the next lease of a fishery, again to two men, was for three years, and 200 'pikerellos' of twelve inches long were taken as entry fine. In 1339 William Pepys and two others were distrained for failing to give their hundred 'pikerellos' in the second year of a lease they had taken up eight years previously.[1] In the very earliest Account Roll (probably of 1257–8 according to Aston) 200 pike were sent to London for the use of the lord. Fish were on occasions sent from Cottenham to restock the ponds at Crowlands.[2]

Waterbeach, much closer to the river bank, and with much of the parish a maze of meres and little waterways where the Cam of those days meandered, had much more important fisheries. Elrington's lease in the sixteenth century helps to identify some of the sites.[3] Marewere mentioned in the Hundred Rolls was in Stretham parish, as was another, Foorde Were. These were presumably on the Cam where it ran through the inter-common area north of Waterbeach, possibly Stretham Mere itself. The same document identifies Bechewere with Clayhithe. The other fishery at Garentre in the Hundred Rolls, is still shown on Jonas Moore's map of 1706, although in its later corrupt form Garden Tree.[4] It was at the junction of Joist Fen and Midload, where the old toll house later stood. The Court Rolls in 28 Ed. III mention a fishery with Weloode and Blakeffen Lake. Three years later they mention fisheries at 'Newlode, Foullode, Blackfen Lake and Half of Little, that is to say from Stonrout unto the Hyes'. In 1427–8 there is a mention of fisheries of 'Horningsea Were unto Bechwere', and from 'Bechwere unto Garentre Were'. This would mean that the convenient stretch of the Cam near the village was engrossed in two demesne fisheries.[5]

In spite of the complete absence of fisheries from Landbeach in the Hundred Rolls fishing occurs in the records of the fourteenth century, perhaps not surprisingly in view of the rise in the water-table. The Extent of Agnes de Bray of 1316, mentions a common fishery worth 2s. At the 1370 Leet of John, Duke of Lancaster, John de Queye and Robert Aubri

[1] *ECA*, p. 379.
[2] CUL Queens' Ad. 29, and Cd. 15.
[3] WPC, Various Documents; cf. EE 12/3/31 Hen. VIII, and Bodleian MS. Gough Cambs., 69.
[4] Bedford Level Collection in CRO, R 59.31.40.13, and Q/RDc. 66.
[5] WPC, WcD.

were presented 'that they had fished in the common fishery with dragnets, contrary to the custom of the town and thus had done great damage' (' *quod piscaverunt in communi piscaro cum Draggis contra consuetudinem ville, et sic fecerunt magnam destructionem* '). In 1362 there were fifteen presentments for breaking the lord's soil with fish-traps. In 1407 John Abell from Waterbeach was caught fishing at Fens End in Landbeach with unlicensed nets. (One of the Orders for Waterbeach cum Denney bans fishing with unlawful nets in 1580–1.) The fishermen do not seem to have respected the bounds and regulations of others: if John de Queye looks like a foreigner from across the river, Roger Sandre junior of Landbeach was one of twenty caught illegally fishing in Cottenham in 1328. But fishing could give rise to obstructions both to navigation and to the free passage of the waters. Fishers not only dug ditches and erected weirs, but also deliberately created artificial shallows. Among the Orders made at a Crowlands Court for cottenham in 1550 was: 'That no fisher put in any mud or sand in mere, dyke or high lake.'[1] This theme is continued in the Orders of 1639:

It is ordered that no person using fishing shall neither lay nor set any engine or net within the fen side of the banks to take any fish nor within ten poles of any Lakes end or in or upon any gull or Breach that shall or may happen upon any man's banks Common place or stopping, in or about the bounds of Cottenham, except they first hire them of the Town Officers…

But in the final versions of these orders, in the last two fen books, which cover the period from the late eighteenth century to enclosure, there is no mention of either fishing or fowling.[2]

Fishers were not the only culprits, but they were the most common; fowlers could be even more destructive. Like other common rights, fowling was customarily limited to supplementing the sustenance of the commoner's household, but it could easily, either through poverty or the expansion of market demand, be developed into a profession. In this area at least, the man who exploited a common right without limit tended to be the most unpopular local figure, and the one whom the local courts fought most strongly to restrain. Fowling before the days of firearms was by its very nature a hidden and almost silent occupation. Little trace has been left in our medieval records of what would seem to have been a traditional fenland way of life. One fowler emerges briefly when his neat is impounded by Kirby in 1549: 'the said poor man being a very poor man living off catching of fowls'.[3] To pastoralists, the fowler might seem

[1] CCCC, XXXV, 145; 121; 126. CUL Queens' Ad. 36: CRO Francis Papers, Crowlands Court Rolls, 4 Ed. VI.

[2] *Common Rights*, p. 232; fen books in the possession of Mr M. Haird of Cottenham.

[3] CCCC, XXXV, 194, 'Injuries done by Mayster Richard Kyrbye by pounding of the inhabitants cattle at Landbeach.'

like Cain to Abel. An entry in the Crowlands Court Roll for 1514 reads:

that Thomas Rogers broke the banks or shores of the river, by which the water came into the common marsh lying there and submerged it so that the lord's tenants lost their use of the marsh, to the damage of those tenants, and further they say that the same Thomas placed in the said marsh a certain engine or instrument for catching fowls. And lest his engine should be destroyed he would not permit the tenants' animals to be depastured there, but drove them away from thence, to the damage of the said tenants.[1]

This appears very much like the description of the building of a duck decoy.[2] The lawlessness of the lonely fowler has a long history in the fens. The wildness of the fowler's ways was remembered by Jacob Sanderson:

There were a great many water fowls in the Fens. Before the enclosure many people made their livings by shooting them in their gunning boats in the nights. There was a dispute between William Munsey of Cottenham and a Wilburton man about some fowls. Munsey, by accident was shot dead. No stranger was allowed to shoot in the Fens, but the townspeople.[3]

This echoes the words of an Order in the Waterbeach Court Book in 1580–1: 'That no stranger hunt or fowl within the manor without licence.' In the Cottenham Agreement of 1596 Hinde is given 'Liberty to Hawk, Hunt and Fowl, not excluding the inhabitants from fowling there.'[4]

The fowls get some mention in the rolls. At the Waterbeach Leet of 1522 one of the orders was that 'none take any fowl, viz. cranes, butters [bitterns], bustards, and heronshaws within the commons, and sell the same out of the Lordship unless he first offer them to the lord of the manor to buy'.[5]

Bitterns were already nearly extinct in the fens in Albert Pell's time in the middle of the nineteenth century. The descriptions of the fenmen that he saw fowling, in his autobiography, are the elegy of a lost world.[6] What centuries of hunting by the wily fenman with his ingenious nets, snares and decoys could not wipe out, and what for the most part survived the popularity of fowling with ever-improving firearms and the massacres of the deadly cumbrous punt-guns, the bird life of the fens, dwindled and almost disappeared after steam drainage, enclosure, and the ploughing of the land.

[1] CUL Queens', Fd 6.
[2] For the best description of a duck decoy, see *Draining*, p. 160.
[3] Notebook.
[4] *Common Rights*, p. 205.
[5] WPC, WcD, 14 Hen. VIII; quoted in *Waterbeach*, p. 14; for Ordinance see under 23 Eliz. in the same court book.
[6] *The Reminiscences of Albert Pell*, ed. T. Mackay (1908).

TURF

If water was the great menace to the medieval peasant in this area in his cultivation of the land, it must also have been a great danger to his personal comfort. Fortunately the fens provided him with the quickest remedy for a soaking – a plentiful supply of firing. Wood for firing must have become less and less available as the fens were improved (as in Cottenham, for instance, Frith Fen became le Smithe Fen). But there is an order against the sale of underwood in Chittering in the Court Book of Waterbeach as late as 6 Hen. VIII.

The mainstay of the peasant hearth, however, was turf. Denson claimed that this was so in Waterbeach until enclosure: 'But a few years ago we could dig our own firing, now the common is enclosed, and we were forgotten in the division of the spoil.'[1]

Miss Page quotes an Agreement of 1344[2] between the lords of Cottenham regulating the cutting of turf in the marsh of Cottenham. Free tenants were to have enough for 'husbote' according to the size of their holding, holders of a full servile land were to have enough for a stack 21 turves high, 4 broad, and 36 feet long. The reductions in scale for the lesser tenants are interesting, not being fully proportionate. For half a servile land 30 feet were allowed, for a quarter, 24 feet, for a croftman 15 feet, and a cottager 10 feet. The restriction does not seem to have much immediate effect: in 1348 forty-three villeins including Thomas and John Pepys were presented for over-digging and for selling the produce illegally out of the manor. Regulations in Waterbeach were very similar in that every commoner could dig sufficient in Joist Fen[3] for his own household, but he had to stack them in the fen, and carry them home before selling any. None without licence were to be sold outside the manor. Presentations for breach of these regulations were very frequent. In Landbeach most of the early remaining court rolls include presentments for breach of customs of turbary. In 1327 there is a case of over-digging to the number of 6,000 and another of 1,000. In 1332 John Tebaud and Robert Attefen were presented for choosing their place to dig in the marsh before the lord had chosen, 'contrary to the lord's liberty'. As well as stealing the lord's corn, John Frerer, the lord's reeve two years before, had misused his turves:

Item they say that the same man kept a foreign woman in the lord's bakehouse at the lord's expense for how long they know not.

Item that the same John sent a cartload of the lord's turves value vid. to the house of John de Waldeseef at Westwyk where Milsent his concubine was staying.[4]

---

[1] Denson, *A Peasant's Voice*, p. 19.
[2] *ECA*, pp. 25–6, and 164–5. The date given by Miss Page is 1345, but it seems quite clearly 1344. Turf has its place in the early rolls, e.g. CUL Queens', Cd 15 (1271–2) where it is sent from Oakington to Cottenham, and Ed 2 (1281) accounts for the expenses of bringing it up from the fen.
[3] See Fig. 6, p. 87.   [4] CCCC, XXXV, 121; see Appendix B.

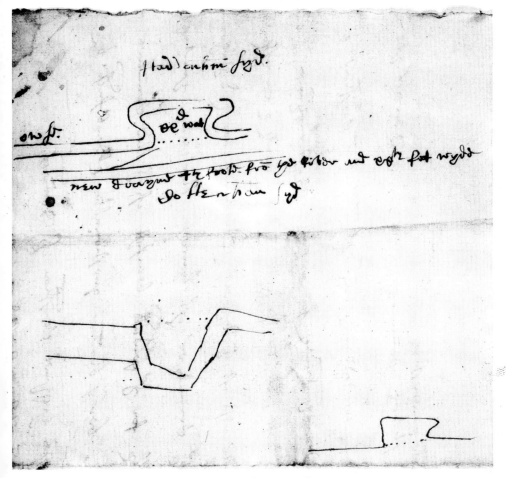

I. Sketch plans for straightening the Old West River: these rough sketches on the back of the record of the Commission of Sewers of 1618 are apparently attempts to illustrate the proposals to straighten the Old West River and to cut a catchwater drain parallel to it. The writing reads:

'Haddenham side.
Ouse   Twentypence water.
New Drain forty feet from the river and twenty feet wide.
Cottenham side.'

(source: BM Add. MS. 33466, fol. 305v).

II. The Cottenham fire of 1850: the mid-Victorian quality of the Cottenham street scene comes from the extensive rebuilding after this fire (source: *Illustrated London News*, 13 April 1850).

After the Black Death the presentations are maintained: in 1359 14 men were presented for digging 1,000 turves each in the marsh where they had no common, and 15 others for varying amounts. There were 21 cases in 1366, and the turf was forfeited in addition to the fines. The same number were presented in the following year. The three cases recorded in 1379 were for 1,000, 6,000, and again 6,000 excess turves.[1]

Very large amounts of turf and other firing appear in the Ministers' Accounts for Denney: in 1325–6 15,000 turves and 1,500 faggots were accounted for as sold. In the next year another 45,000 were made of the lops of willows and the crop of alders, and no less than 20,000 bundles.

Digging had to be closely controlled. The right of digging was strictly confined to commoners, and raiders from outside the village must have been easily detected. In a Cottenham Court of 1454–5 William Fenne of Landbeach, and others from Impington, Longstanton and Rampton were presented for going with their carts into the Turffen and breaking the lord's soil.[2] Even where the amount dug brought in profit to the lord (at Denney it was the ancient custom for commoners to pay the abbess $1\frac{1}{2}d$. for every 10 feet) it was necessary to struggle against over-digging.

Waterbeach Court Rolls have regular presentments especially for selling outside the manor without licence. There must have been a very ready market, and the quantities dug could easily have become a serious danger to banks and causeways. Many orders in the same court tried to control the export. In 1426–7 it was forbidden to sell common of turbary without licence. In the first year of Elizabeth it was ordained:

That none of the Inhabitants of the Manor shall give or sell any turves out of the same manor or marsh thereunto belonging after this said order under the pain of 3s. for every thousand turves; provided that it is lawful for any inhabitant of the same Manor yearly at his pleasure to give or sell one thousand of turves upon notice first given to the bailiff of the Manor aforesaid.

Next year the penalty was raised to 10s. Twenty-two years later digging was causing much concern. Diggers were ordered not to dig up any cartway, and to cut out their bars in the turfpit. The limit for sale was defined as a load in a year. In the following year this was again made 1,000, and the total right for a common re-affirmed as 10,000. Turf-cutting continued to be a valued right until it was banned by the Enclosure Act of 1813, because of the danger to drainage.[3] Even after this in spite of the ban it was the standard fuel on many cottage hearths.

[1] CUL Queens' Ad 26 for Cottenham in 1349; the Landbeach information is in CCCC, XXXV, 121 and 122 under regnal years; for Denney, see PRO SC6 766/13.
[2] CUL Queens' Dd 7.
[3] WPC, WcD, and 53 Geo. III, cap. 59.

FEN CROPS

Turf-cutting was not the only important extractive industry of the fens: they supplied all the main building materials except the best heavy timber, and iron nails, hinges and fastenings. Even some of the large timber could be provided from groves such as those at Denney, but the Crowlands accounts show timber repeatedly imported from Cambridge for major building works and for the bridge at Westwick. Oakington was able to supply a little. Sturbridge Fair, Midsummer Fair, and Barnwell are mentioned as sources in the fifteenth century. In 1442 the vicar of Oakington was employed to ride over as need arose to buy timber at the fair, and was paid 6*d.* for his pains. Lighter timber, *virgae*, was also bought in Cambridge at the same time, but this usually seems to have been available locally. Various kinds of thatching materials and earths were the bulk needs for medieval building, and these the fens produced in super-abundance.[1]

In 1325–6 the Minister's Accounts for Denney mention 1500 bundles of reeds sold for 15*s.*, and this is still far the best material for the body of thatching. An enormous amount of lower quality thatch was provided by the rough hay of the fens, probably containing reed and other coarse plants in its mixture. It was often bought and sold by the acre, as it stood. The quantities used suggest that it did not last long. In 1441–2 'Fenne thak' was bought at Cottenham for Oakington, but in 1455–6, when bought for rebuilding the hall and other buildings of the manor at Cottenham, it is called 'fodyr'. In the latter case it was in addition to 3,100 bundles of reeds. But even fenthack could be relatively expensive. In 1325–6 Denney spent 140 dayworks in cutting, gathering and bundling herbage in Tapping-moor[2] and making two stacks there, and another 40 for carrying these into the barnyard there for the thatching of various buildings and walls. The high labour cost was blamed on the lack of water; this may mean that the nearer grass was not long enough. Certainly, in the next year after gales had damaged the roofs 300 bundles of reed were used for repairs. This had been available in the previous year, 800 bundles of it, but was not used for the less important buildings, and with the 1,000 bundles cut in the new year, 1,500 were ready for sale. In the next account 400 bundles of reed and 20,000 bundles of sedge were supplied for the queen's use to Thomas de Eggesfield. While the manor was in the queen's hands a good deal of running down of stock took place, but essential repairs seem to have been kept up. Waterbeach fens could both meet needs, and provide substantial exports.[3] A very special quality reed was used for making the

[1] CUL Queens' Cd 39; Cd 26a; Cd 61; Cd 80; Cd 74; Cd 66; Cd 83; Ad 8.
[2] Top Moor.
[3] PRO SC 6.766/12; CUL Queens' Cd 80, Cd 39.

frame for daub in the wattle and daub walls, wattlingreeds. The cutting and carrying of reeds in the Frith Fen in Cottenham in connection with local building works is recorded in the Crowlands Rolls for 1267–8 (page 219) and in Smithy Fen in 1455–6. Each of the villages could supply its own ordinary reed, but the wattling reed used by the Crowlands Manors seems normally to have come from Willingham. Laths are not mentioned as being purchased until the days of tile when presumably a better quality was needed, and these then were bought in Cambridge where the tiles came from. The ashes and willows on the banks of the manorial closes and the ditches through the fens would have provided splints for the rest of the wattle.[1]

Sedge was a normal fen crop: Setchel Fen derives its name from this, 'Sedge-Haw' being the early form. It is therefore surprising to find sedge being imported to Cottenham from Milton and Swaffham in 1455–6. Perhaps the demand for the general re-building was too great because eight cart-loads of reed were later brought from Cambridge, and much more was bought from the Cottenham peasantry, like John Pepys. Some straw was used: in this year 'halme', stubble, is mentioned, but this was very small in quantity. In the year 9–10 Hen. VII, straw was recorded in use for thatching peasants' buildings. The main material mentioned in connection with ridging is clay, which again was dug in the fen or elsewhere in the manor. Clay ridging on thatch still survives in the Camargue. But all the accounts make clear that the sedge was used in thatching.[2] It was much more durable for ridging than clay.

All the walling, both of buildings and around the yards was of clay, except for the few paling fences mentioned rarely. There must have been a heavy demand for clay for building purposes throughout the Middle Ages, and it is surprising that more clay-pits are not visible. Probably most of these turned into the ponds in house yards, that are such a feature on the old maps of the fen-edge villages. There was another heavy demand for clay for marling and claying land. In 1327 William Cosyn was fined for carrying away the lord's marl in Cottenham. In Landbeach in 1332 Robert Jordan dug the common in 'Le mor', and marled his land with it 'unlawfully since he has no common right' ('minus iuste quia non hebet communia'). The final phrase suggests that this was normal practice for commoners. George Aikin in the nineteenth century attributed the improvement of the fens to claying and marling almost as much as to steam drainage. There was a very plentiful supply of both gault and Kimmeridge clay in the area, but if the presentments in the court rolls are a reliable guide, the peasantry seemed much to prefer digging their clay from the highway than from the fens, no doubt to avoid the labour of transport.

[1] ECA, p. 219; CUL Queens' Ad 8, and Cd 39; cf. Cd 61, Cd 80, Cd 74, Cd 66 and Cd 83.
[2] Ibid. Cd 39; Ed 26.

There are many cases of this in each of the main sets of medieval rolls.[1]

The area is again very well endowed with sand and gravel, and it would appear that convenience of transport, the nearness of a good main road, decided which site was to be dug. In Waterbeach the major old pits were near the way to Landbeach and the Cambridge Way. In Landbeach they were, and are, north of the green where the main road first moved out of the village on to the gravel.[2] The subsidiary pits out in these parishes were dug for road maintenance after the turnpike was made from Milton to Ely in the eighteenth century, or much later still, particularly after the Second World War, for export to various building sites in the county. During its construction, Waterbeach Airfield took its share. In Cottenham the common pits were out in the fen beyond the Cow Pasture, near the junction of the way from the village and the way to the north-western fens. But the natural inclination to take as easy a way as possible with heavy cartage, gave rise to trouble for the fen reeves and ordermakers:

37. It is ordered that if any man break any ground in between closes any nearer the way that goes from the Bars than is already digged shall pay one shilling per load, and the stuff forfeited to the use of the Town so often as he is found to offend.

38. It is ordered that if any man digs or causes to be dug any earth, slate or sand in the Calve Pasture between the foot road and the Pastures, likewise any nearer the road on the other side thereof, shall pay five shillings per load and the stuff forfeited to the use of the town so often as he is found therein to offend, and the informer, by giving true intelligence of the same shall receive two shillings and sixpence reward to be paid by one of the Officers.

The five shillings and two and sixpence were amendments from two shillings and one shilling which were apparently insufficient. Four similar orders follow this, all directing the places for digging, forbidding digging on waste ground, and ordering pits to be filled in as far as the earth would go. But many of the scars of old workings are still visible today.[3]

The mention of slate strikes an odd note: the local soft, brittle sandstone which often splits into rough sheets is probably meant. There is not much of it, and it barely merits the title 'stone'. Before the general use of brick, stone good enough for the plinths of timber-framed buildings was difficult to get. When the manor house of Crowlands at Cottenham was built in mid-fifteenth century, stones had to be gathered from the fields, from old foundations and from an old well. Large stones had to be imported by barge.[4]

---

[1] ECA, p. 358; CCCC, XXXV, 121; G. Aikin, 'Culture of the Cambridgeshire Fens', Transactions of the Royal Society of Arts, vol. 52 (1838–9); CUL Queens'; CCCC, XXXV, 121–4; WPC, WcD.

[2] To the north of the old Town Pond or Lode Ware. See Fig. 10.

[3] Cottenham Fen Reeves' Books, in the possession of Mr M. Haird.

[4] CUL Queens' Cd 39. Restoration work on nos. 21 and 23 High Street, Landbeach, has exposed earlier medieval plinths of rough blocks of clunch which seem to have been more effective than one would have expected from this material.

One of the lesser, but most lucrative, of the fen products connected with the supply of building materials was osiers. Waterbeach, with its long river frontage close to the village, and with long tongues of low land reaching into The Hollow and Little Hollow, was exceptionally well endowed. The Gough Manuscript Rental lists no less than fourteen osier holts. A glebe terrier of Bishop Wren's time mentions three leys of osier holts there. There is only one medieval mention of an osier holt in Cottenham so far discovered, and none in Landbeach. But in 1727 Robert Taylor noted in the Dukman Book: 'There is a small parcel of Holt Roods not set down.'[1]

Willow could be used in timber frame and thatch construction for many of the minor duties, although ash, hazel or riven oak would be preferred. Wickerwork chairs begin to appear in the local inventories after the Civil War. But its greatest uses were probably in woven hurdles, in the construction of bird-traps and decoys, fish-traps and weirs, and above all in the baskets of all kinds used by the peasantry in farming and at home. A considerable wicker industry flourished on the fen edge until very recent times, and there is an excellent photographic record of its last days in Cottenham and Willingham, where not only all the processes of construction, from the peeling of the wands by children, are shown, but also demonstrations of the variety and strengths of special purpose baskets, have been preserved. The industry received a slight extension to its life when the use of wicker trays as filters was adopted by the local jam factory. But traces of basket-making are now no more than a vestigial remnant. There is still one osier holt remaining in Cottenham at the moment of writing, alongside the Beach Ditch.

When the demand was steady, and that was at any historical period before recent years, osier holts were probably the most profitable use of land in this area. It is difficult to estimate their extent. Individual holts could be very tiny and do not seem to have come into direct cultivation with the demesnes, but to have most often been in the hands of those with the smallest agricultural interests in the village. In addition, they tend to be isolated, beyond the frontiers of other kinds of cultivation, low down on the flood plain close by the river, or on the marginal land where the fen was almost continuously waterlogged. They seem to have been pockets of car fen, subject only to the lightest control so as to select willows as their main growth. The medieval Hollow in Waterbeach was a natural site, as some profit could certainly be taken there from osiers when all other uses became an almost hopeless gamble in the wettest years of the early fourteenth century. Pollard willows still line the banks of the Cam below Waterbeach, and show tenacity of life in this habitat, putting out new

---

[1] Bodleian, Alington Rental, 1542, 17819, fol. 5 (Gough, Cambs. 69); CUL EDR A 14/1; LPC, Dukman Book. Cf. BM Add. Ch. 7060 for osier holts in Cottenham.

shoots and leaves when the trunks, all but the bark, are rotted away. But alongside, the Jesus Holt, at the end of the Car Dyke, the Magpie Holt, and Long Holt, are now no more than awkward-shaped pasture fields, trapped between the railway bank and the river, becoming lakes in time of flood.[1]

Another industrial crop of the fens has left only a trace in odd hedge-rows and banks where chemical weed-killers have not destroyed the few escaped plants: teasels, essential to medieval cloth finishing. Very fine specimens can be found in season on the banks of the Oakington Brook where it forms the Cottenham boundary. These were not a cultivated crop, but could be found in the common when laid out for hay. The only mention of them that I have discovered is a trespass case recorded in the Crowlands Rolls for Cottenham in 1349. Robert Spuer complains that after he had mown teasels on his common, William Goldyng entered with a cart and carried them off. However, the jury cleared William of taking any but his own.[2] As a casual bonus from the hay ground, teasels would not be likely to leave much trace in the records, and their importance cannot be assessed, but they are another example of the bounty of the fens. The frequent references to mowing thistles could refer to teasels.

If osiers were a crop of the frontier between waste marsh and fen proper, hemp could be a crop of the fen's frontier with ploughland. It is a very exacting crop which draws heavily on the reserves of fertility in the soil. On the Crowlands demesnes at Cottenham it appears, like flax, as a garden crop. The labour in fermenting and preparing it after harvest would discourage large-scale production: drying would create excessive demand for fuel. But from the Terrier of Chantry Lands of 1549 in Cottenham it would seem that there were hemplands at the edge of the cultivated area towards Histon. Hemplands are mentioned in 'The Laying Out of the Fens' in the late seventeenth century in the Landbeach Fen Book, again on the margin of the fen. In the 1596 Agreement Christ's College were to have one acre adjoining their close in Ferne Field and Hempland. This would place the hemplands down on the Histon boundary, alongside the watercourse which was several times diverted lower down, and may well have been troublesome in these higher reaches in consequence.[3]

But if the abundance of the fens showed themselves in the variety of the sources of profit that they offered, they showed it even more in the richness of their grass. Tawney never ceased to emphasise that the Achilles' heel of the open-field system was the shortage of grass. Only over-expansion could make this remotely true of the fen and fen edge. In a reasonable winter there was some grass available on the hards, the drier pastures between the flooded fens and the arable, our anonymous Fen-

[1] See Fig. 6, p. 87.   [2] CUL Queens' Dd 4.
[3] LPC; *Common Rights*, p. 200.

man's first class of fen.[1] If cleared of stock when other feed became available, then soon there would be food again for the young stock and their mothers, hence the names Calves Pasture and Cow Pasture in Cottenham. Mitchell, Setchel and Smithy Fen in Cottenham, all had their own small hards, within their boundaries, and so could extend their profitable seasons. Bullocks Haste provided a similar hard reaching out from the Town's End.[2] The delicate and almost invisible undulations of the fen just above and below the line of winter flooding maximised its value as pasture. Mow fens, after they had produced their hay, would, given proper rest from great cattle, soon be covered again with a particularly lush growth from the damp warm ground. This was Cottenham's richest endowment.

A few cheese-presses in village outhouses, the slatted windows of the cheese-chambers in the old upper rooms, and faded memories of some of the old families are all that remains of Cottenham's most famous industry. A Cottenham claim (which seems apocryphal, since the same story from Leicestershire is better documented) is that one of their daughters moved to Stilton, and selling cheese from Cottenham on the main roadside, invented Stilton Cheese. But the village was once famous in its own right. Vancouver wrote of it: 'The cheese so famous through England, by the name of this parish, is made here and in the neighbouring villages; the superiority of which, is not to be ascribed to any particular mode in the management of the dairies, but solely to the nature of the herbage on the commons.'

Albert Pell described its qualities: 'In summer this fen or common was covered with the finest milch cows, and produced a cheese similar to but richer than Stilton, and in autumn a speciality, "Single Cottenham", with the flavour and consistency of Camembert.'[3]

It is possible to glimpse the beginnings of this in the earliest Account Rolls of Crowlands. The demesne herds were specialised so as to concentrate their Cambridgeshire breeding at Cottenham. This is reflected in the dairy items, cheese, butter and, more fitfully, milk. For example, in 1280–1, the bailiff accounted for seven score cheeses from the dairy, produced at the rate of 1 a day from the seventh of May to Michaelmas. The cows did not go back immediately at the festival, and 12 more cheeses were made. Four were allowed for in the loss of weight in the press. Seventy-two were sold for 15s. 8d. Oakington was supplied with 30, presumably for the diets when custom demanded that the lord supply bread and cheese with a day's work, and for use at the lord's table in the

---

[1] See p. 42 above.
[2] For names of the fens, see Fig. 1, p. xii.
[3] C. Vancouver, *A General View of Agriculture in the County of Cambridgeshire* (1794), p. 127; *Albert Pell*, ed. Mackay, p. 73; D. and S. Lysons, *Magna Britannia* (6 vols., 1806–22), *Cambridgeshire*, vol. II, pt I (1808), p. 37.

manor there. Dry Drayton, which had its work needs but did not have to entertain the retinues who went to Oakington for the courts, received only 6. Thirty-two were used in the household at Cottenham. Four were used for the homage when carrying turf and hay from the commons. Others were used by the old abbot, the prior, and by the new abbot when he came from London on his way to Crowlands. In 1288–9 twelve stones of butter were made there, and of these four were sent to Oakington and the rest sold. Sheep would need some of that sent to Oakington for ointment. In 1296–7 three stones are expressly used for the sheep. In 1301–2 there was some sale of milk, but this did not amount to much, only $12\frac{3}{4}d$. worth. The total dairy sales at Cottenham seem normally to have been a by-product of the cattle-breeding, and not a main purpose of the herd.[1]

But the natural advantages of Cottenham meant that in the long run the dairy industry grew both among the peasantry and the lords of the manor. When the market conditions became suitable the village became more and more specialised. As Cunningham pointed out, the 1596 Agreement was concerned with cattle where the previous one had been concerned with sheep. When inventories for the villagers become available after the Civil War, cheeses and cheese-presses are remarkably prominent in them, and not only in yeoman houses. The inventory of Walter Mayle, butcher, taken 20 July 1671, mentions both a cheese-press and a parcel of cheeses. The ejected rector, John Manby, who had returned, had two cheese-presses. William Denson, thatcher, had one and a parcel of cheeses worth £2. John Taylor, junior, yeoman, had one. Stephen Sanderson, butcher, had one, and fifty cheeses. John Rosse, labourer, had one. In these years it is the absence of a cheese-press from any Cottenham inventory that calls for a special explanation, rather than its presence.

The parliamentary enclosure of the nineteenth century began to take away the basis of cheese-making in Cottenham, its great feeding commons and mow commons. But a sizeable herd survived for another generation. The decisive blow fell on it with the cattle plague. Jacob Sanderson lived through both enclosure and cattle plague, and was himself a farmer's son who in course of time took on his father's land. He remembered the hardships in old age:

In 1865 and 1866 the Cattle Plague visited Cottenham by cattle brought from St. Ives Market. 600 head of cattle died and were slaughtered. Whole farmyards were emptied. Farmers never recovered from its effects. We took the cows down Top More. Never lost

[1] CUL Queens' Cd 5, Cd 13, Cd 11; Probate inventories in CUA in year bundles. For the animal husbandry on Cottenham Crowlands, see M. Wretts-Smith, 'The Organisation of Farming at Croyland Abbey, 1267–1331', *The Journal of Economic and Business History*, IV (1931–2), and F. M. Page, 'Bidentes Hoylandie', *Economic History*, I, *Supplement to the Economic Journal* (1929).

one, by the blessing of God, for which Father was very thankful. It was something heart-rending to hear the Dead Cart night and day lumbering through the Town to the playground for two years. Never had so many cows in Cottenham since.[1]

So faded the industry whose method of work was recorded by Vancouver in his *General View*. No cheese is made now, and the detailed recipe is lost.

The neighbouring parishes also shared in the production of 'Cottenham' cheese; in fact it is in his description of Waterbeach that Vancouver places his account of its manufacture. John Denson claimed that it was by use of common rights to establish his own dairy that his father was able to rise from the position of day-labourer. But Masters, in his *Short Account* makes nothing of cheese, although he says that about 300 milch cows were usually kept in Waterbeach to supply butter to the Cambridge market, where the price was usually good. The Drift[2] of 1798 numbered 337 horses, 888 cattle and 18 calves, and 1,934 sheep. Dairy was not the dominant interest in this village as it was in Cottenham. Vancouver mentions the fattening of Yorkshire and Irish steers on Waterbeach Fens. The greater part of them lay beyond the open fields from the village. Here the area which might have corresponded to Cottenham's hards was arable. And in Masters' time the Cam brought Waterbeach in quick easy reach of Cambridge. Subtle differences of topography between these three fen-edge neighbours had much to do with their differences in animal husbandry.[3]

The probate inventories for the three villages between 1660 and 1710 include 202 which give details of livestock, 114 for Cottenham, 54 for Waterbeach, and 34 for Landbeach. The ratios of cows and sheep to horses illustrate how closely the animal husbandry varied with the topography:

	Horses	Cows	Sheep	Ratio
Cottenham	604	1,198	2,267	$1:2-:3\frac{2}{3}$
Landbeach	153	322	1,224	$1:2+:8$
Waterbeach	320	756	1,787	$1:2+:5\frac{1}{2}$

Cottenham is biased towards the husbandry of horses and cattle, Landbeach overwhelmingly towards sheep, and Waterbeach in between. The inclusion of larger farmers and gentlemen in the Waterbeach inventories and their complete absence from those from Cottenham make the average sizes of flocks and herds none too reliable, but the ratios are not without significance.[4]

[1] Notebook.
[2] See glossary. The written list made at the drift is referred to here.
[3] Vancouver, *General View of Agriculture*, p. 129; Denson, *Peasant's Voice*, pp. iii and iv; Masters, *Short Account*; the Drift is in WPC, Masters vs. *Standley* Papers.
[4] CUA, in year bundles for whole county, but with alphabetical lists.

If the sample of flocks and herds revealed by our inventories were reliably representative, the median sizes of flocks and herds might enable easy comparisons with other farming areas at the time, such as those of Lincolnshire. But their value is diminished by the fact that the distributions fail to follow a simple pattern.

Median sizes of flocks and herds in probate inventories, 1660–1710[1]

	Cattle	Horses	Sheep	Number of inventories
Cottenham	12	8	34	114
Landbeach	16	5	9	34
Waterbeach	8	6	10	54

The medians do not reveal that in Cottenham the keeping of cattle was almost universal among the peasantry: out of 114 farm inventories, only 6 show no cattle, while 41 show no sheep. The group with herds of from 5 to 15 amounts to 81. The largest herd in the Cottenham inventories is 30, but this may well be due to the fact that in this village we seem to have no inventories for the largest house-holds such as the lordship. But the picture of the bulk of the peasantry in Cottenham keeping anything from 1 or 2 cows to a modest milch herd is clear and in contrast to the other two villages. In Landbeach no herd appears in the range from 5 to 9, while in Waterbeach, although there are 33 inventories showing herds of from 3 to 12, there are also herds of 40, 70 and 93.

Without horses the activities of a peasant must have been severely limited on the fen edge. In Landbeach we have only 4 farm inventories without horses, as against 11 without cattle and 11 without sheep. In Waterbeach 8 have no horses, 8 no cattle, but 19 no sheep. In Cottenham the cow pastures were so handy to the village that many small peasants seem to have been able to manage without horses, 21 as against only 6 without cattle.

But sheep grazing seems to have been common among small holdings as well as larger: Cottenham had 20 inventories with flocks numbering from 3 to 12, but another 21 with flocks of over 35. But the largest flock to appear in Cottenham was one of 200, whereas Waterbeach had one of 466, and Landbeach one of over 500. Again this difference from Cottenham may be due to the freakish sample of the inventories.

---

[1] These medians for cattle and horses are very close to those found in the Lincolnshire Fenland at a similar period. See Thirsk, *Fenland Farming*, p. 139, which gives medians for the 1690s of 14 for cattle, 7 for horses and 62 for sheep. The Cambridgeshire fen edge had failed to keep up with the growth of the sheep flocks of the much more suitable Lincolnshire fens in the second half of the seventeenth century. Our inventories seem to reflect the turning away of interest from sheep to cattle which was shown by the sixteenth-century agreements in Cottenham.

Our picture of the stock in these parishes must be deficient in that beasts of agistment should not have been included as property of the dead man, but from their obsessive presence in the regulations they must have been of major importance in the economy of many peasant families.

It is by chance that the period over which the inventories have been taken produces totals of beasts that appear to be of about the same order of size as the numbers counted in a single year. Our most complete count, the Waterbeach Drift of 1793, albeit much later, has a fair correspondence with the numbers in the inventories, 906 cattle, 337 horses and 1,934 sheep, compared with inventory totals of 756, 320 and 1,787. Yet the numbers of inventories are much smaller than the households of the contemporary 1664 Hearth Tax, for Cottenham 114 against 215, for Waterbeach 54 against 107, and for Landbeach 34 against 66. Probably there are too many excluded at both extremes, from wealth in another diocese, or from poverty too severe to allow the ownership of beasts. It is also possible that a number of the inventories which have no farm section merely ignore this part of the property.

The numbers of inventories without animals in this period are for Cottenham 19, Landbeach 5, and Waterbeach 8. These were mostly poor widows', labourers', and poverty-stricken landless craftmen's. But even here there is a difference between the villages: in Cottenham some quite substantial yeomen do not have lists of beasts given, but merely a total value for the farm. One of the Landbeach inventories without beasts is for a parson who was also a Senior Fellow of Corpus Christi, and probably his main inventory was made elsewhere. We can hardly feel confident that we have a good cross-section in these inventories while there are such differences among such relatively small numbers.

But there is no denying the presence in each village of a substantial group of modest peasantry, with balanced agricultural interests that nonetheless took advantage of the special endowments of the topography of their own village, and among this group were craftsmen, publicans and shopkeepers most of whom operated from the basis of a peasant holding. On the fen edge the pastoral side of the village economies seems to have been the area in which both peasantry and gentry could most easily seek to take profit from the market.

The mares and foals which, in the later Middle Ages, seemed to fill Landbeach Fens whenever they were emptied of sheep by the murrain, indicate the adaptability of this side of the peasant economy. The opportunities of the rich grass on the fen edge enabled peasant, lord or farmer to exploit market conditions while operating from a relatively unchanging base in the arable.[1]

[1] See p. 166.

63

FEN MANAGEMENT

Probably the best description of Cottenham Fens is that given in a seventeenth-century Book of Sewers which describes some of the effects of early drainage schemes:

We say that in Cottenham there are divers grounds, some half several and some common, both which upon extraordinary floods are sometimes overflown and upon the fall of the river do forthwith drain again as the upland meadows do; but unless the said floods do happen to overflow them in the summer season (which is very seldom) we do find that the said grounds receive more benefit than hurt thereby and are thereby much bettered and enriched: for those grounds which lie lowest, and are oftenest and longest overflown in the winter season are the most fertile grounds, and yield the best yearly value; the snap or forecrop of the said half severals being some of them worth twenty shillings the acre yearly, and some eighteen, some sixteen, some fourteen, and the worst of them all seldom sold for less than twelve shillings the acre, unless it be some dry year when they are not overflown, for then the white fodder decayeth, and the grounds turn much to a small kind of hamer segge which the cattle like not so well, the stuff being much worse. Neither is there scarce half that burden thereof which useth to be in moister years when the grounds are overflown. The commons or feeding grounds are so good or rather better than the severals are, and would yield as good a yearly value if they were used alike; but by reason of their banking and draining of them of late time, they are grown to a smaller kind of grass than formerly they were, so that where in former time they were wont to mow in their common feeding grounds three or four hundred loads of common fodder in a year (which greatly relieved the poorer sort of people among them) (and had notwithstanding plenty of meat for their cattle) there is now scarce anything to be mown and such small store of meat for their cattle in dry years, that they are forced sometime to seek pasture for them in other places; and have been driven to set barn doors overthwart the river to staunch the water, to help water into their ditches for their cattle, the want whereof hath been the cause of so much death of cattle among them, as hath been from time to time observed, whereas in moister years when the cattle have plenty of grass and water they stand sound, and there is nothing so much casualty among them....[1]

If, then, the fens were no worse for being fens but might perhaps be better, as long as they were commons their use had to be controlled, and their use and the controls implied would gradually change their nature.[2] When uncontrolled, their use led to strife and disputes that could only be solved by agreement to regulations. The Wrest Park Chartulary contains a copy of an Agreement dealing with Cottenham Fens unnoticed by Miss Page, strikingly similar to the Agreement which she prints on turf-cutting.[3]

[1] BM Ad. Ms. 33466 fol. 184, anno 1618.

[2] For a modern scientific discussion of the richness of fens, see L. Hoffman, 'Saving Europe's Wetlands', New Scientist, XLVI, no 697 (16 April 1970), 120: 'Often these benefits will be greater than those expected after reclamation.'

[3] Spalding Gentlemen's Society, Wr. Pk. Ch., f. 249 d. The dating of this document is very important, since, if we have agreements made under these circumstances in three years following each other, we might believe that we have evidence here of a village court.

Miss Page gives the date as 1345, but in the text the year is 18 Ed. III, 1344, and the day, the first

In this it was agreed that Smithy Fen should lie in fence from the Feast of the Purification until after cutting and carrying. The laying out of the fen was to be done by the bailiffs of Crowlands and de Lisle, although de Burdeleys bailiff alone might carry his own measuring rod of 16½ feet to check that he and all the free tenants received their proper share. The fen was to be parted into furlongs 40 perches in length. In each of these de Lisle was to have the First Cast, the abbot the Second Cast, and the rest of the inhabitants their proportion in turn.

Agistment pennies for the fens, viz. North Fen, Seghawfen, Charfen, Tappyngmore, and Grekenhilfen[1] were to be collected in a box in the presence of the bailiffs of Crowlands, de Lisle, and Burdeleys. The de Lisle bailiff was to be responsible for the custody but under the supervision of the others. For each 9d. (i.e. 10d. less tithe penny) of agistment money de Lisle was to take 4d., the abbot 4d. and de Burdeleys 1d. The lords of the 'new Fees' were to have nothing.[2] Traces of this survive right down to the parliamentary enclosure, which ended the division of Smithy Fen into furlongs and casts. The Agreement of 1596 seems to mark the change from annual to permanent division of the mowing ground in Smithy Fen: 'Article XIX "That Smithy Fen shall continue and remain for ever dowelled and staked according as it now lieth."'

Landbeach had a similar method for annual laying out of the Frith Fen. The parish fen book gives this in a number of seventeenth-century versions. The first reads as follows:

The laying out of the grass in Fryth fens of Landbeach as it is used in the first year of our Sovereign Lord King Charles by the Grace of God beginning at the end of a foot path on the west near the southwest corner and proceeding in meting [measuring] as the same path lieth toward the low gate or southeast corner using the pole of xiij foot in length throughout as hath formerly been used.

At the end it reads:

Be it known that the next year this order of laying out of the grasses of this Fryth Fen must alter so that you must begin with the acre of the College called Bere's Acre and from that laying the six acres of College Demesne the parson's part and all the Freeholders' whiles you pass Rook's di acre And then begin with John Gunnil's Copy in the Green And

Thursday after the Octave of Easter, i.e. 15 April in 1344. The Wrest Park Agreement gives the date as 15 April in 18 Ed. III, but gives an Anno Domini date of 1343. Since the same people the lords and all the tenants of Cottenham appear in both in the same place, Cottenham church, probably both date from the same time, 1344. Another copy of the Agreement quoted in Page, which has now come into the CRO in the Francis Papers, is dated 1344 also. What appears to have been taking place is a fairly comprehensive review of the use of the fens, this second Agreement dealing with the division of the mow fen, Smithy Fen, and with agistment and trespass in the others.

[1] See Fig. 1, p. xii. These names refer to: Great and Little North Fens, Setchel, Chear Fen, Top Moor, and the last mentioned refers to the area which later became the Undertakers and the Lots.
[2] There were six manors in Cottenham. The three referred to here as new were the knight's fees created by the Norman bishop of Ely.

so forth in order backwards leaving and ending with Giles Annis and Jackson in the end at low gate. The remnant that is left of the meadow is appointed for the Church Lot.

A regular entry in the parish accounts in the early seventeenth century is payment to two men for 'carrying a rope in Frith Fen', probably part of the process of marking the division as measured.[1]

The laying out of the mow fens for hay was only the most obvious form of control necessary for their use. Arrangements had to be made to safeguard the grass in time of growth. The hay ground obviously had to be fenced off in spring until after mowing and carrying, as with Smithy Fen in the above Agreement.[2] The time of opening such land for feed would depend on whether one or two crops were to be taken. This in turn would normally be dictated by the topography and the relative dampness of the different meadows, and also the state of the particular fens, whether they were in good heart or no.

The 1639 Orders suggest that an opportunity was being taken to give Smithy Fen a rest from the regular annual mowing: it was to be several from all beasts only from St Thomas (21 February) to 25 March. No cattle were to be driven over it. This was not keeping it for hay, but merely giving the new year's crop of grass a start safe from the treading feet at the moist, cold time of the year. The Undertakers land, which had been separated out of the commons but was not yet taken over by the corporation, was set aside for hay: it was several from all manner of cattle from 1 March until 10 July, and the meeting for dividing it up was to take place on 10 June. Quite clearly Undertakers was being used as mow fen alongside the Lotts.[3] If parts of the commons were to be taken out of use at certain times the question of alternatives and priorities was raised. Top priority, especially in Cottenham in its great cheese-making days, had to be given to the milch herd, and the lowest to cattle of agistment. It is significant that the new names for parts of the old medieval Aldborough Meadow, Cow Pasture, Calves Pasture, and Bullocks Harste (or Haste), appear with the 1596 Agreement. (In fact we may well have the opposite situation in Cottenham at this time from that which we found in Waterbeach: the lords' and gentry's interests in sheep conflicting with the

---

[1] LPC; these accounts are in the back of the first register. In Over the size of the rod for fen measurement was reduced to thirteen feet in order to increase the leavings, which could then be let in order to save a rate for drainage. See CRO transcript, 65/T1. 'Fen Measure', in Landbeach at least, meant that each fen acre contained two acres, but in the old Meadow Field the selion was kept as a measure.

[2] With the extensive ditches, little fencing needed to be done beyond placing gates (barrs) across the roads at the fens' ends.

[3] *Common Rights*, pp. 235–9. A name for part of the leavings in the meadows of Cottenham, Rampton and Waterbeach was 'Knaveslees'. This is called 'Young men's Fen' in Tudor Cottenham. It was presumably hay ground for those without sufficient property for a common right. CCCC, XXXV, 121, 44 Ed. III, and PRO SC 4, P & M, 3/17.

peasants' interest in cattle, and here, predominantly milch cattle.) The old name, in its corrupt form, Awbrose, still continued to be used for the area as a whole, but it was no longer meadow. The hards, normally winter as well as summer ground on account of the few extra feet of altitude above the Low Grounds, were now even more valuable as pasture for the milking herds since they were adjacent to the village. An expanding market for what had previously been not much more than a by-product of cattle breeding, cheese, and the effects of better drainage, had produced a major change in the use of the common grasslands.

The natural water-meadows in the shape of the low fens, could not only supply the hay, but also especially lush pasture in late summer when the grass of the permanent pastures grew thin; further, they could make an alternative and adequate, if more distant, feeding for the animals excluded from the areas devoted to the milch herd. The other alternative feed to the pastures and Lammas lands of fens was the fallow and stubble of the open fields, and the ways and unsown double furrows which produced grass of a sort. The grazing could only be controlled as a whole, especially as any 'sudden or extraordinary flood' would call for immediate rearrangements of the uses of those commons which had escaped.

There was another factor which brought the control set up for the common fens to extend over the arable: sheep, which could be damaging if allowed to undercrop in competition with great cattle, were particularly valued for their manure on the ploughlands, and the gentle stirring of their hooves was beneficial to the soil where heavier beasts tended to compact it. Thus the ordering of the field paths and grass furrows, the control of entry into the fallows and so of gleaning, the maintenance of the proper size of balks, ways and headlands, all came under the aegis of the ordermakers, who, in turn, appointed the field reeves as well as the fen reeves.

Their power extended over all common rights, and so they became, amongst other things, the sole effective highway authority within the parish, with their own powers to order common labour for maintenance and development. Theirs also was the guardianship of the fens from drowning, as far as it lay in their power. So, too, they took responsibility for banks and ditches, including the waterfurrows and gripes of the arable. The Town Boats were in their care in the early nineteenth century, and they took full responsibility, including financial, for the maintenance and running of the drainage windmills at Chear Fen and Undertakers. Their finances were transferred to the commissioners after the passing of the Enclosure Act in 1842. By this time they had exercised most of the civil economic functions normally performed by the parish elsewhere, e.g. regulating the digging for turf and minerals and the restitution of the surface, paying for the destruction of sparrows and moles, planting osiers, fetching Town wood, viewing the bulls, looking after gates and bars on the ways, providing the fieldkeepers with powder and shot, and even paying for playing the fire engine.

But this did not distract them from their primary duties concerned with the agriculture of the village. They not only looked to the allocation of the commons between alternative uses, and allotted the time and place for each kind of stock, they also saw to the maintenance and improvement of the quality of the ground and of the common flocks and herds. The provision of the right number and quality of bulls was at their direction. The powers and duties of the herdsmen and shepherds were laid down by the ordermakers. Their regulations against diseased beasts on the commons protected the health of the cattle. They prevented the plundering of the store of wealth in the land by overstocking with beasts of agistment or by digging for sale outside Cottenham.

They carried on the work of the medieval manorial courts of watching the encroachment of neighbour on neighbour in the open fields, and the foreigner from outside the village in the commons. The most suspicious of all foreigners to be found in the fens had for long been the butcher. Miss Page quotes a presentment of 1419 which refers to an Agreement laying down the conditions under which a butcher might enter the fens in Cottenham. Bans on their presence in the Waterbeach Fens can be found in the Court Book for 1 Hen. VI, and repeated down to 19 Eliz. In the Orders of 1639 even native Cottenham cattle dealers and butchers lose their freedom of the fens. The herdsmen and shepherds are set on watch against colouring of foreign beasts. A register of brands and the right of the fen reeves to take drifts of all the beasts on the commons was a check both against over-stocking and colouring. At Waterbeach the compulsory use of a Town brand as well as the owners', was a double-check.[1]

The power and range of activity of the commoners' organisation in Cottenham through the seventeenth, eighteenth, and the first half of the nineteenth centuries, a power which dominated the economic life of the village and exercised a conservative control over agricultural development and so over the landscape, was a reflection of the abundance of grass. It was a result of the profusion of natural water-meadow in the fen; and even more of the topography of the fens, which combined these with adequate permanent pastures on the hards near the village, where milking was convenient, or near enough for home milking when necessary.

The skill and flexibility with which the Cottenham ordermakers responded to the vagaries of water-level and climate, is revealed in the surviving order books with their successive amendments to the traditional arrangements. But the system was effective in keeping these traditional arrangements working, not in changing to a new order of things. The

---

[1] Haird Collection, Fen Reeves' Book II; *ECA*, p. 165; WPC; *Common Rights*.

peasant society had adjusted and tailored its way of life to the varied and flexible topography. As peasant power when it had grown, *de facto*, over the fields exercised a strong conservative force, so over the fens, peasant power both *de iure* and *de facto*, anchored the economic life of the parishes to a mode and landscape from the past, a past where the peasant's expectations had been slowly formed over the generations. The separation out of the lord's rights into several closes and sheepwalks in these villages gave freer rein to the conservatism of the peasantry. Apart from the allotments to the Bedford Level Corporation in Waterbeach and Cottenham Fens, each parish had only one major enclosure in its fenland before the great parliamentary enclosure of the nineteenth century, that creating the lord's several or the sheepwalks.

SHEEP

If the suggestion that Landbeach may have begun as a settlement for raising sheep is correct, its subsequent history suggests that, under medieval conditions, it was a particularly good choice. Atkyns in 1604 singled out the quality of Landbeach pasture for sheep: 'They have little fen ground, but between the towne and Denney be good Sheepcourses.'

This is on the better drained gravel soil of the village, and there is a fine flock going there at the time of writing. Vancouver does not suggest a number for Landbeach sheep, but the list of every man's sheepgate in the Dukman Book gives a permitted total for the year 1728 of 3,984. For Waterbeach Vancouver gives 1,000, Masters around 2,000, and the actual number recorded in the Drift Book for 1793 is 1,934. For Cottenham Vancouver gives 2,500, but says that three-quarters were lost by rot in the previous season. Under the wetter conditions of the Middle Ages, disease must have been a continual and serious hazard. Landbeach must have been favoured compared to its neighbours in that, relative to Cottenham, it had so much more gravel soil in easy reach of the village, and that its gravels were, on the whole, slightly, but significantly, higher than those of either Cottenham or Waterbeach.[1]

Miss Page and Miss Wretts-Smith have shown us the picture of the sheep-ranching pursued by the abbot of Crowland, and the part played in this by the Manor of Crowlands in Cottenham. Losses due to 'murrain', an all-embracing term for animal disease, seem to have been such that there was no profit for years. In 1302–3, for instance, in the Cottenham accounts are 72 '*multones*', of which 25 died before shearing, and 12 '*oves*', of which 3 died before shearing. This was not much above the average. The variations in the numbers recorded for this demesne flock only

[1] Vancouver, *A General View of Agriculture*, pp. 126–31; *Short Account*, p. 2; Dukman Book in LPC.

become intelligible in the light of the central organisation of the Crow-lands demesne farms, and the comprehensive section of the central account rolls, 'Bidentes Hoylandie'. Information about other demesne flocks in the area is hard to come by, and even more difficult to understand and interpret. Unfortunately in the Crowlands documents far less information survives for Cottenham than for Oakington, but for forty-odd years Cottenham appears to have played its part in a system organised on the basis of specialisation within the whole group of demesne manors. Cotten-ham, because it was the only one of the three Cambridgeshire manors with water communication to Crowland, became the collecting and dispatch centre for their wool as well as other agricultural products. In 1298, 132 sheep were received at Cottenham.

The end of large-scale sheep farming by Crowlands came in 1322. Then only a few appeared in the dairy accounts at Crowlands; none at all in the Cambridgeshire manors. There is no sign at all of these ever having counted sheep in their dairies.[1]

If topography made Cottenham the loading point for water transport from the other two manors to Crowlands, it also made Oakington the convenient centre for shearing. In the late fourteenth century there was some revival of Crowlands demesne flocks, and in 1392 the Cottenham sheep were sent to Oakington for shearing. In the following year the Oakington demesnes were stocked with sheep from Cottenham. But the scale and specialisation were less than in the earlier period. Then, from the beginning in 1297 or 1298, wethers had been kept at Cottenham and ewes at Oakington. When the male lambs born at Oakington became yearlings they were transferred to Cottenham.

When, in May 1430, the abbot of Crowland finally abandoned direct demesne farming in Oakington and Cottenham, both demesnes were leased on a stock and land basis to local villeins.[2] On each of the manors was a flock of 200 sheep. The tenant had to find for them a shepherd, as well in winter as in summer, wages for the shepherd, and sufficient ointment. Of the sheep-farming in the unspecialised days after the lease of the demesne, the Crowlands Rolls are naturally silent, except for inci-dental mentions in trespass cases. Of numbers and the detailed running of the flocks, no record remains.

Clay gathered together, mainly from Masters' *History of the College of Corpus Christi*, and from his 'Collectanea' in the parish chest, a few fragments on the Chamberlains demesne sheep in Landbeach. The first mention of sheep is in the Charter of 1336 by which Henry Chamberlain granted his brother John the right to fold 120 sheep for life. The lands in this charter look suspiciously like the beginnings of a collection of holdings

---

[1] Page; 'Bidentes Hoylandie', and Wretts-Smith, 'Organisation of Farming'.
[2] *ECA*, p. 444.

including the manor site (or part of it in the earliest years, when the house was probably still standing), the Madecroft, pound for sheep, shippen and shepherd's house. It seems to have been held by Sir William Castleacre in the 1380s, possibly as part of the lease of the whole manor. He leased it to Thomas Bradfield in 1391, and Bradfield's name remained for years as the designation of these lands. Both these gentlemen appear as active sheep-farmers in the Court Rolls of both Landbeach and Cottenham. In 1410 this holding was conveyed from Bradfield to Richard Billingford, Master of the College. After this it was frequently let to the parson. Master Adam held it for years. When the Master of the College was also rector he frequently let it with or without the rectory. It seems to have been an attractive small farm for gentlemen graziers, compounded out of fragments of the demesne, never formally a unit, but with an astonishingly long life.[1]

According to Clay and Masters, the College, after its purchase of the manor, at first leased the demesne, but by the end of the fourteenth century had stocked it and was running it by a bailiff. Sometime after the middle of the fifteenth century, Elizabeth, dowager duchess of Norfolk, and her sister, Eleanor, widow of Sir Thomas Boteler who died in 1466, endowed the College by giving money for the purchase of sheep for the manorial stock, the profits from which were to be divided between the Master and Fellows. This arrangement was still working during the Mastership of Cosyn who died in 1516.

In 1498 we read that Thomas Cosyn and William Rackliffe (then lord of Brays)

hath ordained for the common weal of the tenants of Landbeach, that whosoever suffereth recklessly his flock of sheep to do any great hurt or harm in the meadow or in the field on their neighbour's grass or corn, for each flock the owner of the same flock shall pay to the reparation of the church at Landbeach afore rehearsed xij d.

In his *History of the College*, Masters says that the sheep were wiped out by the rot when William Sowde was rector, 1528–44, but that it was re-stocked by Matthew Parker. The gap would not have been long.[2]

When Mrs Parker sub-let (for almost three times her total rent) part of the lease she had from her husband's half-brother, who had it from Matthew, she kept back most of the grass and the thack of half an hundred sheep. The farmer who eventually got it took also Moor Leys with the thack of another 100 sheep.[3]

[1] CCCC, XXXV, 36; CCCC, XXXV, 101; CCCC, XXXV, 106.
[2] R. Masters, *The History of the College of Corpus Christi and the Blessed Virgin Mary, Commonly Called Bene't, in the University of Cambridge* (Cambridge, 1753), p. 36; cf. *Landbeach*.
[3] CCCC, XXXV, 180, Miscellaneous Documents; cf. J. R. Ravensdale, 'Landbeach in 1549', in L. M. Munby (ed.), *East Anglian Studies* (Cambridge, 1968), p. 107.

When, in 1580, Queen Elizabeth leased the demesnes of Waterbeach cum Denney, she reserved to the Crown:

The yearly herbage and pasture of the aforesaid two hundred acres of land for the flock of sheep of Sir Robertus Chester, Knight...when the same two hundred acres shall be unsown or be with stubble after harvest as the custom hath been used at any time before for the flock of sheep of Denny Abbey...

This had previously been included in the lease of the manor for sixty years to Sir Robert, in 5 & 6 Philip and Mary. So much for the iniquity of separating sheep-gate from house.[1]

The need to fit the grazing of close-cropping sheep into a system that did not starve their larger competitors, meant movement of flocks. This must have been exaggerated by the variable, and often unpredictable, water-table of the fens. In the accounts of Richard Pelle, the reeve for Chamberlains Manor in Landbeach, for Michaelmas 1348 to Michaelmas 1349, no sheep are listed. But in the accounts for the following ten weeks are seven yearlings. For Michaelmas 1345 to St James, 1346, no sheep appear in the stock, but 161 fleeces have been sold, and fells and pells total 157. In Thomas Brotherton's accounts for the year ended Michaelmas 1352, no sheep figure, but in those of Henry Wylmyn for 1356 sheep of all kinds amount to 147. The full story might be more complicated than the obvious simple explanation: a 'Bestial' of 1375, at Epiphany, shows 251 sheep, of which 30 have been sold and two have died. There are signs that the flock had been increased during the year, purchases including 27 from the rector of Landbeach, but of the other stock the pregnant and the young seem mostly to have been sent to Grantchester.[2] One cannot be sure whether this was normal practice at this time, or whether the fen was unusually wet. One cannot be sure whether it was shortage of feed or shortage of shelter which caused this movement. Nor can we be sure how far it was simply due to the economic interests of the de Eltisley family, for the Master of the College and his nephew were about to exchange the livings of Landbeach and Grantchester. We have insufficient information to distinguish between agistment, genuine purchase and the re-shuffling of family property at this point: but it is clear that the movement of animals to and from the demesnes is a considerable feature of the Chamberlains manor. Clearly the full potential of the fen as feeding ground could not be exploited by fixed numbers of beasts. These numbers would vary seasonally, since a good part of the fen would be unfit most winters, but the unpredictable variations of the water-table must have frequently provoked sudden competition for feeding that had been reduced in an unforseen way.

[1] WPC bundle, labelled 'Various Documents'.
[2] CCCC, XXXV, 146. 181, 182.

The taking in beasts of agistment was a continual source of trouble in all three villages. When it provoked an outcry, sheep would be the most unpopular of any foreign animals, because they would so effectively undergraze any great cattle unfortunate enough to be sharing with them. When agistment was banned there was always a good chance of a peasant 'colouring' foreign beasts by including them with his own flock. There is a complaint of illegal agistment of sheep in one of the earliest Chamberlains Court Rolls: 'John Schayl put himself in mercy because he agisted sheep in the town pasture without licence.'[1] This was also one of the graver complaints made against Richard Kirby in 1549: '9. Item, he keepeth in sheep of foreigners to the number of 1200, far above his rate, to the utter undoing of the poor men.'[2]

In Cottenham in 1525 William Whyston 'has taken sheep of foreigners to pasture within this lordship contrary to the ordinances on the subject', ('*cepit oves ab extraneis ad pasturam infra istud dominium contra ordinacionem inde facturam*'). He was in exactly the same trouble two years later.[3]

Orders made at the court of the Manor of Waterbeach cum Denney illustrate the importance and difficulty of this problem in the Tudor period. There are major changes in each of the three years, 24, 25 and 26th Eliz.:

24th E. 'That none shall keep sheep to halves, nor put away his sheep commons.'

25th E. 'That it shall be lawful for them to keep sheep as they did before the last court and to take to halves so as they exceed not the numbers rated them by their tenures, so they have wool and lambs.'

26th E. 'Whereas there is controversy betweene the Farmers of the Joyst Fen, and the tenants, touching the taking in of winter joist by the farmers, and for putting in of sheep into the same fen in summer by the tenants, Ordered that the Farmers shall not put any cattle in before May Day yearly. That all Joist Cattle be avoided on the Common Drift Day except 100, and they not to remain above a week.'[4]

Taking in sheep to halves, which meant taking half the lambs and wool, was very attractive to the poor man with pasture rights but no capital. Commercial farming in Tudor Waterbeach produced the same strains of competition between rich and poor as elsewhere in the period, but at Waterbeach apparently it reflected the rivalry between sheep of the peasants and great cattle of the gentry or yeomen for grass. This was not usual; on the whole it was rich sheep graziers who drew the wrath of the peasantry. Sir William Hinde of Madingley spread his large flocks through many Cambridgeshire villages as well as the City:

[1] CCCC, XXXV, 121, 6 Ed. III.
[2] CCCC, XXXV, 194.
[3] CRO, Francis Papers, Court Rolls of Crowlands.
[4] WPC, WcD.

Item, we find that Mr. Hynde unlawfully doth bring into Cambridge field a flock of sheep to the number of vi or vii Cth, to the undoing of the farmers and great hindrance of all the inhabitants of Cambridge.

Item, we find that Mr. Hynde after the corn be inned and harvest done bringeth in his cattle in great number and eateth up the common to like hindrance.[1]

Mr Hinde could operate on a scale that included the purchase of whole manors in Cottenham and elsewhere to provide room for his sheep. Lesser men had to pick up what they could: in 1539 a Cottenham rectory tenant, Ralf Barrow, and Robert Powell were both presented for bringing in sheep belonging to John Lechworth, 100 and 60 respectively. If the manor court made it difficult for foreign sheep to be taken in, it might be possible to cease to be a foreigner by acquiring a tenement and so 'naturalising' the sheep: a presentation in Waterbeach during the first year of Hen. VIII runs: 'That John Bell, tenant of one messuage and chargeth the Common with sheep, keeping 500 sheep. And that from henceforth he do not surcharge it.' But he seems to have remained and prospered. Eleven years later there is another order: 'Alderman John Bell of Cambridge to move his sheep out of the commons of this town.' His tenement was merely an osier holt down at Clayhithe. An order of the following year seems to have been aimed directly at him: 'That no Foreigner shall purchase any customary tenement within the manor of Waterbeach and Denny unless he brings his family hither to inhabit.' This was followed a few years later by: 'That none take any cattle to agist by colour of his own right.'

An Order of 1495, also couched in very general terms, seems to have been even more of a dead letter: 'That neither the Lady Abbess nor any other tenant from henceforth receive any sheep but their own.'

Shortly after the Dissolution the habit grew up whereby lists of ordinances were drawn up by the court. These appear for the most part to be versions of what had been promulgated piecemeal from time to time as the need arose, and were then undergoing something like codification. One such in the 19th year of Eliz. deals with agistment, and may in fact from the very name of the fen (Joyst short for agist) have been a revival of ancient custom: 'That no foreigner keep any cattle in any part of the Town Common but in Jestffen unless they couch and lie, keep house in the town and pay scot and lot.'

In the following year was added a separate single order which, reinforcing this, must have provided a scheme in which there was some hope of control of agistment: 'That no tenant let his sheepgate or take in any sheep except to halves.'[2] This again may in part have been a revival of ancient custom.

---

[1] C. H. Cooper, *Annals of Cambridge* (Cambridge, 1842–1908), vol. II, p. 37.
[2] The information used in the above paragraphs is taken from the Court Book of Waterbeach cum Denney in the parish chest under the regnal years indicated. WcD.

The size of medieval peasant flocks has been a subject of controversy, and is very difficult to determine.[1] All the evidence for this in the three villages under discussion is indirect and fragmentary. At best we get indications only. Presentations for failure to put sheep in the lord's fold, and for trespass, provide most of the hints in the Court Rolls for Landbeach. In the course of the fourteenth century, presentations for trespass become an obsession to the point where they dwarf all the other business of the court put together. Numbers and kinds of animals involved are usually given, but not always, and there is nothing at all to tell us whether the cases represent the whole of a particular peasant's flock. Nor do they tell whether these are the largest, or average, or smaller flocks. But the Landbeach cases give a strong impression of very considerable sheep husbandry by the peasants, and on the whole this seems to increase until later in the century.[2] But the apparent trend may possibly be in part due to a falling off in respect for law and order, and the attempt of the courts to tighten up the enforcement of agricultural discipline in reply, or simply to collect fines.

The court rolls unfortunately start too late for us to be able to trace the early stages of growth in peasant flocks. At the very beginning there are signs of considerable activity. In 1328 John Haldeyn placed himself in mercy for trespasses with 300 sheep in the lord's pasture; John Sexyne for 200 in the Frith Fen; Henry Sandre for 100 in the lord's peas; William Williams for trespasses on three occasions with 20 sheep and 4 mares; John Judde had been pasturing his sheep in the lord's several in the moor; and Thomas Gunne had put his sheep in the lord's field in winter, and not sent them to the fold. Others are recorded but no numbers given.

In 1332, as well as the case of agistment of sheep by John Schayl mentioned above, Simon le Herne was recorded for failing as pledge to produce William Castleacre for trespasses with his sheep in the pastures of this town. Now William Castleacre of Great Gransden was a knight with interests in Cottenham as well as Waterbeach. Here we already have a hint of the gentleman grazier whose activities extend over a wider area than a single manor, a figure that becomes more familiar in Tudor times, but already present before the Black Death. Professor Miller's injunction to look for rising gentry before the sixteenth century could well take us back at least this far, and take us among the sheep.

---

[1] Cf. Eileen Power, *The Wool Trade in English Medieval History* (Oxford, 1941), pp. 30–2; M.M.Postan, 'Village Livestock in the Thirteenth Century', *EconHR*, 2nd series, XV (1962); R.Hilton, *A Medieval Society: the west Midlands at the end of the Thirteenth Century* (1967), pp. 109–10. The picture in Landbeach seems to be one of large peasant flocks more like those discovered by Eileen Power than the smaller ones of the later investigators. This may be an indication of the pastoral bias of the local fen-edge economy.

[2] The subsequent information on trespass and non-fold cases is found in CCCC, XXXV, 121–126, Court Rolls of the Manors of Chamberlains and Brays, under regnal years and saints' days.

The absence of demesne sheep from the stock list at the end of Richard Pelle's earlier term as reeve in 1342, does not represent a general abandonment of sheep-rearing in the manor such as might have been caused by murrain, for there are several cases of non-fold. A peak is reached in 1347 with 27 such cases. The evidence for the Black Death years shows the existence of numbers of moderate-sized peasant flocks (although these are probably only part flocks). Among 29 cases of trespass in the lord's corn and in the Frith Fen, John Ric(h)ard had 20 sheep in the corn and 60 in the fen. This alone suggests that the figures are not very likely to represent the peasant's whole flock. In the same group of offences Thomas Ric(h)ard had 50, Avicia Martyn 30, John Osebern 20, and John Ward 60. Cases of non-fold in 1349 show John Fenlond with 26 sheep, Henry Sandre with 60, and John Ric(h)ard with 60. These villeins Osseberns, Sexines, Attefens, Martins, were all present in the Hundred Rolls. Roger Sandre was enfranchised in 1377. A Roger Sandre of Landbeach appeared in Cottenham in 1408, and his son was caught illegally fishing there in 1413. But John and Thomas Sandre were recorded as having fled in 1380. Roger was still involved in Landbeach at that date, for order was made to re-possess an acre and a half of demesne which he had occupied without licence. All lands listed in 1459 as having been his were listed as demesne lands. They included two holdings of nine acres each, and a halfland, an old croftland, normally five acres. This would have made him one of the most substantial peasants in the village, representing a living for three villein families. It is not clear whether villein prosperity in Landbeach ended in enfranchisement and removal, or whether villeinage so frustrated prosperity, that it ended in flight. The great villein family of Cottenham, the Pepys, seems to have frequently found ways to make money, and numbered fleeing members among them. Miss Page recorded only four clear cases of simple enfranchisement of villeins, apart from licences to take Holy Orders, and one of these was for John Tankred of Cottenham. It is perhaps significant that a close called Tancred's is listed year by year in the collectors' accounts of the late fifteenth and early sixteenth centuries. But the enfranchisement was in 1389, and there were Thankrets fleeing in 1403, and more in 1409. A prosperous villein denied enfranchisement might well flee, and if no tenant could be found the land itself would become freed. It is not possible to discover which of the two processes produced these big empty tofts in the villages. Fleeing villeins were not necessarily impoverished. For instance, when the goods of Alan, son of Henry Wylmyn, who had gone to live at Dry Drayton, were seized in Landbeach in 1366, he had 44 sheep, 12 lambs, and 30 fleeces, as well as 2 cows and 2 geese. Sheep, in this area at least, for peasant and for knight, could be a means to prosperity.

Office-holding might also help somewhat, but independence of mind more. Henry Sandre, who was fined in 1349 for having 60 sheep out of the lord's fold, as bailiff in 1356 was discovered to have sold the use of the lord's fold to compost four acres. John Osebern whose 20 sheep had trespassed in the Frith Fen in the earlier year seems to have prospered for he admitted a trespass in the lord's corn by 500 of his sheep in the latter year. Not only peasant flocks were involved in offences. Hugo le Bray, lord of the other manor in Landbeach, was accused, on the strength of his holding a bondage tenement of Chamberlains, of failing to send 30 sheep to the lord's (Chamberlains) fold. In 1363 Robert the shepherd of Waterbeach was presented for trespass with 180 sheep. But the bulk of the cases were concerned with villagers. In 1369 some 358 sheep were involved in 7 cases of trespass.

But there are periods when the trespassing sheep suddenly disappear from the court rolls, and the fens seem to come alive with mares and foals; after a few years the sheep reappear, at first a few, then building up quickly. For instance, in 1372, after the enormous numbers of sheep in trespass cases of 1369, there were none at all, but instead 42 cases of horses, mostly mares, sometimes with foals, involving 105 animals. There seem to have been two similar periods in the early fifteenth century. Unfortunately we do not have accounts to tell us whether murrain was at work. Sheep-farming seems to have been not much more certain than arable on the medieval fen edge.

Not only do the court rolls suggest that a number at least of the peasants were prosperous in the late fourteenth century; they also suggest that the spirit of the times filtered through to them in Landbeach in the period of the Peasants' Revolt. In the St Bartholomew Court, 1380, 118 cases of trespass were recorded. Thomas Michel was accused by John Bernard of stealing six ewes from his close. He was also accused of making a practice of turning his swine out into the lord's corn at night. Two years later he was answering for trespasses with 60 and with 40 sheep, and in 1395 for a case with a flock of 100. In 1380 also, the vicar of Waterbeach was presented for trespassing in Landbeach with all his sheep in the lord's oats. A new formula was used from this year. Instead of 'committed trespass' ('*fecit transgressum*') we find in trespass cases, 'who was taken with...in' ('*qui captus fuit cum...in...*'). In these years appeared the two cases of housebreaking in the rolls, one by Thomas, chaplain, servant of the parson. Peasants began to be reported as rebellious against the bailiff. In 1383 Roger Sandre, John Martyn, John Intheherne, John Sweyn and Roger Wylmyn rebelled against the order of the reeve at the turning out of the lord's sheep. At the following court in the same year, the same six, together with John Symme and John Fen, were accused of being rebellious again in refusing to do their carrying services to the lord's brew-house in Cambridge. If this 'independence' is the fruit of apparent moderate prosperity and hope of more, there is not much doubt that the sheep played its part in creating it. Such flocks as were numbered in the 108 cases of trespass in 1395, amount to a total of 1,900; many other flocks were mentioned with no figure given.

With such numbers there was likely to be a problem of over-stocking. The first known attempt in this area to remedy this by stinting, regulation of the numbers of animals that could be stocked, came from Cottenham in 1285. At the Assizes in Huntingdon that year, a case claiming over-stocking by the other lords and tenants was brought by one of the Crowlands freehold tenants in each of Oakington, Cottenham, and Dry Drayton. In Cottenham it was alleged that Walter de Pelham, who had 24 acres of land in demesne and villeinage constituting a manor, kept 60 head of stock and 400 sheep there, and that each of the six others named had a great number of animals and flocks in the pasture over and above the number which they ought to have according to the size of their tenements. The complainant, Symon le Waleis, a lord in his own right as well as tenant of the abbot, said that by reason of the thinness of the pasture of the said village the pasture there would hardly suffice each hide of land an allowance of 6 oxen, 2 horses (this might constitute the local plough team), 6 cows, 80 sheep, and 15 geese. Order was given that the commons should be so measured.[1] There are limitations, too, in the first mentions of sheep in Landbeach. When in 1336 Henry Chamberlain granted to his brother John the right of folding 120 sheep on his land for life, he made the proviso that John should keep only one fold and no ram, and that if John broke this agreement, Henry should have the right to destroy the fold and take away the overplus.[2] In Waterbeach the commonest form of restriction on the amount of stock is written into one of the earliest court rolls, 1335: 'It is agreed by the homage that no freeholder within the said manor ought to have common for more cattle than he can keep in the winter.' This was repeated in 1432–3 with a reference to this roll of 1335. A much clearer regulation was introduced in the second year of Elizabeth's reign: 'None keep above one sheep for every sixpence rent and that no cottager of the town or village shall keep above ten sheep in number.'[3]

This particular regulation survived a long time. In the 'Articles of Agreement for the Use of the Commons' of 1683, it appears as part of the arrangements for control of the commons. This was to be by regulated stint, supervised by two fen reeves elected by a meeting of commoners:

Item that for each and every common every owner or occupier shall or may feed fifteen milch cows or dry neat cattle and ten sheep, and the owner of every half commonable house proportionably. And if he or they shall not think fit to keep so many cows then he or they may keep ten cows and five mares or geldings, but not to exceed the number of five mares or horse beasts, and to abate a cow for every colt after it is a year old.

[1] PRO JI 1/186.   [2] CCCC, XXXV, 36.   [3] WPC, WcD.

'Item that three weanling calves of the first year shall or may be kept in the place and stead of one cow, and two yearling neat cattle in lieu of one cow, and so proportionably for every cow.'

The fens, wastes and commons were to be spared from Lady Day to May Day from being depastured by any cattle, sheep only excepted.[1]

The Act for the Draining of the Waterbeach Level in 1740 reduced each of the $119\frac{1}{2}$ common rights to fifteen head of great cattle with eight sheep. The Act of 1790 reduced this from fifteen to twelve head of great cattle.[2]

Landbeach tried to solve its share of the mounting problems of sheep in the mid-sixteenth century by stint. In 1548:

First it is ordained that no tenant or inhabitant of the aforesaid town shall keep upon the commons there above the number of three sheep for an acre under pain to forfeit unto the lord xx d.

Item, it is ordained that no tenant shall take in to feed upon the commons of this town the sheep of any stranger above two sheep for an acre and to take of the lord's farm three for every acre upon pain to forfeit xl d.[3]

This regulation was the product of crisis, when the troubles in Norfolk had their miniature counterpart in Landbeach. The leet was held on the second of November 1548. Had its terms been accepted and observed by Richard Kirby, the lord of the Manor of Brays, the disturbances which resulted in the next year from his over-stocking could scarcely have taken place.

Whether sheep-farming was on good or bad times, the seigneurial monopoly of folding must have been irksome to the peasantry. Miss Page tells of the kindness of the abbot of Crowland in the hard years around 1322 when he relaxed the right at Dry Drayton, allowing the homage to fold half their sheep on their own lands for twelve successive years.[4]

But more often the right seems to have tested the lord's powers of control over the peasantry. Eleven years after the sale of part of the lord's right of folding by Henry Sandre, bailiff, in 1356,[5] another bailiff was presented for letting it at farm. In the previous year the lord's shepherd had failed to place it for one week. In 1401 Roger Sandre, John Fen and William Sweyn raised an unlicensed fold instead of putting their sheep in the lord's. When the Manor of Brays was let to farm, the lord seems to have been unable to enforce his right. Thomas Letes, his farmer, was presented regularly from 1408 to 1415 for illegally sub-letting it. Five years later the court rolls record an ordinance that the lord's farmers (there were now three) must fold on lord's demesne lands only. Even when his

---

[1] CRO transcript no. 12.
[2] *Waterbeach*, p. 19.
[3] CCCC, XXXV, 134.   [4] *ECA*, p. 50.
[5] See above, CCCC, XXXV, 121.

direct interest in cultivation had gone the lord remained jealous of his right to the tathe of the sheep for the demesnes. When the abbot of Crowland let the manors of Oakington and Cottenham in 1430 it was an important duty of each tenant to maintain a flock of 200 sheep. A Crowlands Ordinance for Dry Drayton of 1523 asserts the farmer's duty to receive and look after the peasant sheep in the fold, and the peasants' duty to help him feed them in times of drought.[1]

This complex ordinance illustrates how closely interwoven were the problems of agistment, stint, foldage, and sheepwalk on the commons. There seems to have been less trouble in the villages once the lords had acquired severals for their share of the fens. This happened first in Waterbeach. In 1438, according to an extract of Cole's from the Court Rolls of Waterbeach cum Denney (an extract that does not appear in the version in the parish chest) the abbess had enclosed common land:

The ministers of the Lady have enclosed the Hye Meadowe and the Marish called the Frithfenne with Ditches and Hedges as the Several of the Lady to the exclusion of the Commoners of Waterbeche who claim them to be common from St. Michael to Candlemas and desire that they may be opened that they may have their common there. To which it was answered them openly in full court, that it is clearly found by sufficient evidence viz., before the foundation of the Abbey of a certain Exchange made between the Master and Brothers, Knights of the Order of St. John, Templars in England, Lords of the manor of Denney, of the one part, and Mary Lady Munchensey, Lady of the manor of Waterbeche, of the other part, in which evidence, publicly shewn and clearly read is contained, That by an Exchange and Covenant between the parties aforesaid made, that the said Templars, Lords of the manor of Denney may enclose the said meadow and marish, as their own several by the year; absque hoc that any commoner of the Towne aforesaid at any time of the year ought to common there, as in the said Evidence is more fully contained. And so it appeared to the Chief Pledge and all commoners That they had unjustly and maliciously put in the said presentment. Therefore with general consent they humbly entreated the Steward to disannul the presentment and to expel it utterly from the Books.[2]

We cannot date the creation of the Landbeach Sheepwalks, which absorbed the greater part of the fen, so precisely. The first indisputable reference is in Serjeant Bernard's opinion of the mid-seventeenth century:

In this waste ground there hath been time out of mind four several sheepwalks, distinguished and certainly known from one another. The College hath one, Sir John Barker two, and the College copyhold tenants in that town hath a fourth.
The bounds of those sheepwalks are so certainly known that the sheep that are in one of the walks never have used to come into either of the other, but when or how their waste ground was thus divided into several sheepwalks; there is no mention, neither is it certainly known to which manor any part of this waste ground, where these sheepwalks are, do belong.[3]

[1] CCCC, XXXV, 124; *ECA*, p. 444; CUL Queens' Dd 2.
[2] BM Ad. MS. 5837, fol. 148d.   [3] CCCC, XXXV, 176; cf. Masters' Collectanea in LPC.

At the end of the parish copy of the field book of 1549 there is a note of Clifford's of the customs of the parson at his entry there in 1565: 'In primis, the parson is to have the course of ix score sheep in the College flock, paying to the shepherd ij d. for every sheep.' This is of course not a complete proof of the physical division of the ground having taken place to correspond to the division of the flocks, but at the very least this half of the process of separation of sheep-grazing has happened. The parson's ration remains the same in Masters' time on the College Sheepwalk.[1]

There are a number of other inconclusive early references to what may be the Sheepwalks. In 1622 the tenants certified that the late William Ridlie and his predecessor William Lane had always kept their sheep from their ground on the 'College Sheepcourse'. A Court Roll Order of 1578 dealing with the ditching of Frith Fen refers to a '*pastura ovium*' in a place where we can locate the Town Sheepwalk on the eve of parliamentary enclosure. The Lease Books of Corpus Christi College contain several references from 1563 to 1667 to rights for sheep in Landbeach, but the wording seems deliberately vague, conveying customary rights of which there is precise local knowledge, and leaving them undefined in the written leases. In 1563 Robert Norgate conveyed to William Norgate 'liberties of sheepwalks and foldings'. In 1609 this became, 'their moor ground or soil called the College Sheepwalk and the whole liberty of Sheepwalk and fold course'. There can be little doubt that the Sheepwalks as permanently separate enclosures from the fen were in existence by this time, but they may well date from the previous century.

There is a confusing difficulty with the local terminology. In Landbeach and Cottenham sheepwalks were permanently separate pieces taken out of the fen. The term seems to have been used in Waterbeach as the entitlement to a fixed number of sheep in one of the three flocks, Denney, Town, or the parson's. This is also an alternative use for it in eighteenth-century Landbeach, but in Waterbeach there seem never to have been permanently separate areas as particular sheepwalks.[2]

The word 'foldcourse' creates even more difficulties because of its association with a highly-specialised East Anglian system. In criticising Allison's account of the Norfolk foldcourse, Simpson suggested that the arrangements in Cottenham under the Agreement of 1596 represented a similar system, and that the foldcourse represented a survival of the lord's monopoly of foldage.[3]

As Cunningham suspected, there was an earlier stage at Cottenham. In the reign of Philip and Mary, after enclosure and fence-breaking, agreement was made in the Court of the Star Chamber for Sir Francis Hinde, as

---

[1] LPC, Field Book, and CCCC, XXXV, 178, Pemberton–Masters Correspondence.
[2] CCCC, XXXV, 139, 135, and College lease books.
[3] Allison, 'The Sheep-Corn Husbandry of Norfolk', p. 12; Simpson, 'The East Anglian Fold-course', p. 86.

lord of the Manors of Crowlands and Lyles, to maintain two several sheepwalks in Longhill, Marehill, and Tylling. In exchange all the other customary sheep pastures were to be devoted exclusively to the inhabitants, and Hinde was to confine his to the specified enclosures. But so far from being a development of the seigneurial monopoly of folding, the agreement of the tenants effectively bought out this right; the sheep masters and the fold reeves were to order the same folds as before for the composting of the lands *as they should think meet and convenient*. The record makes it clear that this was an innovation.[1]

Cunningham gives the subsequent history of this Agreement being disputed and renewed up to its final confirmation by a Decree in Chancery in 1597. The Agreement then seems to have lasted until parliamentary enclosure.[2]

Cunningham also printed the Orders of 1639 in the same *Camden Miscellany*. It is possible to trace something of the history of these orders right up to parliamentary enclosure. The two last fen reeves' books survive in private hands. They are large ledger books in which all the orders currently in force are carefully entered, and cancellations, amendments and new orders added from time to time, usually with the dates noted marginally. The end papers have been used for rough work, mostly voting records of changes, sometimes with the names recorded, 'For' and 'Against'. The receipts and expenditures reveal not only a lively social side, so that ordermakers' days were like an additional feast, but they also show how extensive were the powers of these officials.

The Agreement of 1596–7, as Cunningham pointed out, seemed to have been rather more concerned with great cattle than sheep. It was to solve problems of the commoning of great cattle also, that Landbeach completed a similar pattern of fen management. In this case regulated stint and its control were the immediate issues. Proposals for an Agreement, in the hope of securing a Chancery Decree were drawn up in 1735. The College, its farmer, the rector and two tenant farmers stood together to block it. But in 1738, after the College farmer had shown signs of changing sides, Chancery granted the Decree.[3]

Five ordermakers were to be elected each year at an annual meeting of commoners. Cattle were stinted to eleven head per common, those below two years of age only counting as half. Joysting was to be allowed to make up the numbers.

One hears curiously little of the ordermakers in later years at Landbeach and Waterbeach. The 1748 Orders are headed 'Mannor of Waterbeach with Denny', and are made 'At a Court Leet General Court Baron and

[1] PRO SC 4 P & M 3/17.
[2] *Common Rights*, pp. 177–9.
[3] LPC, Collectanea, quoted in *Landbeach*.

Customary Court', by the jury impanelled there. In 1779, since the Act of 1740 was being flouted in that persons with no common right were putting beasts into the commons, a general meeting of the commoners was held at 'The Rose and Crown'. In future it was decided that all beasts must have a Town brand as well as that of their owners. The brand, and a register were to be kept by Edward Mason, innkeeper, who was also to have the paid duty of going daily into the fen to inspect the herd. The order is signed by Robert Masters, vicar, and ends, characteristically, with an arrangement to charge a flat rate agistment tithe, whatever the charge made by the commoner.[1]

Thus each of the three villages solved the problems arising from the conflict of interest among those raising sheep by a solution which embraced something far wider, the whole common rights. Each evolved a similar machinery, but each had its own variations. No doubt each influenced the others by example. There would probably be more justification in talking of a 'fen-edge system' than there is for some of the other systems that litter the pages of agrarian history. Some of their problems and solutions have similarities derived from their topographical similarities like the possession of fens; some from wider economic currents, such as the shift of the centre of stress from sheep in the mid-sixteenth century, to cattle later. A good deal of the variation in the machinery was a function of their small but important topographical differences, as in Landbeach's more elaborate Sheepwalks. Some was indirect, through the influence of topography on social structure. But whatever the formal arrangements, it could never be simply the system or conditions that determined the issue in a village where Robert Masters was vicar, or Matthew Parker rector.

For the last century or more of the open fields in each of these villages there was a stability, in the general working of their commons and fens. Perhaps, as suggested in other connections, this was due to the shift of power from the lords to the peasantry on the land. Article XXV of the 1596 Agreement may have held much of the answer: 'No laws to be made in any of the lord's courts.' This certainly created a powerful and effective all-purpose authority.[2] Perhaps the last word on the commons should go to the shrewd observer, a lord of a manor across the Old West River from our parishes, Albert Pell:

The right to graze the ways with cows was confined to a limited number of persons, the commoners. Horses, goats, geese, sheep, were not commonable animals. The sheep were in three limited flocks, the first belonging to the manor, the second to the rectory, while the third was an independent one, the rights of which could be bought and sold. These three rights of grazing were called sheep-walks. The sheep in each had its shepherd, who stalked ahead of his flock, the dog bringing up the rear and every now and again rushing in, police fashion, at any ewe that ventured to snatch a bite from the corn that grew on the

---

[1] WPC, Tithe bundle. [2] *Common Rights*, pp. 212–13.

ends of the 'lands', which, unprotected, bordered the green 'ways' between the cropping. The commoners' cows, about twenty-two in number, were 'flitted' or tethered with rope and shackle out of reach of the corn. After harvest on a given day the commoners' cattle and pigs roved all over the stubbles to pick up the 'shack'. They also stocked an inter-parochial waste or common at all seasons of the year, and it was the commoners, not the lord of the manor, who resented and resisted the intrusion of the 'public' claiming or attempting to turn stock on to this land. Sometimes the trespass was summarily stopped by ham-stringing the unprivileged animals. The vulgar idea of the general public having rights of any kind on the waste or commonable land was never for a moment admitted.[1]

[1] *Albert Pell*, ed. Mackay, p. 95.

III. (a) North-east view of Denney Abbey, engraved by S. and N. Buck, 1730. The refectory of the minoresses became a barn in the farmhouse period.

(b) Masters' engraving of Denney Abbey which appeared as the frontispiece to his *Short Account*. The windows of the first farmhouse after the Dissolution were replaced by Georgian sashes after the date of this engraving (1795). The farmhouse consisted of the remains of the romanesque church as adapted by the countess of Pembroke for her own quarters.

IV. (a) Stukeley's sketch (19 May 1731) of Lordship House, Cottenham: this was the house of Katherine Pepys, and the formal garden, which vanished long ago, probably dates from her time (source: Bodleian MS. Top. gen. d. 14 fol. 30v).

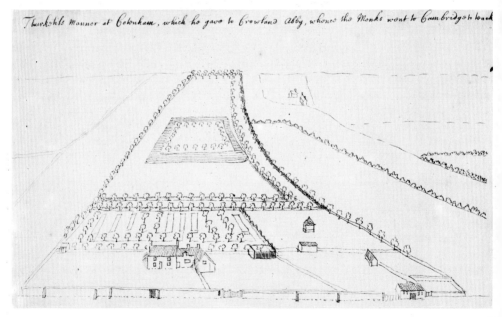

Thurketils Mannor at Cotenham, which he gave to Crowland Abby, whence the Monks went to Cambridge to teach

(b) Stukeley's sketch (28 August 1731) of the Crowlands manor of Cottenham: this house is still perfectly recognisable under slate roof and stucco (source: Bodleian MS. Top. eccles. d. 6 fol. 20r).

3

THE FIELDS

In his thesis on 'The Open Fields of Cambridgeshire', M. Postgate made a survey of the fields on the eve of parliamentary enclosure, and showed a very complex picture which seemed to bear little relation to traditional views on the pattern of Midland open-field farming. For the county as a whole it appeared that the final result was the outcome of two opposite movements, the creation of new fields by assarting, and the absorption of such fields into a regular cropping system. In earlier years assarts and fields multiplied, but as the plough neared the boundaries of potential arable fewer fresh ones could be created, but assimilation still continued. On the whole the earliest documents suggested that two- and three-field systems, like those of the Midlands, were common, but later evidence suggested a proliferation of fields, which were in turn somewhat reduced in early modern times. But there were numerous paradoxes which cast doubt on the neat simplicity of the explanation offered. For instance, the Ely Old Coucher Book for Willingham suggested what appeared to be an orthodox three-field system in 1251, while Fen Ditton apparently had something much more informal with sixteen fields listed.[1] Yet on the eve of enclosure a three-field system was operating at Fen Ditton and what Postgate interpreted as six fields at Willingham.

Postgate based his thesis mainly on the lists of names of fields which he gathered from a vast amount of material, especially terriers. Its validity depended very much on the meaning or implied meaning of the terms used in the documents. The Berrycroft in Willingham was counted as a field because it appeared in a terrier as 'Every year land', but crofts attached to manor houses or peasant houses, and cropped on completely separate individual lines, have always been accepted as running alongside open-field systems.[2]

Recent local research has increasingly exposed a further difficulty; terriers, particularly terriers contained in indentures, frequently contain far more field-names than are recognised by contemporary eye-witness descriptions of the local farming practice.[3] With this in mind, it seemed worth

[1] BM MS. Cotton Claudius CXI; Gonville and Caius College, MS. No. 485/489; CUL EDR Liber R. The copy in the BM is the best.
[2] E.g. CCCC, XXXV, 121, mentions 'three stetches of croftland'. Berry or bury is common in this area for crofts by manor houses or for sites of former manor houses. Cf. CUL Queens' Ad, 26, 25 Henry, Abbot, 'two butts of arable land in a croft' ('*duas buttas terre arabilis in croftam*').
[3] This was brought out very clearly by Dr Margaret Spufford in her essay, 'Longstanton', for the Nicols Essay Competition at Leicester University. I am most grateful to Dr Spufford for the loan of this work.

while to examine all the written and visual evidence for a small area, relating the names to the detailed topography and the development of the systems of cultivation. For the three parishes chosen, Postgate found on the eve of enclosure, five fields at Cottenham, four (formerly five) at Landbeach, and eight at Waterbeach. This seemed to offer a good opportunity for testing his hypothesis. Part of Postgate's argument depended on the assumption that when an improved assart was brought into the common cropping scheme of the arable, a field-name would be lost. But as long ago as 1897 Maitland had shown that this was not necessarily so: when discussing the Cambridge East Fields he showed that the four fields, each with its own distinctive name, cropped as three, those on the extreme north and south running together as one ('*pro uno campo*').[1] Field-names need to be examined both in their relation to the local topography and to the cropping system before we can discover the pattern of the arable farming.

THE OPEN FIELDS OF WATERBEACH

For the arable farming of the open fields in Waterbeach, Postgate's method now appears to have suggested complications which were absent in practice. The three-shift system which Maitland found in the four Cambridge East Fields seems, on closer examination, to have been very like that which operated in Waterbeach from the early thirteenth century right up to the parliamentary enclosure of the nineteenth: three shifts only, in spite of more numerous field-names.

Field-names for this parish have been examined from medieval charters, from extracts from the now vanished Court Rolls of Denney and Waterbeach, from the series of glebe terriers and terriers of glebe lands, from the papers in the tithe dispute in the late eighteenth century between Masters and Standley, and from the Award Map and Schedule of the Parliamentary Enclosure in 1813. When carefully examined all this evidence is congruent with the observation of Vancouver; 'The common husbandry of two crops and a fallow prevails in this parish...'.[2]

In his list of open fields for Waterbeach, 1638–1813, Postgate gives: (1) Bannolds Towne, (2) Denney Bannoll, (3) Haverstock Towne, (4) Denney Haverstock, (5) Winfold Town, (6) Hill, (7) Fannes Close, (8) Hall. These names are apparently taken from the Glebe Terrier of 1638, where they are used as sectional headings, but the other sectional heading,

---

[1] F. W. Maitland, *Township and Borough* (Cambridge, 1898), p. 55. Even more complicated was the division of the four Cambridge West Fields into three seasons.

[2] Charters in *Liber Eliensis* as detailed below; extracts of Court Rolls, WPC, WcD, supplemented from Cole MS., 5837; glebe terriers in WPC and CUL, EDR H1/5 & 6; *Masters* vs. *Standley* in CUL, EDR A 14 and WPC; enclosure award and map, CRO Q/RD 28 and Q/RDc 31; Vancouver, *General View of Agriculture*, p. 129.

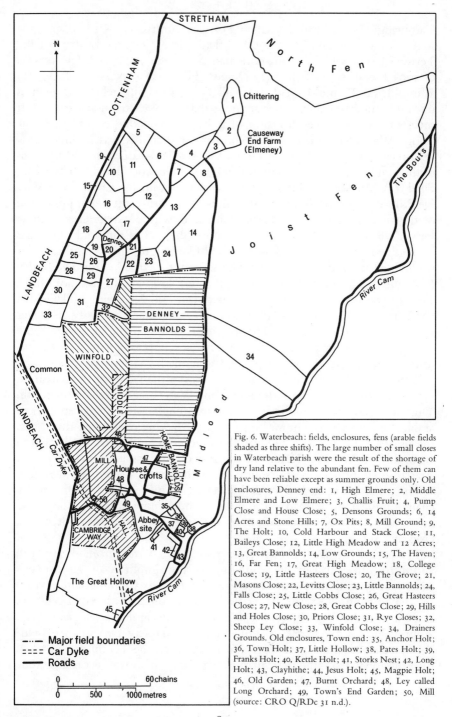

Fig. 6. Waterbeach: fields, enclosures, fens (arable fields shaded as three shifts). The large number of small closes in Waterbeach parish were the result of the shortage of dry land relative to the abundant fen. Few of them can have been reliable except as summer grounds only. Old enclosures, Denney end: 1, High Elmere; 2, Middle Elmere and Low Elmere; 3, Challis Fruit; 4, Pump Close and House Close; 5, Densons Grounds; 6, 14 Acres and Stone Hills; 7, Ox Pits; 8, Mill Ground; 9, The Holt; 10, Cold Harbour and Stack Close; 11, Baileys Close; 12, Little High Meadow and 12 Acres; 13, Great Bannolds; 14, Low Grounds; 15, The Haven; 16, Far Fen; 17, Great High Meadow; 18, College Close; 19, Little Hasteers Close; 20, The Grove; 21, Masons Close; 22, Levitts Close; 23, Little Bannolds; 24, Falls Close; 25, Little Cobbs Close; 26, Great Hasteers Close; 27, New Close; 28, Great Cobbs Close; 29, Hills and Holes Close; 30, Priors Close; 31, Rye Closes; 32, Sheep Ley Close; 33, Winfold Close; 34, Drainers Grounds. Old enclosures, Town end: 35, Anchor Holt; 36, Town Holt; 37, Little Hollow; 38, Pates Holt; 39, Franks Holt; 40, Kettle Holt; 41, Storks Nest; 42, Long Holt; 43, Clayhithe; 44, Jesus Holt; 45, Magpie Holt; 46, Old Garden; 47, Burnt Orchard; 48, Ley called Long Orchard; 49, Town's End Garden; 50, Mill (source: CRO Q/RDc 31 n.d.).

Cambridge Way Furlong, which Postgate omits, seems to have equal status in the original with the other field-names. This is also true of the Terrier of 1661 which has the same names, in the same order. The version of 1704 lists only six fields: (1) Denney Field, (2) Haverstock Field, (3) Winfold, (4) Bannold Field, (5) Mill Field, (6) Hill Field. The next is undated, but internal evidence suggests that it comes from about 1715. It reverts to the seventeenth-century list, but changes the seventh to Cambridge Way *Field* Furlong, thus confirming that this was intended as a field-name. Masters' Terrier of 1765 uses six field-names as sub-divisions of the arable: (1) Bannold Town Field, (2) Haverstock Field, (3) Winfold Field, (4) Mill or Hill Field, (5) Denney Bannold, (6) Cambridge Way Field. In case this should suggest a mid-eighteenth-century simplification of the field system, it should be compared with a terrier in Matthew Parker's Field Book for Landbeach.[1] Near the end of the book there has been added 'A Rental of the copy called Cheryngtons in Waterbeach for the arable land only', dated 1580. This sets out the lands in four fields only: (1) Hylle filde, (2) Have stack filde, (3) Winfold Fylde, (4) Bannold filde. The equivalence shown by Masters between Hill Field and Mill Field is confirmed by the topography and local vernacular: the only hill ever mentioned by the older inhabitants of the parish in the area where the open fields once lay is Mill Hill, and it takes the eye of a native of the fens to detect the slight rise in the ground so named.

A glance at Fig. 6[2] shows that Denney is in the north of the parish, in fact beyond the north end of the arable, and Waterbeach Town in the south. Thus 'Denney' as an epithet bears the meaning 'north' when applied to arable, and 'town' or 'home' means 'south'. The local usage thus has a means of adding precision to location of pieces of land, particularly within Bannold and Winfold Fields: in the rest of the arable, which does not stretch so simply north and south, but rather curls around the west and south of the town, such finer definition seems more effectively given by changing the name instead of the epithet. The naming of sub-divisions was intended to help exact location of pieces of land, not to represent a cropping system.

The earlier medieval evidence, consisting of charters from the twelfth and thirteenth centuries, has something of the simplicity of Vancouver's statement quoted above. In 1176 or earlier Robert Chamberlain gave to the Benedictine cell at denney certain lands, 'in the township of Beche...ix acres, in each field, iii' ('*in villa de Beche...ix acras, in unoquoque campo iij*'). Aubrey Picot's gift carries a similar phrase, 'namely two in each field' ('*scilicet duas in unoquoque campo*'). In 1207, when the Templars had taken over the abbey from the Benedictines, a grant to them was recorded as nine

---

[1] LPC, Field Book.
[2] See p. 87.

acres in Wulfholes, two acres and a half in Rudichefeld, and two acres and a half in Baneholefeld.[1] If Rudichefeld means Row Ditch Field (i.e. the Old Tillage or Car Dyke) the outlines of the three fields as identifiable later, were already established. Winfold on the west and Bannold on the east ran north from Waterbeach village towards Denney. The third field ran south and east from Winfold Common, past the mill and its hill, along the back of the peasant crofts that lined the road, across the old Cambridge Way, to the site of Waterbeach Abbey (Hall Field or Close), and so to The Great Hollow. Any of these features could have given a name to the field or part of it: at some time or other each one did so.

The bulk of the medieval evidence, consisting of extracts from the Court Rolls of Waterbeach cum Denney,[2] offers a great profusion of field-names. These extracts are copied in a much later secretary hand, and since Cole seems to have had access to another fuller version,[3] may well be copied from another copy rather than the lost originals. Some of the variations in spelling, which shade off into separate names, may thus be the result of multiple transcription. But even after due allowance for this, there is still considerable variety (see Table 2).

As far as these field-names can be identified they reveal a marked difference in usage from those of the terriers. The earlier Baneholes and Wulfholes appear clearly in their transition to the Bannold and Winfold of the last days of the open fields, but even at the end of the court book the designation of areas within these fields (Denney and Town), which we found in the terriers, is absent. But the old third field of the charter, Rudichefeld, is absent except under the names of some of its constituent parts or alternative names. Some of these names disappear, like Croft Field which vanishes in the reign of Henry VIII, and may well have been replaced by the alternative 'Cambridge Way Field', since this way ran between the crofts and the Hall Close on which Croft Field in part abutted. The great rival to Cambridge Way as a field-name, Haverstock, also makes its appearance about the same time, in the form Hallfeldstoke. The Halough Field mentioned under 31 Ed. III would again appear as an alternative since The Great Hollow forms the southern boundary of this third arable field. In the dispute between Masters and Standley, Middle Field was given as an alternative to Havistock, but both survive as useful place-names into the enclosure award, when they seem to have helped the commissioners to give precise locations without the use of furlong names. In fact the commissioners omit the general name, Havistock, in favour of

---

[1] Clay's date of 1176 (in *Waterbeach*, p. 89) seems too late. He appears to have taken it from Cole, BM Add. MS. 5837. Blake gives the full text, *Liber Eliensis*, Charter 139 (Robert Chamberlain), pp. 387–8, 1133 × 1169, and Charter 140 (Duke Conan), p. 389, confirmation; Charter 141 (Albericus Picot), p. 389, 1160 × 1169. Templar deed of 1207, Clay's *Waterbeach*, p. 89.

[2] WPC, WcD.

[3] BM Add. MS. 5837.

TABLE 2. *Field-names in the Court Book of Waterbeach cum Denney*

6 Ed. III	Hawfield
21 Ed. III	Hillfield
22 Ed. III	Crosse Field and Baneholes
22 Ed. III	Crosse Field
27 Ed. III	Croft (?) Field
28 Ed. III	arable mentioned in le Holough
31 Ed. III	*(Cole) field of Banehale, Wolfhale Field, Halough Field
36 Ed. III	le Melnefurlong, Letlewayfurlong, Overshuttefurlong
46 Ed. III	Crosfield (× 3), Croftfield †(× 2)
48 Ed. III	1 acre in inlond
49 Ed. III	Wolfollfield
5 Hen. V	Wynfollfield
8 Hen. V	Banall, Hillfield Hallfield
9 Hen. V	Hillfield
4 Hen. VI	Bannallfield
5 Hen. VI	Cambridge Field, Hillfield
7 Hen. VI	Joyn Field, Croft Field
9 Hen. VI	Croftfield, Waterbeach Field
11 Hen. VI	Bannallfield, Hillfield, Fourthfield, Croftfield abutting on Hall Close
14 Hen. VI	Croftfield
18 Hen. VI	Croftfield, Bannallfield
6 Hen. VIII	Banalfield
7 Hen. VIII	Wolfhaven
13 Hen. VIII	Wynfield
15 Hen. VIII	Bannallfield
16 Hen. VIII	Hallfeldstoke
18 Hen. VIII	Croftfield, Banallfield
18 Hen. VIII	mention of a messuage with land in three fields of Waterbeach
18 Hen. VIII	Bannallfield...in the field near Halfwaystoke
18 Hen. VIII	Halfwaystoke Field, Bannall Field, Wynfold Field, Cambridge Field
18 Hen. VIII	Bannallfield
18 Hen. VIII	Wynfole Field
18 Hen. VIII	Halfewaystoke

(In this period 'near Cambridge Way' appears frequently instead of a field-name.)

38 Hen. VIII	Cambridge Field (× 2)
1 Mary	Bannallfield
10 Eliz.	Cambridge Field, Bannallfield
13 Eliz.	Wynfold Field
14 Eliz.	Haleswysake, Cambridgeway
6 Jas. I	12 entries: Hillfield (× 3), Haverstock (× 5), Bannellfield (× 7), Wynfold (× 4), Cambridgefield (1)
10 Jas. I	Winfold (× 2), Cambridge Way (× 3), Bannold (× 2), Haverstock (× 1).
11 Jas. I	Cambridgeway (× 2), Mill (× 1), Haverstock (× 3), Wynfold (× 2), Bannall (× 4)
13 Jas. I	Hill, Wynfold, Haverstock
6 Chas. I	Bannall, Haverstock, Wynfold.

Notes † (× 2) means two entries this year; etc.
* (Cole) means in Cole MS. but not WcD.

the names of the appropriate sub-divisions, Middle, Mill, Cambridge Way and Hall Fields.[1] These areas were extensively sub-divided for the allotment, but Winfold Field went entirely to the lord of the manor and its sub-divisions were not used, although both Denney Bannolds and Home Bannolds appear in the schedule.

Further evidence on the open fields of Waterbeach comes to light in the tithe action brought by Robert Masters against Standley, lord of the Manor of Waterbeach cum Denney, from 1765 on. Robert Masters had the instincts and habits of a scholar, as his history of the College, his brief description of the parish of Waterbeach, and his Collectanea in Landbeach Parish Chest prove.[2] He was also cantankerous and litigious. One of the results of this not uncommon combination is a very useful collection of historical material which he prepared for this tithe action.

In appraising the value of the lordship crops for tithe purposes, he gives us a four-year cropping sequence as shown in Table 3.

TABLE 3. *Four-year cropping sequence*

	1760	1761	1762	1763
Bannold	*W	B & P	–	W
Denney West	B	–	WM & P	B & P
Denney East	–	W	B & Bns	–
Low Grounds	O	O	O	O

Note * W=wheat; B=barley; P=peas; M=mixed corn; O=oats; Bns=beans.[3]

Here at least is a core of an open three-field system, cropping on lines that might, with its fallows bare, have seemed ultra-orthodox and old-fashioned in the fourteenth century. The Low Grounds, sown with oats every year varied from 17 to 31 acres in this period. The higher and more reliable demesne arable (for Waterbeach) amounted to:

	Acres	Rods	Poles
Bannold	81	2	20
Denney West	64	0	5
Denney East	98	0	15
Total Lordship arable	243	3	0

Although the evidence of the glebe terriers and court rolls might make us reluctant to believe in any systematic rotation of open fields in Waterbeach, the petitioners' proofs submitted by Masters against Standley leave us in no doubt. They also highlight the usefulness of counting open fields by counting names. Brigham's evidence was clear: '...that in the said parish there are three common fields and that it has been generally usual to sow two of these fields with corn and grain, and for the other to lie fallow alternatively.'[4]

---

[1] See Fig. 6, p. 87.
[2] Masters, *History of the College of Corpus Christi*; *Short Account*; LPC, Collectanea, a manuscript book containing an impressive collection of transcripts and some original documents relating to the history of Landbeach.
[3] WPC, copy in Masters' hand of a letter from Mr Jas. Day to Mr Philip Burton, Attorney at Law.
[4] CUL, EDR, A 14/1; WPC, *Masters vs. Standley* bundle.

His father had farmed the lands of Denney Abbey, and Brigham gave the names of the fields as Winfold, Havistock or Middle, and Bannall. It appears certain from the acreages that he quoted that his Winfold was Masters' Denney West, and his Havistock or Middle was Denney East.

In his deposition, Wiles mentioned 'three common fields of Water-beach, called Bannall Field, Havistock Field, and Winfold Field'. But later on when he described Peck's Farm, he said that it was 'about seven score acres of land lying dispersedly in the three common fields of Waterbeach, called Cambridge Field, Hall Field and Mill Field'. His description of the cropping fully corroborated Brigham's. Hemington gave the same names to the fields as Brigham. Peck did likewise when he began his evidence, but in the course of it he spoke of Bannall, Havistock and Middle. All their evidence was in agreement as to a three-field system: it was only at variance in the use of alternative proper names. The witnesses, when making their first considered statements invariably used the names of the great fields of the three shifts, Bannal, Winfold, and Havistock or Middle, but two of them slipped into using lesser names when led by lawyers. This should be a very cautionary example when so many of the documents from which we draw our knowledge of the open fields, come from lawyers. William Hall, a commissioner of the Waterbeach Level as well as a farmer, refined the description of the cropping, as first year wheat, second year barley, and the third year fallow. Peck gave the size and composition of his own farm, about 172 acres arable, 41 pasture, and 93 meadow.

The evidence in this case, not great in quantity, has produced seven of Postgate's field-names, but it has also shown conclusively that these seven names did not mean that there was not a recognisable three-shift system operating in the parish, and it is interesting to see that Hall, a local substantial farmer, thought of its cropping in the simple terms of wheat, followed by barley, followed by fallow, when Masters' tithe appraisal showed more variation in practice.

The open fields of Waterbeach formed an arable core to the cultivation of the village's land. From the late twelfth century right up to the parliamentary enclosure in the early nineteenth century this was worked on a three-shift system, and those concerned with its working thought of its arrangement as lying in three fields. Two of these field-names remained constant, merely suffering normal corruption with age, while the third underwent several changes. The constancy of the system over so long a period is surprising in face of the risks of flooding: in 1770 Cole wrote, 'This is the third time within six years that my estate has been drowned, and now worse than ever.'[1]

---

[1] *Waterbeach*, p. 18, quoting Warburton's *Life of Horace Walpole*, vol. II, pp. 371, 375, 377.

The open fields contained all the regular arable. Outside this there were areas of special risk where attempts could be made to snatch a quick spring-sown crop if the ebbing away of the winter waters of the fen seemed hopeful. But these areas, Denney Low Grounds, severals in The Hollow, and later the Drainers Grounds,[1] could never be incorporated into the regular field system of the permanent arable.[2]

The proliferation of field-names in Waterbeach can hardly have been due to assarting in the way Postgate's thesis would have suggested: furlong names would have a much stronger claim to this, and many of the field-names appear far too late for such an explanation to be plausible. The simplification of the field-names which Postgate thought would come about after the imposition of a cropping scheme did not happen in Waterbeach even after an unconscionable time. But two problems still seem to call for further attention: the differences in treatment so often accorded to Havistock Field compared with the other two; and the differences in the usage of field-names between different classes of document.

Bannold and Winfold, even in their earliest form Baneholes and Wulf-holes, seem so much a pair that they may well represent an earlier two-field system, but if the difference in the treatment of the third field originated in this way (and there is nothing in the earliest evidence, the charters, to suggest that it did) such a simple historical explanation can hardly account for its persistence. The reasons are more probably topo-graphical. We can scarcely claim that its systematic cultivation was more liable to disturbance from flooding, even though its southern reaches must frequently have been under threat from the waters that inundated The Great Hollow: Bannold was even more vulnerable. Topographically Havistock was the most varied field, containing much of the highest as well as much of the lowest arable in the parish. This may well have made it especially attractive. It had further virtues in that, compared with the others, it could be reached by very short journeys from many access points in the west of the village where the greater number of peasant crofts seem to have been concentrated. A disproportionate number of the court roll entries which give rise to field-names refer to tiny fragments of land in this field, not often balanced by equal amounts in the other fields. Still more signs of the activity of the peasant land market relate to scraps of land in various conditions in the Hollow. The bulk of the Waterbeach peasantry seem always to have had only very tiny arable interests which can only

---

[1] *Short Account*, p. 2, mentions the Drainers Grounds as illustrating this point: 'from time to time let out as Severals by the Corporation to such as are disposed to become adventurers in that way; for the undertaking is rather hazardous, they being liable to be drowned by breaches of banks from immoderate rains, in wet years...The severals are sometimes ploughed, and bear very plentiful crops of Oats, Coleseed and flax'.

[2] For a fuller discussion of these lands, see Chapter 2 above.

have been supplementary to their main sources of income. For them a scrap of land in Havistock would have been far easier to work than one in Denney Bannolds or Denney Winfold, and would have been in every way more desirable. The multiple names seem to correspond to something like miniature natural regions from the point of view of this type of peasant.

The different systems of nomenclature in the different classes of document seem to be a simple reflection of the purposes of those who drew them up. In the glebe terriers the parson wanted to establish a precise claim to scattered pieces of land, hence the breaking down of the field-names into smaller areas for more accurate location. The operation of the peasant land market discussed above would often call for even more detailed definition, and so account for the even greater number of names in the court rolls. The charters were concerned with early attempts to endow a monastic house with a viable estate and so emphasise the equal distribution of the land between the three main fields. For tithe the parson was concerned with the crops of all the fields, and so the documents bring out the collective system of common field agriculture very clearly. We can almost see Masters sitting in his Landbeach study and viewing the fields of Waterbeach in his imagination, producing his own system of description, Denney West for Winfold, Denney East for Havistock, and Bannold. This is hardly a good piece of topography, but it served his purpose, the assessment of all the crops on the Denney Abbey estate in the open fields.

The use of field-names in the different classes of document, taken together and in context, have much to tell of the way in which the system operated, but the indiscriminate listing of names is confusing at best and at worst misleading.

THE OPEN FIELDS OF COTTENHAM

Cottenham is the only one of our three villages for which we have strip maps. The map of the Pratt estate in Cottenham has recently come into the CRO, and there also is an excellent first draft of the enclosure award map.[1] This indicates every strip, as distinct from selion, at both ends and middle, and, except for one small area, gives each a reference number. Surprisingly few strips consist of more than one selion, and so this definition is extremely detailed. Fields are clearly named, and their boundaries distinguished in red, but unfortunately the furlongs bear no names, and many are sub-divided by ditches, similar to boundary ditches. Copies of Alexander Watford's Terrier survive for at least two farms, one the largest

---

[1] 'Plan of the *Estate of Edward Roger Pratt, Esq., at Cottenham Cambridges., 1802*', CRO R/61/5/1. *Cottenham Award Map*, 1842, Alexander Watford of Cambridge, Surveyor, CRO 152/P9.

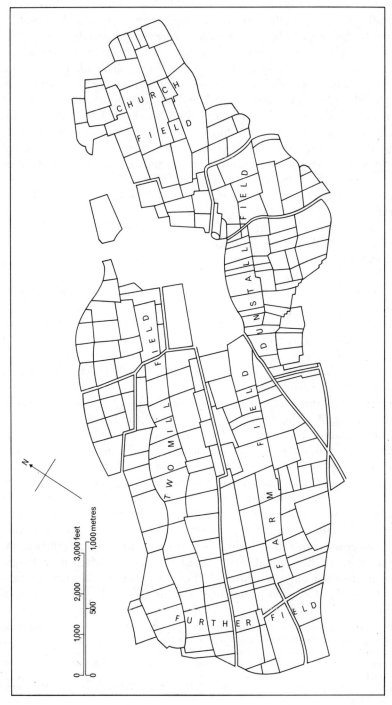

Fig. 7. Cottenham: open fields. This map indicates field ditches rather than furlong boundaries. The furlongs varied considerably in size, but the drainage required ditches to be more evenly spaced (source: CRO 152/P9).

in the village. This gives the reference numbers to each strip and so enables most of the furlongs to be identified by name on the map.[1]

At the time of the enclosure, Cottenham's 1,576 acres of arable lay divided into five open fields; Church Field, Dunstall Field, Farm Field, Further Field, and Two Mill Field.[2] In the Middle Ages there had been only three, Aldeburghfeld, Foxholes, and Lowfeld or Loumilnefeld. These are recognisable under various spellings in the Crowlands Court Rolls until after the abbot gave up demesne cultivation in 1430.[3] The transition from three to five fields proves exceedingly difficult to date. Various documents, taken together where some of them alone would be misleading, enable us to trace the five fields back to the reign of Edward VI.

1 The Pratt map shows: Church Field, Dunstall Field, Farm Field, Foxall or Farther Field, and Two Mill Field.

2 Glebe Terrier, 1780, mentions: Two Mill Field, Church Field, Dunstall Field, Fern Hill, and Foxall Field.

3 Crowlands Admission, 1645: Millfield, Loumillfield, Foxen Field, Ferne Field, Church Field.

4 Glebe Terrier, 1638: Ferne Field, Banhill, Churchill, Church Field, Dunstall.

5 Rectory Terrier, 1630: Fearne Field, Two Mill or Bannill Field, Church Hill, Church Field, Dunstall Field. (The Lots are listed with the arable here.)

6 Award in Chancery, 1596: Dunstal Field, Foxall Field, Ferne Field, Church Field, Farm Field.

7 Terrier of Chantry Lands, 1549: Church Field, Dunstall Field, Ferne Field, Foxham Field, Lowmyll Field, Lyles Lane Feeld.[4]

Without careful topographical identification of the names listed it is again very difficult to see a five-field system running through the whole of the period covered by the documents cited. The confusion between Further Field, 'ferne' in Middle English, and its neighbour Farm Field, has been too much even for the Ordnance Survey, which amalgamates them still in its latest edition as 'Further or Farm Field'. Church Field appears in all the documents: the fourth and fifth lists, more concerned with full listing of property than with cultivation, detail separately Church Hill, that part of the field detached to the west by the northward encroachment of the village on to a series of furlongs. Only the Crowlands Admission omits Dunstall, but it gives a Mill Field as well as Loumilne: there was another mill in Dunstall as

[1] See Westrope's *Year Book – Cottenham, 1913*; the other belongs to Mr M. Haird of Cottenham, to whom I am indebted for the loan of this and other documents.
[2] Act of 1842, 5 Vict. sess. 2, cap. 3, and award 28 October 1847.
[3] *ECA*, pp. 240–3, and 442ff.: *ECA*, p. 336 has three examples of half-acre holdings lying in three places each.
[4] 1, CRO R61/5/1; 2, CRO Cot C 35, 1; 3, CRO Cot C 31/7; 4, CRO Cot C 35.1; 5, CRO Cot C 35.2; 6, *Common Rights*; 7, CRO L 1/198.

well as the two in the field usually described as Two Mill. The Rectory Terrier of 1630 gives Bannill as the equivalent of Two Mill, the name of a furlong serving as an alternative field-name as it does in the Glebe Terrier of 1638. The omissions of Further or Foxall Field from the Terriers of 1630 and 1638 seem to be accounted for by the note in the Glebe Terrier of 1780 that there is no glebe in Foxale Field. The Lyles Lane Field mentioned among the Chantry Lands in 1549 appears quite clearly from abuttals to lie in the northern part of Two Mill Field. The omission of any mention of Two Mill Field from the 1596 Agreement is simply because that document was concerned only with closes, and the only close in that field, Pelhams Close, lay between the field proper and the village, and needed no field-name to identify it.

The absence of glebe from Further Field suggests that this, as its name implies, the remotest from the village, was assarted last, after the glebe was complete. But this south-western expansion of the arable had reached the parish boundary before 1315. In a tithe dispute in that year between the vicar of Oakington and the rector of Cottenham witnesses not only asserted that butts existed on both sides of the way dividing Westwick from Cottenham, but that certain selions from Cottenham, as well as one from Westwick, crossed the road.[1] This strongly suggests that the change from three to five fields must have been the result of re-arrangement rather than fresh assarting: in 1315 Cottenham ploughs were already up against the fen and the parish boundary. The only possible place for expansion would have been on the eastern fringes of Dunstall in the marginal lands where the now extinct watercourse had been diverted. Here the Terrier of Chantry Lands of 1549 mentioned Hemp Lands both inside and outside the field boundary. But the cutting of the watercourse, by disturbing natural drainage, may have made defensive operations necessary here in order to hold the frontier with the fen, and keep what was traditionally arable. There certainly was considerable drainage activity here in the late thirteenth century, with no apparent expansion of the fields as a result.[2] This could have been the beginning of the general rise of the water-table, and if so, the mid-sixteenth century may well have been a suitable time for the reconquest of ploughland lost to the fen, but it cannot have been on a large scale given the topography of the area.

It is possible to identify the general lay-out of the Cottenham fields in the Middle Ages,[3] and so to see the nature of the subsequent re-organisation. Foxholes is identifiable by Foxholes or Godfrey's Close, and

---

[1] BM Add. MS. 5887, f. 25f.: Cole's transcripts from the now missing Oldfield Register of Crowlands.

[2] CUL Queens' Cd 5, 1282–3 (or 1283–4 in Aston's dating), mentions a hundred perches of new ditches at 'le Estlondes', and Cd 3, 1285–6, accounts for making of ditches towards the 'more'. For the stability of the demesne area see *ECA*.

[3] See inset, Fig. 1, p. xii.

the survival of its name on the Pratt map, as embracing the south-eastern sector between the Histon road and Westwick Way. It cannot in medieval times have included the south-western sector across the Westwick Way as this clearly belonged to Loumilne Field. Loumilne was the mill in West-wick hamlet in the parish of Oakington, and the Cottenham field named after it must have reached the Westwick boundary.[1]

The three medieval fields would have been divided from each other by Westwick Way and the Histon road; Loumilne on the west, Foxholes to its east, and Aldeburgh Field to the north of Foxholes and the village. To form five fields from this, Aldeburgh Field divided into Church Field and Dunstall Field, along the line of its central way; Farm Field was created from the northern part of Foxholes; the remainder of this, now called Further Field, gained the southern part of Loumilne Field; and the northern part of the latter became Two Mill Field

The difficulties in reconciling the variations in the documents with the same field system between 1549 and enclosure seem to spring from two main sources, the custom of using the name of a part, a furlong, for the whole field when a preciser location is wanted, and the survival of the traditional names in popular usage even when field boundaries have changed.

The name Foxholes, whose survival from the medieval system to its successor makes the dating of the change so difficult, lasted so well probably because of its descriptive powers: its southern boundary is still the most likely place in the area on a quiet evening for the sound of a fox's bark.

There are hints in the field-names of some of the nearby villages of two-field systems which developed into three. In nearby Oakington Osmoorfield (or the Moorfield) suggests addition to the earlier pattern before the documentary evidence begins. In Waterbeach the three fields are clearly established in the twelfth-century charters, but Bannold and Winfold look very much like a pair, and the other, which may have been the third field, never settled down to a universally-accepted name. In Cottenham we can only conjecture from the topography and the pattern of the village as it expanded over open field furlongs: a scheme of a north field and a south field is very plausible, but there is no proof of this.

Tithe returns of the late seventeenth century, since the glebe was leased, appear to give the total arable under crop in each year. The sequence for 1691–5 enables field sizes to be calculated:[2]

---

[1] CUL Queens' Dd 1: William Pepys, senior, testified in court: 'The mill of Loumilne…which mill as is said is within the parish boundaries of Oakington' ('*molendinum de Loumilne…quod molendinum, ut dicitur, est infra limites parochiales de Hokyton*'). Cf. BM Add. MS. 5887.

[2] Westrope's *Year Book – Cottenham, 1911*, p. 11. The general figures from Watford's Survey for the enclosure commissioners, and for the Ivatt estate are given in the same publication for 1913, p. 27.

	Acres	Fallow	Tithe
1691	1,318	289¼	2/9 per acre
1692	1,346	261¼	3/– per acre
1693	1,308	299¼	3/4 per acre
1694	1,304	303¼	3/– per acre
1695	1,153	454¼	3/4 per acre

The imbalance, whereby the largest field is nearly twice the size of the smallest is still apparent in the holdings of one of the largest farmers on the eve of enclosure, Mr Thomas Ivatt. His field land was as follows:

	Acres	Rods	Poles
Church Field	11	0	21
Dunstall	12	2	31
Farm	18	0	21
Further	17	0	2
Two Mill	10	1	26

The total acreage suggested by the tithe figures, 1,607¼, is near the total given by the enclosure commissioners almost two and a half centuries later, 1,576 and 11 perches. The difference could in fact be due to rounding in the calculations from the tithe figures: a comparison between the old enclosures which the commissioners found on the eve of enclosure and those of the Award of 1596 shows them to be identical.

This remarkable stability in the fields after the change to five makes the dating of that change the more important. Postgate recognised that the five fields were there in the Terrier of Chantry Lands in 1549, although he omitted to mention the problem of the inclusion of the sixth, Lyle's Lane Field. By this time references to field-names in the court rolls are few, but both the Rectory and Crowlands Rolls mention some of the old names in the reign of Henry VIII.[1] Unfortunately Foxholes continued to be used under the new system and therefore cannot help us, but '*Campus voc*' *holborowfild*' occurs in the Crowlands series under 4 Hen. VIII, 'lowmyll feld' under 8 Hen. VIII in the Rectory Rolls, and 'loughmylfeld' under 12 Hen. VIII. The change must have taken place between 1521 and 1549. It seems to have been the only major change in the field system of Cottenham during the seven centuries for which we have documentary evidence of how its open fields were managed.

THE OPEN FIELDS OF LANDBEACH

For Landbeach there are no contemporary open-field maps except an extremely rough pencil sketch by Masters, found in a bundle labelled 'Miscellaneous Papers' in the Archives of Corpus Christi College, Cam-

---

[1] Rectory Rolls, CRO, R50/9/3; Crowlands Rolls from 1509 to 1727 with gaps, in the Francis Papers; new acquisition and unindexed at time of search.

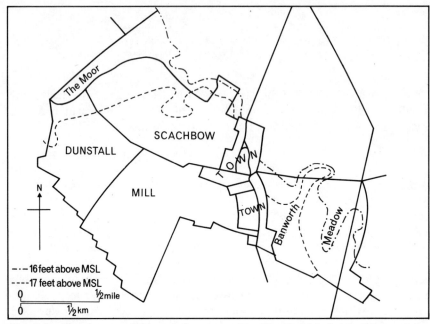

Fig. 8. Landbeach: open fields and the water-table. The situation in the Extent of the Lands of Agnes de Bray in 1316 implies a flood reaching a line between these two contours. (Based upon the Ordnance Survey map of 1878. Additional source: Great Ouse River Board's 1″ contour map.)

bridge.[1] The schedule on the enclosure award map, however, enables us to work out the general location of the previous fields, and there is a most helpful attempt at this made by the Rev. Bryan Walker before the tradition of the open fields was dead among the villagers.[2] But Landbeach more than makes up for the paucity of maps with a profusion of descriptions of its open fields. Three early field books, beginning with that of Simon Greene in 1477, lead up to Matthew Parker's Book of 1549; two parts of an Elizabethan Field Book survive; and there is yet another complete version for 1727 in the Dukman Book.[3]

When the open fields of Landbeach came to an end with the Parliamentary Enclosure of 1813, four fields were listed, Mill Field, Dunstall, Scachbow and Banworth. These are the same four fields as those of the

[1] CCCC, XXXV, not assigned further catalogue number at time of writing.
[2] CRO Q/RDz7, pp. 26–83, 1813, Award; Q/RDc18, award map. Rev. Bryan Walker's 'Landbeach – Collectanea II', is now in the Parker Library, Corpus Christi College, Cambridge: X.4.3.
[3] CCCC, XXXV, 163, 164, 170, 173, 174, 175, 177; 173 is clearly part of the same survey as 175 and belongs to the time of Copcott's Mastership, 1587–90. The 'List of tenements new built on the Lord's waste' on the back of 173 applies only to the two names below, and not to those inside, which are holders of strips. Postgate ('The Open Fields of Cambridgeshire', p. 101) appears to have counted the latter as houses and so produced the absurd total of 179 new built in Landbeach.

Dukman Book for 1727. In a mid-seventeenth century legal opinion on the Sheepwalks, the first article reads: 'There are four several open fields of arable land in Landbeach, which in their several seasons according to the custom of the Town are commonable for sheep and other cattle.'[1] Here then, superficially, seems to be a four-field system. If we go back to Matthew Parker's Field Book of 1549 there is a fifth also, Meadow Field. Some of the early charters seem to be describing parts of a three-field system in the twelfth and thirteenth centuries.[2] Thus the main field-names in the documents seem, at first glance, to suggest that Landbeach affords a simple example of the working out of the process described by Postgate. A closer examination of all the evidence suggests something at once more complex, and yet closer to the essence of older ideas on the subject.

In the archives of Corpus Christi College, Cambridge, there are over 120 charters relating to Landbeach, and a number of these have detailed references to fields and furlongs. There are also the very detailed Extents of the Lands of Agnes de Bray in 1316 and Alice Bere in 1356. Further, there is a considerable amount of information about the fields in the fourteenth century in the Court Rolls of the Manors of Chamberlains and Brays, and Reeve's account rolls for three years for Chamberlains.

Table 4 brings together the field-names in the charters and extents during the period of the development of the fields. It is not possible to date the origin of a field by its first mention in a charter, but the sequence of appearances may give an echo of the process by which Landbeach acquired its fully-grown field system. The first suggestion made by the table is that Banworth may well be a late-comer as open-field arable. If the hypothesis that Landbeach was first settled from Waterbeach as a subsidiary out-station for sheep is correct, Banworth, whose name means 'bean enclo-sure', may be where the shepherds first began to supplement their pastoral activities by raising beans. The element 'worth', the mention of 'le Benelond' in 1229 and of a 'gardinum de Banworth' in 1354, indicate something different from open-field cultivation, and a possible survival of such alongside a developing system of open arable fields. Field-names containing 'bean' elements are so common in Cambridgeshire that the whole question is worthy of special study.

The name Acrefeld is the only field to include 'acre' as an element in its furlong names. The first field to appear in the charters appears to be deliberately named to differentiate it as arable ridge and furrow from the area of primitive bean-growing. Its gault, as distinct from Banworth's gravel, its higher elevation, and its closeness to the settled area, would have made it the natural first choice for beginning cereal cultivation. So it would represent the development of colonisation beyond the lighter soils

<hr />

[1] CCCC, XXXV, 176; cf. LPC, Masters' Collectanea, p. 28.
[2] E.g. CCCC, XXXV, nos. 2 and 4.

TABLE 4. *The names of open fields as they appear
in charters and extents of Landbeach*

Ch. no.	Date	
2	12th cent.	Acrefeld (includes Bremliacre) Tunstalfeld, Scarchbowfeld
4	1229	Scachbowfeld, Scaceboyfeld; Tonestalfeld, Dunstallefeld; Stratefeld (includes Brembelaker)
	Extent 1316	Skachmowefeld (once only; Skachbowefeld many times), Stratefeld; Tunstallefeld; Banewurthfeld
19	1317	'in campo vocato Banwurth, iacent' iuxta le ffloed'
26	1327	Scachbowefeld; Stratefeld; Tunstalefeld
27	1328	'in campo qui dicitur Blakelond'
28	1328	Scachbowefeld; le Milnefeld; Dunstalefeld
33	1331	'in campo vocato le blakelondforlong'
34	1333	Stratefeld; Scachbowefeld
43	1354	Banworth (as abbutment only), 'gardini de Banworth'; Tonstallefeld
	Extent 1356	le Stratefeld; Dunstalefeld; Skacchebowefeld
91	1384	(French) Stratefeld; Dunstalefeld; Scachebowefeld
93	1384	(French) Stratefeld; Dunstalefeld; Scachebowefeld
94	1384	Banneworthfeld; Stratefeld; Dunstalefeld; Scachebowefeld

worked by the Roman–Britons; and on the gault, it may have represented also the first clearance of dense hardwood forest.

When Acrefeld becomes Stratefeld the furlong called Bremliacre is still there as Brembelaker, but it soon disappears. The brambles that would have been a memorable feature if they bedevilled a new assart would in time disappear too with cultivation. With the development of a multiple field system the name Acrefeld would have become confusing; all the open-field arable would deserve the title. By this time the first field had presumably developed across the Roman road, and this naturally became its main access way. Access ways are a very common source of field-names, and so Acrefeld became Stratefeld. After the windmill was built it would be the natural landmark to give an alternative designation to the field.[1] The Roman road also runs through Scachbow, even though it is not well placed to become the main access to the field. Thus in time, the alternative name won and lasted as Mill Field, although Strate Field lingered in the charters until the late fourteenth century.

The other field-names in this period may well be pre-assarting names, taken over and used to identify the new fields. 'Tunstal' is read by Reaney as 'farm-steading'. If so it would have applied to some small subsidiary settlement for forest or marshland grazing in the inter-common towards Cottenham. The Stodfold in the meadow, which leaves its name in the field books, may have been similar, but taking advantage of different natural conditions for another special purpose. Dunstall gives its name to its neighbour when the new fields are created in Cottenham in the mid-Tudor period.[2] For Scachbow *English Place-Name Elements* enables

[1] CCCC, XXXV, 145, Extent of the Lands of Agnes de Bray shows a mill already there in 1316.
[2] Reaney, *Place-Names of Cambridgeshire*, p. 151.

TABLE 5. *Extent of the Lands of Agnes de Bray*
(CCCC, XXXV, 145, Michaelmas 1316)

Scachbow	Acres	Rods	Poles
le Dole	16	3	0
le Dole per le Grenewey	5	0	0
Thwershlondole	4	2	0
Skachbowefurlond	1	0	20
Skachebowehavedyn	1	0	0
ult. le Renneles	2	2	0
per le Grenewey	2	2	0
Morefurlonge (?)	11	2	0
*Goosebrichdole**	*3*	*0*	*0*
eodem campo	*7*	*1*	*0*
eodem campo	*5*	*1*	*0*
Colyversdole	*2*	*2*	*0*
le Cleydole	*2*	*0*	*0*
le Pambyle	*1*	*0*	*0*
abb' super le Pambyle	*2*	*2*	*0*
abb' super le Renneles	*1*	*2*	*0*
Bradelondes	*9*	*0*	*0*
Dunstall			
29 pieces	53	1	0
Reynbowe Furlonde	*9*	*2*	*0*
Stratefeld			
abb. s. altam stratam	27	2	0
s. Thwershlond Blakelond and mormetefurlongs	23	1	0
Dufhowsfurlong and Thryttiacrisfurlond	18	2	0
Banworth			
in Banworth field	20	0	0
Banewurthfurlong	*18*	*3*	*0*

*Note Italics indicate 'and is or are common unless sown' ('*et est (sunt) communia(e) nisi sominata(e)*).

	Acres	Rods	Poles
Total area (maximum?) arable land in any year (Summa acrarum terr' arabil' quolibet anno)	186	3	0
Total area of 'pasture except when sown' (Summa acrarum pastur' nisi quando seminatur)	63	0	0

us to offer a satisfactory meaning, 'the curving frontier of field against the fen'.[1] 'Skachmowe' of 1316 is tantalising, but is probably a slip on the part of the scribe, since it seems never to be repeated in the many instances of this name, either in this document or elsewhere.

The general impression left by the appearance of the names in the charters is that, once the development of arable cultivation began, it rapidly produced a three-field system by the twelfth century, and that this in turn grew more complex from early in the fourteenth century.

[1] A. H. Smith (ed.), *English Place-Name Elements*, Pt II (1956), p. 99, *Sceaga, scaga*, OE, 'a small wood, a copse, a strip of undergrowth or wood...OE *sceaga* is equated with Latin mariscum, "marsh"...Like NFris *skage* "the edge of cultivated land"'. Pt I, p. 40, '*boga*, OE, a bow, an arch, something bent'.

Beyond Dunstall lay the moor; beyond Banworth, the meadow; and beyond Scachbow, the fens. The middle of Dunstall was crossed by the twenty-foot contour; part was above and part below. Through the lower part ran the Rennels Brooks. Heavy clays made the soil subject to water-logging. Mill Field was well above the twenty-foot contour, and almost entirely above the twenty-five. It stood up above the tofts and houses of the village. Part of Scachbow, next to the village, in a triangle based upon Cockfen Lane, stood proud of the level subject to the severest floods, but the far greater part lay below. Banworth lay beneath, but most of it only just beneath, the twenty-foot level. A good deal of this field, particularly that in the south adjacent to the tofts, is so near the height of the road, which here runs almost exactly at twenty feet, that it was above the critical level for this period.[1] The tenement named 'le floed' lay in a slight hollow below the cross-roads where the spot-height reads 19. In the southern half of Banworth is a site prolific of late-Roman sherds, and any Roman farm of that period would have been sited above the line of the disastrous floods of the third century, according to the conclusions of Mr John Bromwich. This topography helps us to understand the Extent of the lands of Agnes de Bray, made in 1316, the great famine year.[2]

If we total the acreage shown (Bray's demesne arable) in each of the fields we arrive at the following:

	Acres	Rods	Poles
Scachbow	78	3	0
Dunstall	62	3	0
Strate field	69	1	0
Banworth	38	3	0

This accords well with the idea of an earlier three-field system to which Banworth has been added, when Scachbow met the fen or the fen encroached on Scachbow. The total that can be sown in any year, is this total acreage less Dunstall. If we range the fields in order of their proportion 'common unless sown' ('*communia nisi seminata*') we get (1) Banworth; (2) Scachbow; (3) Dunstall; (4) Strate Field. This is precisely the order we get if we range the fields in order of their proportion below the line reckoned safe from even the severest floods. In a period of notoriously deteriorating weather and rising water-table, when we find that the land '*communia nisi seminata*' is valued at nothing although the rest is 9*d.* per acre, there can be little doubt that the cause is flooding. Apparently about a quarter of the arable is unlikely to be sown even in due season. The general nature of the comment suggests that this is more than a

[1] Cf. Jurgen Klasen, *Vergleichende Landschaftskunde Der Englischen Marschen* (Cologne, 1967), p. 331: 'microrelief is proving everywhere [i.e. everywhere in the marshlands] to be the decisive factor as regards the natural landscape'.
[2] See Table 5, p. 103.

matter of one year only, but the uncertainty of it suggests that the land may or may not be sown sometimes. If it ever is common, then this would be when the flood subsides too late for even a spring sowing. In other words about a quarter of the arable has become subject to severe winter flooding. This means that it has almost reverted, temporarily or permanently, to the condition of fen.

The Great Ouse River Board has marked up some maps of the area with contours at one-foot intervals outside the built-up areas. These enable us to refine the analysis. The sixteen-foot contour shows that if water rose to this height, Scachbow's expansion would be checked, and the field would be invaded by fen. The seventeen-foot contour shows that if the water continued to rise a lake would form well inside the boundaries of Scachbow.[1]

We appear to have a series of three peaks in the rise of the water-table: the first probably caused the development of open-field arable, Acrefield, to begin in Landbeach when Waterbeach fields would have been submerged; the second would have checked the development of Scachbow, and called for compensatory assarting in the drier south of Banworth, the meadow and the moor; and the third and highest peak (the highest for which we have evidence in this area during historical times) would have produced a situation like that shown in the extent of 1316. This seems to have been a disastrous year for flooding generally in Western Europe:[2] in an area prone to flooding, 1316 must have been a peculiarly catastrophic year.

The frontier between fen and ploughland was at the end of Scachbow, and Scachbow was certain to lose first if the fen advanced. The most obvious place to recoup such a loss of arable would be that part of Banworth which lay highest, conveniently behind the houses and tofts, with a soil that drained more quickly than any other in the parish. If Banworth was turned into open field arable to replace losses in Scachbow, it would be natural for them together to do the duty hitherto done by Scachbow alone.

From the acreages given in the 1316 Extent we can only arrive at the 'total area arable land in any year' ('*summa acrarum terr' arabil'* quolibet *anno*') of 186 acres, 3 rods, by adding up the *maximum* possible for all the fields but Dunstall. If this total is meant to be the maximum that can be cropped in any year, then it must mean that Banworth could not stand fallow alone, for if it did the total would be twenty-four acres more. Banworth seems to have been altogether insufficient as a course in itself

[1] This lake may well be the unidentified feature, 'le pambyle', which is several times mentioned in the early fourteenth century as lying towards Cottenham from Landbeach.

[2] R. H. Bautier, *The Economic Development of Medieval Europe* (1971), pp. 188–9, 'The bad harvest of 1314 was followed by two years with so much rain that catastrophic floods occurred more or less everywhere.'

even when it all could be cultivated: it was not even fully able to make up for losses in a bad flood, for it could then only provide twenty acres while Scachbow alone would lose thirty-four. From this time on right up to the parliamentary enclosure, every scrap of evidence that sheds light on their cropping shows Banworth and Scachbow running together as one shift. They are usually counted together and totalled together in the Survey of 1722 in the Dukman Book. They appear at first glance to be separate in 1345–6, when Banworth is fallow and there are some peas in Scachbow, but these amount to less than nineteen acres and it has become the practice by this time to sow some peas in the fallow. In their next fallow in 1348–9 both are under beans, peas and vetches. In the only other Reeve's Account Roll which we have for Landbeach (Thomas Brotherton's of 1352–3) they form the 'winter field' and are under wheat and maslin together. The court rolls are illuminating at this point: at the St Denis Chamberlains Court of 1346 a tenant has surrendered a ten-acre holding to reduce its size. The lord is then to choose an acre and a half of the better land 'in three fields' ('*in tribus campis*') and the said Robert then to choose one acre and a half of land 'in the said three fields, of the better sort, namely in every field, half an acre' ('*in dictis tribus campis de meliore viz. in quolibet campo d'i acre…*'). In spite of the fact that the system was then at its most complicated, crops being sown in six fields (Milnefeld, Fortemade, Sckachbowe, Tunstallfeld, Madefeld and Morefeld), those concerned thought of this as not merely in three seasons but in three fields.[1]

What is clearly happening in 1345–6 is that the Millfield is the winter field sown with wheat, Dunstall, the spring field sown with dredge and a little oats; part of the fallow, Scachbow, is sown with peas. But this is being supplemented by ploughing in the meadows and moor; seventeen and a half acres of maslin are sown in Fortemade (the meadow area where Milton, Landbeach and Waterbeach meet, Hardmede in later documents). This allows the pure barley, ten and a half acres to be sown in Millfield. It is not clear whether this barley was winter sown, but in 1352–3 there were four and a half acres under barley and dredge 'in skacchbough de seisona yemale'. If Fortemade, the dry meadow, could be used to supplement the winter field, the moor and other damper meadow could be spring sown for oats and dredge.

Unfortunately the acreages are not divided from Dunstall, so that we cannot be sure of the scale. In some past years trespass cases have shown that supplementary incursions by the plough have been taking place, at least on a small scale into the meadow and moor.[2]

---

[1] CCCC, XXXV, 182, for the Account Rolls of Richard Pelle for 1348–9; CCCC, XXXV, 181, for his Roll for 1345–6 and Thomas Brotherton's Roll for 1352–6; CCCC, XXXV, 121, 20 Ed. III, St Denis, for Court Roll 1346.

[2] CCCC, XXXV, 121, 12 Ed. III, St Edmund, King, 1338, 'in the lord's corn in the meadow' ('*in blad' d'm' apud le made…*'): similarly trespass cases can show Schachbow running with Banworth, e.g. CCCC, XXXV, 121, 6 Ed, III, St Michael, shows dredge in both.

But 1346 is the first time in our records that these intakes have been dignified as Meadowfield and Morefield. They do not appear in 1352–3 when Dunstall is fallowing; they were cropped with it 1346, and so appear to be joined in its shift. The only supplementary cropping in the later year is four and a half acres of peas somewhere undefined in the fallow ('*in warect*').

So was born the Meadow Field of the field books, and also the Scachbow in More Field and More under Dunstall of 1549. Meadow Field can be listed simply as a field, but More Field is part in Scachbow Field and part in Dunstall Field. Thus, superficially the whole system of field nomenclature appears to have been reduced to chaos: in fact the names have evolved to cover the extremely sensible practical measures, that have been taken to preserve the old system and shore it up under the appalling conditions of the early fourteenth century. Like shoring round a building, the new appearance is untidy but the structure may be saved.

If the bringing of new areas under the plough in the fourteenth century was an emergency measure in response to the deterioration of the climate and water-table, we might expect them to revert to their old conditions in better times. This in fact happened, although dating the change is not easy.

The Account Roll of 1352–3 showed that there was very little supplementary sowing, only four and a half acres in the fallow. It also showed that the plough had passed over once more to the counter-attack on the encroaching fen: an acre and a rod were sown with oats 'in Scachbow on empty land cultivated anew this year' ('*in skacchebough de terra frisca hoc anno de novo cult*').

More under Dunstall and Scachbow in Morefield of the 1549 Field Book are absent from the fifteenth-century field books,[1] but in the Dukman Book appear in part as arable under the names More Furlong and Morleys Furlong. Their arrangement in 1549 bears witness to their origins as intakes from the lords' waste: they are divided in blocks, five selions to the armiger (the Manor of Brays), and six to the College, rotating in order, interrupted only by the occasional two or three selions of the most substantial freeholder, T. Lane, who held the only big house ('*mansio*') in the village. These are the only parts of the field for which the acreage is not given. One is not convinced that at that time they were not down to grass, and the same suspicion attaches to Meadow Field.

Meadow Field was no longer arable by the mid-seventeenth century. In addition to the opinion of Serjeant Bernard mentioned above, there is a 'Survey of Real Property in 1665' in the Fen Book,[2] in which the total area of the 'laies' proves to be that of Meadow Field. There is a note in

---

[1] LPC, Field Book; CCCC, XXXV, 163 and 164; LPC, Dukman.
[2] LPC, Fen Book.

Clifford's writing in the parish copy of the 1549 Field Book (on what was originally the outside), referring to Banworth Lees. They are divided between the two farmers of the two manors and the inhabitants. The acreage amounts to 179, and if one adds to this the six and a half acres glebe land in Meadow Field in the terrier of Cliffords, we arrive at the total of 185½ acres. This is much too great to be part of Banworth Field, which is only 117 acres altogether, but Meadow Field is given as 185 acres 3 roods. There can be little doubt that this field, created out of Banworth Meadow, is back again to grass. There is one earlier hint of this: in the College archives in the bundle, 'Miscellaneous Papers', are two Terriers dated 1558 (or possibly 1554), neither of which has any land in Meadow Field, although there is separate meadow.[1]

This takes us back so close to Parker's time that it seems possible that Meadow Field was already back to grass in the Field Book. Parker was concerned to establish exact property rights over every piece of land, and this meant looking back. The ridge and furrow in the field would still make the essential property boundaries perfectly clear in a more permanent and economical form than the normal method of annual marking out, and so be the logical way of recording the Meadow Field. (House-plots taken out of the arable centuries before are still measured as selions in the 1549 Field Book.) Cropping details from this period would be invaluable, but unfortunately do not seem to exist.

Any changes from grass to arable and back again that we can trace seem to be due to the flooding of the early fourteenth century, and the slow recovery from this. In any case the changes seem to be confined to the original meadow and moor, outside the open fields of the period when the flood struck except in so far as flooded land could be used as temporary pasture. The nearest thing to convertible husbandry are the later changes of Scachbow Leys and Moreleys back to arable, but this was only marginal to the system as a whole, nor have we any evidence to suggest that the change was repeated, let alone frequent or regular.

CONCLUSIONS ON THE FIELD SYSTEMS

The evolution of the open fields of each of our villages took its own course, and in none did it conform to the pattern suggested by Postgate.

In Waterbeach the system of cultivation seems to have been based on three great open fields at least from the mid-twelfth century up to enclosure in the nineteenth century. Contrary appearances of complexity

---

[1] CCCC, XXXV, 172; cf. CCCC, Lease Book, which has a series of leases the manor including Scachbow Leys and Moorleys, beginning with the lease to John Gotobed on 29 December 1553 of 'certain void leys'.

and confusion arise from the changing name of one field (a common enough phenomenon), and the use of names of lesser units; not from changes in farming practice. This use of names seems to have arisen in part directly from topography and partly from the preponderance of small arable holdings among the peasantry. This again was largely due to the peculiar topography of Waterbeach. As far as Waterbeach is concerned, the facts that Postgate was trying to explain are a documentary illusion.

In Cottenham the increase in the number of common fields from three to five was not due to assarting, which had been completed centuries before, but to re-arrangement for more intensive exploitation of the arable. This was made possible by the abundant supply of farmyard manure, a by-product of the scale and topographical peculiarities of Cottenham Fens. The date of the increase in the number of fields, not before the beginning of the sixteenth century, is too late to fit into Postage's scheme.

In Landbeach the increase in the number of fields in the early fourteenth (and possibly late thirteenth) century *was* due to assarting, but not as part of a steady expansion of ploughland towards the parish boundary. Most of it was an emergency operation in face of the rise of the water-table at that period. But this never disturbed the rotation, which the villagers thought of as in three open fields.

The detailed investigation of the fields of these three villages in no case produces a result that conforms to Postgate's hypothesis. Close examination of the documents suggests that the picture which he found may be in very large part due to the varying usage of proper names for field land in the classes of documents which he consulted. We can never be quite sure what field-names represent until we can relate them to documents concerned with the actual cropping.

FURLONG AND SELION

The enclosure of Cottenham was so late, the Award not being made until 1847, that living memory still reached back to the open fields when interest began to increase again in the system. In 1905 Jacob Sanderson jotted down his memoirs,[1] which took him back to his boyhood days when he had worked on the open fields after harvest, minding his uncle's pigs. A few years later, in 1911 and 1913, *Westrope's Year Book* recalled the fast-vanishing signs of the days before enclosure in the words of one who still remembered them functioning.

In all cases it may be stated, the different 'furlongs' lay in such directions that one end of them was higher than the other. This excellent arrangement was for drainage purposes.

[1] *Notebook.* I am grateful to Mrs Norman for permission to read and quote from this notebook.

This was most important and was most effective, as the 'lands' were narrow. A 'furlong' was mostly about ten chains in length, though sometimes less, giving as near as possible average plots of half an acre each. These holdings were never ploughed flat, as is the custom at the present time, but had from time immemorial been 'ridged' much more often than they were 'cast'.[1]

This suggests an unusual pattern for the open fields of Cottenham, and this indeed is what strikes one most in studying a strip map of the village: by comparison with one of the strip maps for, say the neighbouring Rampton,[2] Cottenham's furlongs seem unusually long; they run for by far the greater part parallel north-east and south-west, and the 'grain' of the lands is at right angles to the main Westwick Road. The road runs along the spine of a very low watershed between such natural drainage lines as there are in this flat ground. Even today in a flood on frozen ground, a gale can move water over the top of the ridge. So the plough's furrow took the rainwater as fast as possible away from the ridge, the deep water-furrows between the lands brought it to the gripes alongside the furlongs, which took it to the common drains, and hopefully towards the fens and the Old West River. Natural surface drainage was so slight that every possible advantage had to be taken of it.

The best surviving selions of the old pattern in this area are on the heavy clay land near the fen edge, close to Belsars Hill in Willingham. There they are still carrying out their original function on the most difficult ground. The local name for them is 'winding lands' from the aratral curve, and it is reckoned nowadays that it takes a good man to plough them.[3] When two adjacent selions have been ploughed there is naturally a double, or open, furrow between them. This is then deepened by ploughing it outwards again, and in wet places a further mole furrow may be put down the centre to deepen it once more.

Such furrows would form excellent boundary marks that would not be easy to move, and if moved would be impossible to conceal. These were probably the 'amplas culturas' referred to in the twelfth-century charter for the division of lost lands in Dry Drayton.[4] In the ordinances in the Cottenham Rectory Manor Court Rolls of 17 Eliz. it lays down: 'Each to plow a water furrow by his lands in the fields before St. Thomas the Apostle, and these to be of the fashion of the lord's work.'[5]

Such entries tend to be still more frequent in the Landbeach Court Rolls; and in Waterbeach, orders to scour or make all manner of ditches and banks in field, fen and town are an obsession.

[1] 1913, p. 19.
[2] E.g. CUL, MS. Plans, 177 (R), 1754.
[3] I am grateful to Mr Dennis Jeeps of Willingham for this information. Belsars Hill is at TL 423703.
[4] ECA, p. 162: Wr. Pk. Ch., fol. 242 (18).
[5] CRO C 1–9.

Water furrows or ditches between neighbour and neighbour were under constant observation by an interested party, and not likely to suffer much from encroachment without being noticed and reported to the court. Common ditches and balks were a different matter. In the second Fen Reeves' Book of Ordinances in Cottenham[1] for the early nineteenth century, some of the orders still have a faintly biblical ring about them:

42. It is ordered that if any person or persons shall plow or dig up any of the common baulks in any of the fields to engross it to themselves shall for every such offense pay 3s. 4d. and plow or cast the same back again, and no baulks, grass furrows or furlong ends to be mown or fed till harvest...

Informers were to be paid to enforce this in medieval fashion.

45. (1807) It is ordered that the headlands in all the fields shall be set out by the officers and order-makers and stulped[2] at the expense of the town, and them that are too big to be reduced to their proper standard and those that are too little to be made as big as they ought to be.

References to encroachments in this area are not so common as the frequent cases of trespass; and references to boundary markers of any kind very rare. The word 'mere' also meant a boundary, and mere-stones were boundary markers. One of the local names for the Roman road is still the Mereway, and this is a very old usage.[3] The balk existed as a field path, and where it lay it certainly marked a furlong boundary. When it was longer it was usually called a dole, as it was the custom to include the grass of the paths and the unsown water-furrows in the precious herbage of the village. A field path could, when untrodden, in the appropriate season apparently be allotted as a dole in the meadow. The name seems to imply this, although no direct evidence of this practice seems to be forthcoming for the three villages here discussed. Evelyn-White found much evidence in Rampton of the letting of such grassland as a regular source of income to the township.[4] But the above order, the charter referred to earlier for the division of lands in Dry Drayton mentioning 'certis metis', and other references all seem to imply that sometimes other markers were used than balks and furrows. Among the Landbeach peas-

---

[1] Part of the collection of Mr M. Haird of Cottenham. I am most grateful to Mr Haird for the generous way in which he has made documents available to me.

[2] Stulped, staked, and dowelled are local equivalents for marked boundaries; cf. *Common Rights*, p. 207, Article XIX, 'that Smithy Fen shall continue and remain for ever dowelled and staked according as it now lieth...the stake or landmark for the parcels of the said fen...'

[3] CUL Queens', Fd6, 5 Hen. VIII, 'a certain common mereway called a common balk' ('...*quoddam communia mara vocata a Common Balk...*'), cf. *Common Rights*, p. 237, refers to cattle after harvest on 'Baulks, forrands or furrows in this Town's Fields'.

[4] Rev. C. H. Evelyn-White, 'A Book of Church Accounts relating to certain "Balks" in the Common Fields of Rampton, Cambs.', *TCHAS* I (1904), 142–210.

ants' complaints against Kirby in 1549, they say: 'He blindeth in their bounds the meres and the doles by his covetous dealing.'[1] In Landbeach again we find the rector, only a few years before enclosure, searching to find his lost lands, and providing painted oak posts with anchor pieces, to mark all the glebe lest it be lost again.[2] He marked each field in its fallow year. Common lands were much more vulnerable to encroachment except where the lord of one of the manors was interested in preserving them: where he was interested in making the encroachment himself there might be little protection. Kirby managed to include in a yard of his, a lane and a row of willows whose loppage had provided the township of Landbeach with a small annual income.[3] This is still identifiable on the ground. Perhaps the most impertinent peasant encroachment was recorded in Cottenham in 1442:

The jurors say that William Warde stopped a certain ditch in Cottenham which was a boundary between Henry Arneburgh and William le Wode and planted willows in the midst of the bottom of the same ditch appropriating the same ditch to himself where it was the boundary between the fee of the lord bishop of Ely and the fee of the lord Abbot.[4]

But such instances were not altogether uncommon:

The jurors present that the same William [Cosyn] made an encroachment against the lord appropriating to himself the lord's soil next the manor namely in length eight perches and in breadth three feet. Therefore he is in mercy. And order is made to the jury that in the presence of the said William, if he wishes to take part, they themselves place boundary markers there that right may be done and the said encroachment altogether be done away.[5]

But in our villages there is very little sign of permanent encroachment of any kind, and little of either consolidation of strips or of enclosing arable to turn it down to grass. Enclosures of this kind, apart from the very early expansion of the villages on to open field furlongs, tended to be on a relatively small scale to provide home paddocks for the lords and substantial freeholders in order to exploit the fens more fully. Cottenham had a few small enclosures on the boundaries of the open fields, but these dated back to the sixteenth century at least. A feature on the strip maps of some of the nearby villages are 'Pieces', whole furlongs consolidated and enclosed down to grass. These are prominent in Rampton, a village with only one lord, but no less so in Dry Drayton which had two. Landbeach and Waterbeach have one such enclosure each, in the former the Thirty Acre Piece of the College on the margin of Scachbow and the fen, and in

---

[1] CCCC, XXXV, 194.
[2] LPC, Tithe Book; where a landlord gave up cultivation and became a rentier there was always the possibility of losing lands, cf. *ECA*, p. 282, Cottenham in 1529, 'no income because it was not known where it lay' ('*nullus exitus pro eo quod ignoratur ubi iacet…*').
[3] CCCC, XXXV, 194.
[4] CUL Queens' Ad 36; Appendix B.   [5] *ECA*, p. 358; Appendix B.

the latter the part of the village on the east of the High Street, which has left its name in Pieces Terrace, and must once have been a very convenient adjunct to a farmhouse in the village centre.

But there were no major losses from the medieval arable right up to the parliamentary enclosures, and both the strip maps for Cottenham and the Field Books for Landbeach show little consolidation.

Matthew Parker's Field Book of 1549 gives the complete details of fields, furlongs, strips and selions, with ownership and past and present occupation, and acreage by strips. It includes also the built-up area of the village as the first selion in each of the three fields that adjoin the houses and crofts. Deducting the latter we arrive at the figures shown for the arable.

TABLE 6. *The open arable fields of Landbeach*

	Quarentele	Seliones	Acres	Rods	Poles
Banworth	8	246	112	3	0
Mill Field	10	571	278	3	20
Meadow Field	13	372	185	3	0
Dunstall	16	535	259	1	0
Scachbow	11	460	229	0	0

The local name for a pair of selions side by side ploughed as one is a 'broad' or a 'broadel selion': none are mentioned here, but in 'More under Dunstall in Dunstall Field' (which we saw was late assarted land and contained some of the few blocks of demesne selions) there are two notes: 'ij ac go through' and 'they go through'. This would appear to mean a double selion arranged end to end. In Stretham Glebe Terriers the name 'a throughout' is given to such, and the more familiar side by side double selions are called a 'twilstitch'.[1] The record of More under Dunstall bears a note: 'all the selions in this furlong are divided among the tenants' ('*omnes seliones istius querentule solent divisi inter tenentes*'). This is where the plough has finally reached into the old moor against the parish boundary. Their appearance in blocks is quite different from the rest of the furlongs. Even the nearby 'Histon Barrow' in Dunstall Field, although it is, uniquely, entirely owned by the College as lord of the Chamberlains Manor, has its ten selions in seven different tenants' hands and formerly in eight. In the seventh furlong (*quarentela*) in the Meadow Field, selions are measured in 'buttes', three such making an acre according to a note inserted by Masters into the Dukman Book.

Selions proper vary in recorded size from a rod to an acre, but a substantial majority are of the standard half acre that we found in Cottenham. As is clear from the list above, there is no significant difference in selion size with difference in soils. What difference there may have been was probably in the height of the ridges. Local tradition has it that the

[1] CUL EDR H/1/5, Glebe Terriers, Stretham.

worse the drainage, the higher was the ridge. The local name for such ridges as are left today is high-backs, but purists say this should properly be kept for the steepest, all of which seem to be on stiff clay.

Of the furlongs proper in the arable fields the variation in size is very great. All fields except the Meadow have a furlong containing less than four acres, and the largest, the seventh in Mill Field, at 82 acres is well over twice the average of about $36\frac{1}{2}$ acres. In one area a whole group call attention to themselves by their tiny size. The set in Dunstall Field, labelled one to five 'in Renels' (or 'in Ropes'), begin with the largest under seven acres, and decrease to the smallest which is less than two. These would appear to have been fitted in between the two branches of the stream before the junction. This must have been difficult ground.

All the furlongs were numbered within their respective fields. Not all appear to have had names. Sometimes the name appears in each of two fields for adjacent furlongs, e.g. Redland in Dunstall becomes more often Blackland as time goes by, although its neighbour in Mill Field is always Blackland. Perhaps its soil improved with long cultivation and dropped its old 'assarting' name, 'Ridland'. There is a Lamcothyll in Meadow Field as well as Banworth.

Sometimes the names are sources for the field history in themselves; in Chapter 1 Lamecot and Hammys were suggestive of a shepherds' settlement in the Dark Ages. The rest of Meadow Field names are more obvious, but are confirmatory, nevertheless: Twenty Swathes, Redemedowe, Ravensmedowe, Wellfurlong, Langlond. Short Furlong, Fenn Furlong and Butts in Banworth are a little more closely identifiable on the map because of the names. Some of the names are plainly informative about the fieldways as well as the position of the furlong, like Dovehouse Dole; some intriguing, like Morman's Furlong which becomes Norman's Furlong later. This adds the first faint addition to the suggestion that there may have been an isolated farm or hamlet in the Dark Age moor, reabsorbed as the ploughland grew, leaving only its name in Dunstall. Near where the furlong Perecourt once was, wild pear still flourishes in the boundary hedge.

CRISIS, CHANGE AND STABILITY IN THE OPEN FIELDS

The early fourteenth century seems to have been the great testing time for our villages. Even Cottenham with its arable above the twenty-foot contour did not escape the flooding. In 1314 four tenants were in mercy, on account of a watercourse in the fields; in 1322 twelve acres of demesne in the fields were flooded in June;[1] in 1328 the Court of Landbeach

---

[1] *ECA*, pp. 343, 241; CUL Queens', Ad 26, 14 Abbot Henry, St Gregory.

Chamberlains found a new formula for reporting floods; and by 1337 there seems to have been some reversion since four butts which had been cropped in the recent past were now mowing meadow. But then, as now, floods from the fens may have repaid any loss by enriching the soil: there is little sign of falling fertility. Miss Page's tables show little if any sign of falling yields. I have come across only one reference to worn out land, and that had been over-cropped for hay, not corn, in Landbeach moor.[1]

But the trials of the farmers in this period were far from confined to flooding. Second only to the land they relied on the tractive power of the plough teams. On the Crowlands manors the team seems to have consisted of two horses and four oxen.[2]

Crowlands cattle-breeding centre for Cambridgeshire was Cottenham, and normally if an Oakington team were short another would be transferred from Cottenham or bought on the open market. But in the return for milk for 1321–2 the Oakington Roll has, 'and no more because the cow was helped in the plough', and the Cottenham Roll, 'and no more due to plough-work'. This conjures up the picture of a peasant community on the verge of complete collapse. This was the year of the June flood mentioned above, and in Oakington an additional reason for the low return on milk was the wetness of the season. Hay had to be spread and dried in the courtyard. At the sowing of peas, paid villein labour had to be called in while the 'staff' ('*famuli*') worked on the carts and on throwing water over the ploughs. Over half the pig herd was lost in what looks like swine fever. The pay of the '*famuli*' was short because of the dearth of corn this year.[3]

But the instability of the weather in these years faced the communities with something worse than simple deterioration. The Ministers' Accounts for Denney for 1325–6 show that all the oats were lost from drought, and the hay scarcely grew at all in some meadows. The next year not only had problems from drought and heat again: westerly gales stripped the thatch from large areas of the roofs of the church and farm-buildings, and the little enclosure walls of mud, as well as their thatch, lost the top two feet.[4] It was in face of such disasters as this that the changes in rotation, and improvisations to maintain production were made.

The court and account rolls show the management responding with increased attention to detail: work such as sowing and lifting the hemp in

[1] CCCC, XXXV, 145, 1316.

[2] *ECA*, p. 239, 'expenses of ploughing' ('*custus carucarum*'), 1322–3 (Aston dates this 1321–2): 'the shoeing of 2 stotts and 4 mares' ('...*ferrura ii affrorum et iiij Iumentorum...*') *ECA*, p. 444; the 1430 lease of the manor of Cottenham has 'four oxen and two horses in each plough' ('*iiij bobis et ij equis in qualibet caruca...*').

[3] *ECA*, pp. 238–46.

[4] PRO Ministers' Accounts, SC/6/766/12 and 13.

the garden, and making ditches to save the leeks, formerly included in gross totals is now itemised. What appeared to Miss Page writing almost forty years ago, as the wildest confusion[1] in the arable rotation, seems now to have been sound farming practice in face of the greatest difficulties. It is a remarkable tribute to the manorial administration that so much survived through the famines and pestilences of the century. The improvements in managerial techniques which had begun on the large estates in the thirteenth century, appear to have been exploited to the full in the early fourteenth century, not only by Crowland Abbey, but in Waterbeach and in both the Landbeach manors as well (see Table 7).

In the cropping recorded in these tables, Denney, then in royal hands, seems to be the most conservative. But the kind of changes which can be traced later and further in neighbouring Oakington are already under way. The area under spring crops is increasing, and these are occupying part of the winter field in Cottenham and Landbeach. In Landbeach some of the barley appears to be winter sown. Legumes are sown in part of the fallows in Cottenham and Landbeach, and in the waste in Waterbeach.[2] Mixed grains are replacing much of the pure seed. But substantial amounts of wheat are still sown; its progressive replacement by the high yielding barley, even in the form of dredge, scarcely seems to have begun at this stage; and oats, especially when included in dredge, have not yet lost an important place. In the later Middle Ages oats seem to have been grown mostly on cold lands, and wet soils on the fen edge would have been particularly suitable. Oats were sown on the part of Scachbow which had been newly ploughed again after being retaken from the fen. Oats were to be the normal crop from the Adventurers Lands when the water subsided in time for any crop at all. They were to be the chief first crop later still when the fen was first broken up after enclosure. They would have been the last cereal crop that could be sown with any hope of harvest in a season delayed by late flood. It is significant that where we have comparative accounts for the Crowlands manors in Cottenham and Oakington, the decline in the importance of oats proceeds much faster in Oakington, away from the fen edge.[3]

Again slight differences in topography may account for some of the differences between cropping changes on different manors. Denney Account Rolls for 1324–5 show sixty-five acres

of demesne land in the fallow and other seasons let this year to various men to sow vetches, beans and peas as is shown in various items

[1] *ECA*, p. 119.
[2] Cf. G. Duby, *Rural Economy and Country Life in the Medieval West* (1962), trans. C. Postan (1968), p. 348, where he reports that bare fallows had disappeared in Flanders by 1328.
[3] *ECA*, pp. 175–6, 177–8, 313–14, 220–1, 225, 232, 235, 242, 250.

TABLE 7. *Crops sown in certain years in the fourteenth century*

Denney, 1325–6

	Acres	Rods	Poles	
Wheat	110	0	0	'on the Mill Field' ('*super le mellefeld*')
Maslin	16	0	0	'on the Mill Field' ('*super le mellefeld*')
Peas	15	0	0	'in a heath' ('*in uno Heth*')
Barley	3	0	0	'in the Spring season' ('*seysona quadr*')
Dredge	60	0	0	'in the Spring season' ('*seysona quadr*')
Oats	81	0	0	?
	285	0	0	

Cottenham, 1321–2

	Acres	Rods	Poles	
Wheat	23	3½	0	in Aldeburghfeld
Maslin	44	3	0	in Aldeburghfeld
Beans and peas	13	0	0	Lowefeld
Dredge	40	2	0	(probably Lowefeld from quantity; so in *ECA*)
Oats	40	0	0	Aldeburghfeld
Barley	9	0	0	?
	171	0	20	

Landbeach Chamberlains, 1352–3

	Acres	Rods	Poles	
Wheat	33	0	0	Banworth and Scachbow
Maslin	29	0	0	Banworth and Scachbow
Peas	10	0	0	'5½ in Mill Field and 4½ in the fallow' ('5½ *in Melnfeld and* 4½ *in Warect*')
Barley and dredge	41	3	0	37¼ in Melnfeld and 4½ in Scachbow winter ('*hiemal*')
Oats	17	3	0	'16½ in Mill Field and 1¼ in Scachbow in empty land cultivated anew' ('16½ *in Melnfeld and* 1¼ *Scachbow in* 'ter' frisc' cult' *de nove*')
	131	2	0	

Cf. Landbeach Chamberlains, 1348–9

	Quarters	Bushels	
Wheat	10	7	in le Milnefeld
Maslin	2	5	in le Milnefeld
Beans and peas	32	1	Scachbow and Banworth
Dredge	25	5	Dunstall
Barley	6	5	Milne
	77	7	

Note: Hemp and flax are included in small amounts in the stock for Landbeach, and from the Cottenham '*opera*' account we learn that hemp was grown in the garden.

Sources: PRO Ministers' Accounts, SC6/766/13; *ECA*, pp. 240–2; CCCC, XXXV, 182; CCCC, XXXV, 181.

and in the following year fifty-four acres were let in the same way. Some of this area may well have been the same Denney Low Grounds which were being sown year after year with oats in the late eighteenth century. The peasants here were taking the risk, and the lord the residual fertility.

In trying to see how rigidity came to replace the adaptability and flexibility of this system in the fourteenth century, perhaps the key change is the return of bare fallows.

Bare fallowing with double ploughing seems to have been regarded as essential for conditioning the soil for a winter crop. In 1356 the Chamberlains bailiff in Landbeach was presented by the homage for failing to double plough three acres of fallow, with the result that they could not be sown with wheat,[1] but since pure wheat sowings had decreased, this would not preclude spring crops in at least part of the fallows. For Oakington Miss Page dated the return of bare fallows, except for the occasional cleaning crop, to 1391. The reason for this assertion is not clear since the rolls show sequences of years with bare fallows in the 1360s, the 1370s and the 1380s; they also show sequences with legumes in the fallows in the early fifteenth century. In the leases of the demesnes in Cottenham and Oakington in 1430[2] fallows are specified, of which part is to be double ploughed, part composted with carted dung, and part dunged by the sheep-fold. The practice of bare fallowing seems to have lasted on to parliamentary enclosure. The Tithe Appraisals for Cottenham show bare fallows throughout the five-year period recorded, 1691–5.[3]

A note in the Dukman Book in the Landbeach Parish Chest has the same implication, 'in all the said fields, which put it into three parts, two corned and one close...'[4] This is dated 1727, and Burroughes seems to have been able to mark the glebe in bare fallow fields on the eve of enclosure there. Masters' Tithe Appraisals for Waterbeach in the late eighteenth century are likewise unmistakable,[5] as is the rest of the evidence cited above from the *Masters* vs. *Standley* case. In his *General View* Vancouver states directly of Cottenham:

The rotation of the crops is first fallow, with sheep-folding: second year, wheat; the wheat stubble winter-fallowed and highly manured for the third year's crop of barley; fourth year peas and beans; fifth year, barley, produce

28 bushels of Wheat
30 bushels of Barley
20 bushels of Peas and Beans

[1] CCCC, XXXV, 121.
[2] *ECA*, pp. 438–48.
[3] Westrope's *Year Book – Cottenham, 1911*.
[4] P. 54.
[5] WPC, Tithe bundle.

No turnips, clover, tares, or other green crops are cultivated, though it is evident from the soil that they might be brought to a very great perfection.[1]

This did not last in quite as rigid a form for the few years of life left to the old system. In 1905, Jacob Sanderson, who had worked as a lad on the old open fields before the enclosure, gave full details of the rotation in its last days:

One course was Dead Fallow. Second course was Wheat. Third course was Barley. Fourth course was Beans. Fifth course was a cross crop of roots, turnips, potatoes or corn: if turnips were wanted they could be grown on the bean field. Sheep were allowed to be folded on the dead fallows any time in the summer (that is, the owner's sheep).

All the manure was put on the wheat stubble for barley and carried out before the harvest on the waste places in the field near the town, ready to be put on after the harvest. The wheat to be sown before the Feast (Shrove Tuesday); the beans before Candlemas Day, February; the barley as late as May when the threshing was done. The cow dung carted and carried out after the 13th May when the Commons were stocked.[2]

The period of flexibility and experiment in our open fields seems to have been the time when the lords showed most interest and initiative in direct cultivation. With the removal of population pressure, peasant power grew as lordly interest waned. The peasantry seem to have been able to make necessary minor changes quickly to keep the system going, but to have been able to avoid any major radical alteration.

Parallel to the loss of managerial interest from lords over much of the arable, was the increasing interest in stock on the part of those particularly eager to make money. If much of the battle of the first half of the century for subsistence against the often unfavourable odds had been won, the numbers interested in and able to accumulate wealth had increased. For many, arable could have only provided a relatively stable base from which to operate in more lucrative pastures. Unfortunately we do not have the sources to examine such possibilities closely in the three villages under discussion, and a fully satisfactory answer could only come from the kind of detail that was never written down about the farming operations of the peasants.

The disappearance of the fallows, and their re-appearance later, raises a problem of some interest in view of the recent controversy about the 'common field' system. Before the fallows were eroded and disappeared, they were undoubtedly common, as the 'Inquisitiones Post Mortem' of the time usually specify. There is even the hint in the 1316 Extent of Agnes de Bray that any arable that could not be sown became *ipso facto* common while in an unsown state. There is plenty of evidence from the later period

[1] Pp. 126–7.
[2] Notebook.

5-2

to show the fallows again subject to common. As Mrs Thirsk[1] so rightly emphasised, in this later period it seems to be the right of common on fallows that provides the biggest barrier to change. In Landbeach it was the lord of Milton's right to common merely on the mown lands of the old Meadow Field that held back the final enclosure.[2] Yet such difficulties were clearly not insuperable in the fourteenth century. As with our maps, so with other documents, one can read back far too much from the end of the open fields into the medieval period.

[1] Joan Thirsk, 'The Common Fields', *P & P* no. XXIX (1964), and 'The Origins of the Common Fields', *P & P* no. XXXIII (1966); cf. J. Z. Titow, 'Medieval England and the Open Field System', *P & P* no. XXXII (1965).

[2] LPC, Collectanea, *P & P* Masters' Correspondence.

4

VILLAGE PATTERNS

The first impression of the pattern of Cottenham village that one gets today on passing through, is of its unusual length. Ignoring recent ribbon development outside the area of the old village, its length from Green End to Church End is well over a mile (see Fig. 9). There are houses from the first half of the seventeenth century, if not perhaps earlier, on the side of the green, and others of similar age to be noticed intermittently all the way along the High Street to the church. Here then, at first glance is an example of the geographer's street village, running from church to green, and only marred from perfect simplicity of pattern by the dog-leg formed by two right-angled bends in the middle. The farmhouses stand at the road-side, and their long yards stretch out behind them like generous crofts and tofts. One seems to have a medieval pattern almost perfectly preserved. If, however, one goes off the High Street down Denmark Street (the old Chequers Lane) there are other houses of similar age, showing that development in this area, away from the single street, had taken place well before parliamentary enclosure.

On any map of the village which shows the property boundaries, the shape of the plots clearly differentiates the village into three main sections. This appears most dramatically in Alexander Halford's map made at the time of the enclosure.[1] The centre of the village is a large rectangle around which the High Street is diverted on its dog-leg. Here the plots are irregular, inclined towards short rectangles, but fitted together on no consistent pattern, and divided by sinuous lanes. North and south of this, for the most part, on both sides of the High Street, the properties run back from the road in long strips. Some of the boundary lines, if projected across the street, flow smoothly on to those on the opposite side. If one also looks at the boundaries at the back of these properties it becomes clear that these were once open-field furlongs.

To the north the High Street runs almost straight to the church. To the south it almost bisects the furlong, until the Histon road forks left and the Rampton and Oakington road swings right, leaving the green as a triangle in the fork. The outline of the central rectangle, and the property boundaries in the area of strips, fit neatly into the general pattern of the open fields of the village, with its axes approximately north-east south-

---

[1] CRO 124/p42.

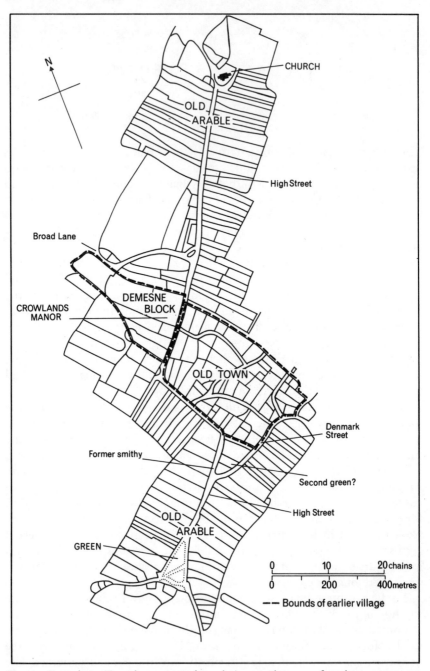

Fig. 9. Cottenham Town's property boundaries on the eve of enclosure: property boundaries differentiate the patterns of older and later development during the medieval period (source: CRO Q/RDc 31 c. 1845).

west, and north-west south-east. The line of the High Street from the village centre to the church appears to be imposed slightly diagonally on this, as does the Histon Road from the apex of the green.

It has been argued elsewhere that the sites of the churches in these three villages were chosen as the first convenient spot of firm ground above the peat soil and the reach of the flood-waters, and that the heavy stone was transported to them by barge along the lodes. This might well involve a change of site from that of a previous wooden church, and the legend that sometimes enshrines the memory of the change of site has survived in Cottenham. It was intended, so the legend runs, that the church should be built on Church Hill, much nearer to the village centre and adjacent to the closes of the principal manor, Crowlands. However, although the good inhabitants placed the stones there during the day, each night the Devil moved them to the new site, and in the end in exhaustion they accepted the Devil's choice. Jacob Sanderson in his memoirs has a slightly different version in which not the Devil, but the Aborigines were responsible.[1] This has an echo of the Celtic-speaking demons who tormented St Guthlac, the founder of Crowlands in another part of the Fens.

If there really were a change in the site of the church when it was first built in stone as the legend implies, then the fragments of re-used stone with Norman tooling and decoration in the walls suggest that this was not later than Norman times. We know too that a Cottenham Lode was available in the early Norman period for the Conqueror to use in his assault on Ely.[2]

The major change of village pattern which resulted in the northwards extension through the open fields to the new church probably began in the Norman period. The central rectangular area would seem to have been the late Saxon village.

The southern expansion of the village plan could well belong to the same period as that in the north. The site of the manor house of Burdlaries or Harleston lay well to the south, against the village green. This manor was one of the new fees created by the Norman bishop of Ely.

There may have been another village green taken from former arable where the High Street approaches the squarish heart of the old village. The apex of the triangular area formed there still has a fragment of common around the war memorial, where the village smithy formerly stood. When village feasts were still held Cottenham had two, Church End and Green End, but as far back as we can trace it, the traditional site of the Church End Feast, and also of the fair granted to the rector in 1265, was Broad Lane, much nearer the church and rectory.[3]

[1] Notebook.
[2] *Liber Eliensis*, p. 182.
[3] W. Farrer, *Feudal Cambridgeshire* (Cambridge, 1920), p. 34.

The part of the village not so far discussed is the area across the High Street to the west and north of the central rectangle. Here was the demesne homestead of Crowlands Manor in medieval times, and by the time of Katherine Pepys in the eighteenth century, and possibly originally, the demesne homesteads of at least two other manors. Lordship Lane, Lordship House, and Pelhams Croft Close formed a consolidated block. Around the Crowlands site there is a convergence of some of the boundaries towards a square elevation in a moat. Beyond this, across the joint ditch was once a much larger rectangular moat.[1] This presumably held medieval warehouses and other out-buildings. The square site is presumed to have held the hall, although since it is now an orchard and planted with daffodils, no remains can be looked for. Leading up from this towards the High Street, until the recent levelling by bulldozer, was a raised roadway between two shallow ditches. A small lode runs from the northern corner of the larger moat to the Cut, and so, via The Waits to what was once Cottenham Lode. This moat was where the abbot of Crowland's small barges could take aboard the produce of his manors of Cottenham, Oakington and Dry Drayton, for shipping off through the fens to the abbey. Cottenham was the malting centre for the three: was the medieval malting in the large rectangular moat, and did the Oakington bailiff bring his barley down the now extinct roadway? When the demesnes of Cottenham and Oakington were leased in 1430 and the rents delivered in malt, no longer did the Oakington farmer need to bring his sacks down the road through the Cottenham farmer's yards.[2] Broad Lane seems obviously designed for loading from the north side of the moat, and it was malt, not barley for malting, that now came to Cottenham.

In the Collectors' Accounts for the Cambridgeshire Crowlands manors for 1454–6 there are details of extensive rebuilding of the manor farmbuildings at Cottenham;[3] in the first year, hall, granary, kitchen and bakehouse, and in the second, kilnhouse, great barn and sheephouse. This suggests a complete adaptation of the site to the needs of the lay farmer. It may also be the shifting of the farmstead and house from the moated sites up towards the village street. The present 'Crowland House', which under its stucco and slates is reported to have gothic windows hidden, and which well deserves detailed investigation whenever a major renovation takes place, stands back from the building line of the other houses on the High Street. It quite possibly contains some of the structure of the new hall referred to in the account roll, and very probably indeed marks its site.

[1] There is a good Stukeley drawing of this house and moated site on 28 August 1731, in Bodleian MS. Top. eccles. d. 6, and another of what appears to be the Lordship House in the same year in MS. Top. Gen. d. 14 fol. 30v. See Plates IV(*a*) and (*b*).

[2] *ECA*, p. 438.

[3] CUL Queens', Cd. 39 and Cd. 83.

All the other old houses stand near or upon the line of the sidewalk and appear to have long done so. The 1596 Agreement, Article XXXVII, regulated 'any Pales, Walls, Hedges, or other fences standing before their houses towards the Street', 'so that they which shall be hereafter made shall not stand further into the Street than without the compass of the outmost part of the eaves' drop of the house'.[1]

The village suffered a large number of fires in the nineteenth century, the worst of which was in 1850. An engraving in the *Illustrated London News* of the time (see Plate II) shows a great tract of the High Street as a series of exposed chimneys surrounded by smoking debris. The extent of the rebuilding necessary in Cottenham at this time gives a unity of style to the numerous yellow brick houses and shops all re-built in a short space. But what is more remarkable is that this was when enclosure had just made it possible to build away from the village centre, out on the farmlands. This did not happen. The tradition of the nucleated village was still at full strength, and several much older chimneys emerge from the tops of yellow early Victorian villas, the houses having been rebuilt around what little was left by the fire. Such older houses as remain may often date from the rebuilding after the earlier great fire of 1676.[2]

The hards in some of the commons appear to have offered possible sites for squatters' houses in the Tudor period, but the Agreement of 1596 put an end to that. Article XIV forbade the erection on the commons of any 'Houses, Hovels, Sheds or other like buildings' except for one little cottage or shed for the keeper of the fen, and ordered all those then standing to be pulled down.[3] On the eve of enclosure the pattern of the village was very much as it had evolved in the Middle Ages, with little in the way of general alteration in lay-out having come since. The medieval pattern itself was, as we have seen, a compound, but this must reflect both periods of change and periods of stability. From the high Middle Ages stability seems the dominant note in the pattern of this village even more than it was in the pattern of its fields.

After enclosure it was expected that the village would disperse over the old open fields and commons. The rector was so sure of this that he claimed that land should be set aside to pay for the erection of new churches and chapels that would be needed to serve the groups of people who would move to new homes remote from the old religious buildings.[4] He failed to win his point, but the village failed to spread. It was not until after the First World War that much development took place outside the

---

[1] *Common Rights*, p. 221, Article XXXVII.
[2] R. L'Estrange, *A Sad Relation of a General Fire at Cottenham, Four Miles Distant from Cambridge* (1676).
[3] *Common Rights*, p. 204, Article XIV.
[4] CUL, DOC 630.

old envelope. Some ribbon building came along the Histon road, the Rampton road and Lambs' Lane, but there was plenty of land for growth by infilling. After the Second World War most of the new estates have been built on the periphery of the old. Enclosure made surprisingly little difference to the village pattern for well over a century: the fields remained empty of buildings except for the three corn mills; the pumping mills on the far edges of the fens came down but were replaced by engine houses. The few farmsteads along Twentypence Road and the other droves, and 'Gravel Diggers' which eventually turned into a farmhouse, scarcely break the emptiness of the fens even after the new intensity of cultivation that followed the ploughing up.

Perhaps the greatest change of the enclosure at the village centre was the addition of the strips of field land south-east of Lambs' Lane to yards of houses on the southern part of the High Street. Some of these houses have quite a moderate frontage, but back garden stretching right to Lambs' Lane, containing over four acres, a parody of medieval croft and toft.

LANDBEACH

A trip to Landbeach before the recent rash of new building, would have revealed a great contrast to Cottenham and a great similarity also. The contrast is in the relative size: for Cambridgeshire, Cottenham is an exceptionally large village; Landbeach exceptionally small. The similarity is in the immediate impression of old village patterns: Landbeach again appears to have been a simple street village in the past. All the houses of any age stand close to the village street, or to the edge of the old green at the north end, and this itself appears to the eye to have been little more than a widening of the road (see Fig. 10). All the houses away from the main street, with a single exception, date from the nineteenth and twentieth centuries.

There is a profusion of evidence in documents as well as in property boundaries, buildings and earthworks, which indicates the phases of change in the vlllage pattern. We can proceed in the manner of Maitland, stripping off layers of change, and by so doing we come to a very differently-shaped village in the high Middle Ages. The pattern which at first glance looked ancient was a product of the early modern period.

As far as the medieval topography of Landbeach is concerned, our great medieval survey is the Rental of 1459. The surviving copy appears to have been made two years later for the collector of the Manor of Chamberlains, and was kept in a bag at the manor at Landbeach. It is endorsed in a hand that looks suspiciously like that of Robert Masters, 'An ancient bagged roll very curious', and seems to have been neglected by him when he gathered together so many local sources. For the next fifty years and more

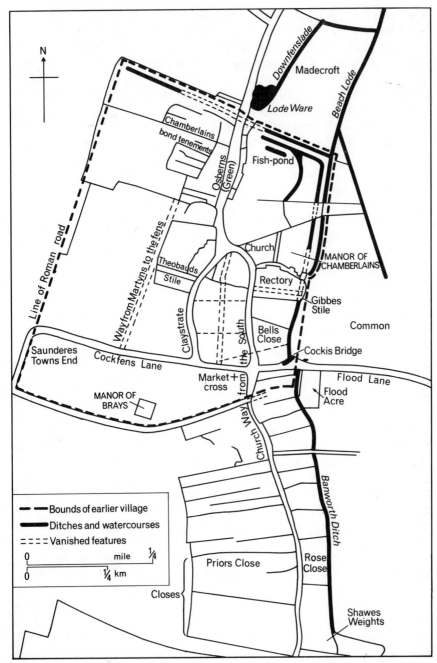

Fig. 10. Landbeach: development of the village. The development from a squarish to a linear pattern was the net result of both expansion and contraction.

it appears to have been the Domesday on which all later collectors' accounts were based. It describes in minute detail all the lands of the Chamberlains manor, venturing into geometrical terms at times, but by its abuttals makes possible the identification of the bulk of Brays tenements as well.[1]

It shows an older village, almost square in plan, to which had been added, at a more recent date, ribbon development along the present High Street to the south. The accretion will be shown by other evidence to be the product of the period of the great expansion of medieval population, which came to an end around the beginning of the fourteenth century.

The older squarish village lay between the Roman road, the medieval Beche Street, on the west, and Banworth Ditch and its continuation, Beach Lode, on the east. Its northern boundary ran across what is still called Green End, and was defined in the fourteenth century by a ditch, much of which still remains. On the south are two possible early boundaries. One is Cockfens Lane, but there were three medieval homesteads south of this, Saunderes Towns End (or Fens Close), Martyns and the Manor of Brays in its square moat. Another way ran south of these three homesteads and formed a back lane, but tongues of open field, still visible as ridge and furrow penetrated between them to Cockfens Lane. They may therefore represent an accretion to the village plan before the date of our earliest documentary evidence, and before open-field ploughing came to Landbeach. Alternatively they could represent part of the great phase of expansion of the medieval village, a not improbable period for a manor house to move out to a moated site.

From early in the fourteenth century the village lay defended on its north and east by ditches, and double ditches and banks at its north-east corner, yet on the south and west it was stitched into the ploughland, for there was another furlong of arable east of the Roman road between peasant tofts. This makes no sense at all as defence against any human enemy, with all its strength concentrated at one corner while flank and rear are left open. But the gradients, slight as they are, make the purpose quite clear: it is the lowest corner that was protected, and the invader was the black fen water.

The central section of the northern ditch is now filled in where the present road crosses its old path, and for a short distance further on the west. Here it has become a lane with a seventeenth-century cottage standing on what was once the bank. Originally it was probably a tapping ditch and catchwater drain, taking the water from the springs in the gault and diverting it outside the banked enclosure which might otherwise have been outflanked by the run-off. Behind it the double bank and extra ditch

---

[1] CCCC, XXXV, 150, Rental of Landbeach, 1459.

could hold off several feet of flood-water, and further back, the great capacity of the fish-pond could have held much of the drainage from inside the moats.

Flood conditions, such as we found when discussing the fields in 1316, would have called for defences in exactly this place, and in all probability what we have in this part of the village are the remains of the attempt to fight against the rising water-table of the early fourteenth century. We know of no other flood in historical times which would have justified such measures.

At very first glance these earthworks strike one as impressive even by Roman standards, and are quite exceptionally extensive for medieval domestic works. They guarded the demesne homestead of Chamberlains which formed a block in the north-east corner of the village. North of the church and rectory lay the manorhouse, yards, barns, pound, paddocks and fish-ponds, with Madecroft, the lord's several pasture, running out beyond the ditches towards the fen. All together this made a well-appointed home for a country gentleman.

West of this, the remainder of the northern part of the plan was filled by bondage tenements of Chamberlains, one of them, on the site of the later green, lying across the heads of the others. Their few extra feet of elevation saved them from the need for protective flood-works.

For the rest, the greater part of the plan was laid out along ways that formed a grid-iron, scarcely discernible in the degraded fragments that remain today. There were no less than six ways running north and south: the Roman road; the way 'from Martyns unto the fens' (a back lane between tofts and field land, still traceable today after ploughing); Clays-trate (now Spaldings Lane); Brays Church Path (the sunken way still visible bisecting the great grass field in the centre of the village;[1] Church Way from the South (the modern High Street); and a way east of Banworth Ditch, through the common to the fen bars.

There were anciently more ways running east and west, too. The former southern boundary of the rectory garden was a path called Gibbes Stile. This was continued by the sunken track that still cuts clearly across the central field of the village. In medieval times one could go on this way, cross Claystrate to another track, Theobauds Stile, and so across the way from Martyns to the fens, to the Roman road. To the south, and parallel to these, ran Cockfens Lane, and further south still, the sunken back lane behind the Manor of Brays, Martyns, and Fens Close. Only Cockfens Lane has been preserved as a right of way.

At this time a tongue of the common spread out around the cross-roads

---

[1] This way is described, listing the tenements between which it passes, in a Court Roll of the Manor of Brays, CCCC, XXXV, 124, 9 Hen. V, 1421–2.

as a green.[1] A still surviving fragment of this was recorded by Matthew Parker in his Field Book in 1549 as 'a little piece of common called "The Tree at the Cross"' ('*parva pecia communis vocata the arbor at the cross*'). Some idea of its earlier extent is given away by the apparently meaningless kinks in the four roads as they come together today, and also by the swelling of the grass verges. The Waterbeach road of today was merely a field path, an unnamed balke in the Tudor books. But here stood the market cross of stone and, in later times at least, the village smithy.

The development of the village from this shape was determined mainly, but not exclusively, by changes both in the water-table and in population. In Cottenham pressure of population caused the village to overspill on to ploughland both to the north and to the south: in Landbeach the fen barred the way to the north. Indeed it may already have caused some shift from the developed north end when the advance south began. The Fen family whom we found living at the highest point of the whole housing area seem to be the Attefens of the Hundred Rolls of 1278–9. When they moved, they moved well away from the water.

In the south, where the High Street ran practically along the twenty-foot contour, the water offered no impediment. All the tenements on the west of the High Street south of Brays demesne closes appear to be compounded out of open-field selions. So also do the last plots on the other side of the street, from Rose Close south. Even in some of the gardens there today it is still possible to detect signs of ridge and furrow both from the ground and from air photographs. Fortunately we do not have to rely for confirmation of this merely from the suggestive property boundaries: centuries after the houses had moved on to old ploughland, the Landbeach Field Books still measure these tenements, and only these, in selions, as well as acres. All the house plots are listed with the adjacent fields, but those not cut out from old furlongs are never counted in selions. Some of the tenements made from selions have 'havedens' among them, a local term for an open-field access way rather like a headland. Although the block of Chamberlains bond tenements in the north-west all ran back from the road in narrow strips, for these there is no sign of aratral curve and no mention of selions. They may date from the foundation of the village.

Tenure offers further help in distinguishing the earlier from later housing areas: scattered through the area taken from ploughland, and also from the area taken for houses by encroachment on to the old green around the cross, are tenements held by charter. This seems to imply land enfranchised from its earlier state, to something distinct from ancient

---

[1] The part of this enclosed by Richard Kirby in Tudor times kept the name 'Green Croft'. LPC, Dukman Book.

freehold or copyhold. Such tenure is unique to those parts of the village where change of use can be proved.

From the start, on the west side of the High Street any expansion had to take place on to a furlong of Mill Field. In the previous chapter Banworth appeared as a latecomer as an open field, and our first example of it as a field-name was in 1316. The greater part of the expansion south along that side of the High Street had run its course before encroachment started on the new field. Expansion of the housing area seems to have come to a halt at about the time that pressure of population ceased. The southwards expansion of the village belongs to the great period of increase in the medieval population.

Perhaps the last flicker of the expansive phase of the development of the medieval village is recorded in Matthew Parker's own hand in the margin of the Corpus version of the 1549 Field Book (on its first page). Here he refers to a charter of Henry Chamberlain and others dated 1313, granting an acre at the 'Flood' for a tenement to maintain the Mass of the Blessed Virgin Mary. The unfavourable conditions soon halted further expansion for housing, and the pause in the erosion of this first village green seems to have lasted for two centuries.

There is reason to believe that the great Black Death of 1348–9 and perhaps later pestilence struck Landbeach and its neighbours savagely.[1] An immediate effect is shown by the robbing of building materials from empty tenements in the village, and failure in maintenance of walls and fences. By the time of the lists of the fifteenth century the third town's end has effectively gone: Cockfens and Martyns are empty closes, and the listing is done as if Landbeach were already a street village. The desertion of Fens Close and its change of name to Cockfens seems to represent the passing of a family while a topographical location stays. Its final emptying may perhaps be represented by the enfranchisement of Roger Saundre in 1377.

Incidental references in the Rental of 1459 to Brays lands in the newer, southern part of the village show empty tofts for Richards, Hache, Leffe, John Fen and William Trewe. The prior of Barnwell's tenement has become a close leased to the farmer of Chamberlains. House property is at a discount: in 1461 John Lane took Hache's cottage rent-free for the first year, on condition that he repaired it.

There seems to have been a centripetal force operating in this first phase of the shrinking of the village. In 1433 Henry Attelane was listed as one of the gentlemen of Cambridgeshire. In 1459 he or his son was recorded with 'terre et mansio' east of the High Street very near the parish boundary with Milton. This must represent almost the high-water mark of the expansion of the housing area. By 1477 the family and the mansio (the only one in the

---

[1] See below, Chapter 5.

village) were to be found across the road and up nearer the heart of things, next to Brays home closes, very near the site of the present Worts farmhouse.

The north-eastern sector of the village, the part nearest the flooding fen underwent the most drastic change early. There had stood the manor house of Chamberlains. By the time of the rental it no longer held the home of a man of some social consequence. The hall had gone and its site had become a yard. Now it was primarily a home for sheep. 'Schepen' and 'insethous' for the shepherd, and a 'shepcote' had taken the place of the great house. The area within the double moats had become a pinfold for sheep 'a pen for sheep, in English a pinfold' (*'unius carcerali ovili anglice a pynfold'*). The space between the moats which still shows ridge and furrow having been cultivated by licence of the two lords, was down to grass again. Adjacent lay the great demesne pasture, Madecroft, and beyond that another pasture, Bradfields, purchased when Billingford was master of the College (1398–1432).

Thus, early in its ownership, the College had converted the central demesnes into a sheep station from which to exploit its rights of common on fen and arable. For a time it appears to have done this directly through a bailiff, but by 1459 the manor had long been farmed out to Master Adam, the rector. As far as the Manor of Chamberlains was concerned, once the College had bought it, the great house was the rectory, since the Master or a Senior Fellow was normally rector.

The vulnerability of the whole north-eastern site to the fourteenth-century floods may account for the willingness of the Chamberlain family to part with it. The depth of the ditches and the height of the banks where the house once stood suggest that it was subjected to very extensive foundation robbing. Nearby, across the road at Beach Farm and North Farm, several outhouses and yard walls are constructed of good dressed clunch blocks. Some of these, too, are in the foundations of the brick-built Beach Farm, but more are of the even more precious (in this area) Northamptonshire limestone. Some of these show pink calcining, as if from a building destroyed by fire. The last days of the Chamberlains house may have been more sudden than we can tell.

Next to the demesne block of Chamberlains an even more startling change of use had taken place even earlier. Here on the site that was the village green at enclosure, lay the bondage tenement of the Osbern family, transversely across the heads of the other Chamberlains bondage tenements. Upon the death of William Osbern it fell vacant. His godson, John Sweyn, cultivated it for a few years, and then it again fell vacant into the hands of the College as an empty green. At first it was known as College Green, but as the earlier green disappeared it remained simply 'the Green' until split up by parliamentary enclosure. It is still a major visual feature of the village in the long front gardens made from its western side, and the wide verge and charity cottage plots carved from its eastern half. Documentation of the creation of a village green is so unusual that we quote the relevant sections:

Item, for a certain ancient bond-tenement with a croft, formerly called William Osberns, now an empty green [*viretum*] of the said college and lying in the hands of the said college next the demesne of Chambreleyns now in the tenure of the College on the east part, and the common watercourse on the west part, whose south head abuts on that highway which goes across between the bond-tenement commonly called Denys now demesne of William Keterych and the foresaid green now demesne of the college. And the north head abuts on the ancient watercourse which runs between the demesne of Chamberleyns and Maydecroft otherwise the tenement of Thomas Bradfelds purchased for the college.[1]

The detail of its creation is given in another passage:

the college green which was formerly William Osberns the Godfather of John Sweyn, which John cultivated the whole of the said green for several turns, witness Master Adam and Dominus Thomas, parish priest there [i.e. before and after 1429 when Master Adam succeeded Thomas Bodneye].[1]

Elsewhere in the same document, the green is described as common. John Sweyn died in 1439, and so the village green of Landbeach was created either in that year, or not very long before.

Thus the village, which on its old plan had two manor homesteads roughly at opposite corners, for about a century at the end of the Middle Ages had two greens. There was a tendency for the village to develop two *foci*. Around the cross-roads, when the common green was nibbled away by enclosures, the market cross still stood until the eighteenth century, and the village smithy until the twentieth. Just south of the College green the village pound still remains in a north corner of the churchyard, with the village pump just across the road. Nearby, in 1528 was built the guildhall which stood there for at least a century. By the time of the building of the guildhall what might earlier have been a balance had become polarisation inside the village.

The homestead of the Manor of Chamberlains was sited as near as possible to the common pastures and fens, which offered such enormous possibilities for exploitation by flocks of sheep. As we have seen, the Chamberlain family were interested in this as far back as 1336, and the whole demesne block around the homestead of the manor had been converted to a base from which to exploit the common grasslands by the time of the 1459 Rental. The Manor of Brays came to this more slowly.

With the very general revival of the interest of Cambridgeshire

[1] See Appendix B.

landlords in the possibilities of sheep-farming in the late fifteenth century, the Chamberlains demesnes were well prepared. Their complex of home closes, which could provide the necessary care and shelter for extensive flocks, had been created at a time of low population and land surplus. When the lords of the Manor of Brays tried to follow suit they coveted land that was desirable again, and with the topographical situation of their house, the most desirable land of all, in the built-up heart of the village which had decayed less than the fringes. The climax came under Richard Kirby who was lord of Brays in 1549, when he came into head-on conflict, not only with the peasantry but also with Matthew Parker, Master of Corpus Christi College, as the other lord and also rector of the parish.[1] Although resident, Kirby was vigorous and fitted well the stereotype of the ruthless, acquisitive gentleman grazier that the moralists of the time fulminated against. More than anyone else he was responsible for building up the series of grass closes which ran across the middle of the village out of common land, small fragments of open field, and most of all from peasant tenements.

Witnesses claimed that he and his predecessors had allowed all their copyhold houses to fall down, so that the only dwellings left on the manor were those of his four freeholders and his own. The death of William Sowde, one of Parker's predecessors probably prevented him from concluding an exchange which would have allowed him scope for larger-scale clearance in the village centre.

His progress seems to have been halted, but only after he had changed much of the village. Of the six peasant tofts in the centre of the village, only one is tenanted in 1549, and all the houses appear to have gone. At some later date the four southernmost tofts were ploughed in ridge and furrow. These selions appear in no field book, and in 1727 were certainly down as one grass close. The ploughing may date from the Napoleonic Wars: on the Enclosure Award Map of 1813 the two northern tofts of this group, which were never ploughed, are hedged off from the rest.

In Kirby's later years he showed increasing signs of the approach of the general paralysis of the insane, and occupied himself chiefly in cheating his daughters and sons-in-law, and fighting law-suits against them. But he has left his mark on the village as surely as slower impersonal forces.

By the time that the Field Book of 1727 was drawn up the process of change had been accepted by those who might have had power to prevent it. Further exchanges, combinations and extensions had rounded off Kirby's dream. What had been the heart of the old built-up area now presented quite a different picture. After the eight College tenements still lying as they had in the earliest records comes:

---

[1] Ravensdale, 'Landbeach in 1549'.

	Acres	Rods	Poles
Two closes of pasture	6	0	0
One close of pasture next the Cock Fen Lane	8	0	0
At the west end of the said closes a pightell	1	0	0
Next to a pightell of the aforesaid first closes lyeth a Tree Close			
Thos. Sparrow Thos. Christmas	1	0	0
A tenement Coll. Thos. Sparrow Thos. Christmas	1	0	0
A tenement Coll. with a croft Mr. Alington Hutch Willson	1	0	0
Two closes called pightels next the lane on the east head and south side which lane leads into the field	5	0	0
A croft called the Nut-Tree yard or Moal-Yard of the College farmer	[not given]		
A tenement with a croft Mr. Barkers lying between the aforesaid street and aforesaid lane Mr. Day	1	0	0
One close called Raye's next the lane leading from the street into the field against the Cross	4	0	0
The Manor House of Brayes Mr. Barkers	Sir John Barker, gent.		
A close called Dovehouse Close and three more closes called Cockfens next to the lane on the north part, and on the west part and south side Mill Field, and also the Nuttree Yard and a close called Green Croft next the common street are Mr. Barker's now Days. All these pastures lay for 16 acres	16	0	0

Further south Priors Close, Townend Close, Rose Close and other empty tenements had continued the process begun by the Lanes moving their mansion next to Brays.

The opportunity to create these empty closes where medieval houses had once stood had been in part at least the consequence of the decrease in population. By 1727 this had been completely reversed, but social conditions had changed as that there was no pressure to build on the empty ancient tofts again. On the one hand there was a demand for improved farmhouses. The Manor of Brays was divided between three substantial peasant farmers. The timber-framed houses at 'The Limes', the later 'Black Bull' public house, and Worts Farm were all skinned and extended with brick. Some of the peasant families had become yeomen, even on occasion calling themselves gentlemen. This was reflected in the village landscape even before the Civil War. A handsome brick house, Beach

Farm, had been built on one of the bondage tenements to replace the peasant house good enough for earlier generations. Its building and ownership until after parliamentary enclosure symbolised the rise in status that could come from the engrossment of peasant holdings and taking demesnes on lease.

Where the new society felt the need for more houses to hold its increased population these could be provided very economically in terms of land. Houses for the poor could be built on the lords' waste and be exempted from the operation of the Elizabethan Cottage Act which normally required four acres of land to be attached. Six such exemptions for Landbeach are found in the minutes of the Quarter Sessions for 1666, but the building of cottages goes back much further. Scribbled on the back of a 'Survey of Beach' made in Copcot's time (in the 1590s) is a list of 'Tenements new builded on the lord's waste', two in number.[1]

By 1639 such cottages had become a prominent feature of the village landscape. The rate list of that year shows no less than eighteen of them, on the eastern side of the green, on the fringes of the common from near the parsonage barn to the area around the cross-roads, and on tiny slips of land on the way to Waterbeach. From the two which survive today they appear to have been little smaller than the normal peasant's house in the village. Richard Foote, who had been a substantial peasant, and Thomas Weyman, who had been village herdsman, seem to have retired side by side as neighbours. Richard Foote would not have reduced his standard of housing much by moving to the cottage, but would have been freed of the burden of an acre of garden.

This was soon to change. Two of the charity cottages built by Robert Masters in the second half of the eighteenth century still survive, the clerk's house and the widow's or schoolmaster's.[2] These are two-roomed cottages with no chambers, and originally with only one hearth each, much meaner than the houses for the poor of the previous century.

In the list of houses for a rate for the wages of the parish clerk in 1639, there are 63 houses. The Hearth Tax of 1664 gives 66. But the numbers appear to have fallen in the eighteenth century, 55 in 1727 and 49 in 1781.[3] More poor households were being squeezed into less space.

The big expansion in the number of houses appears to come after the Enclosure of 1813. Some of the new small brick houses in the south-west sector of the village were built a few years after this around small courtyards, several being fitted into the frontage of one old peasant tenement. Recent demolition has shown that only the external walls were

[1] CCCC, XXXV, 175; this is clearly part of the same survey as 173.
[2] The clerk's cottage roof was destroyed by fireworks on 4 November 1972.
[3] 1727 figure in LPC, Dukman Book, and the Speculum in CUL, EDR B8/1; 1781 figure in LPC, Masters' Collectanea.

of brick: internally they were made of clay bat. But a good deal of the large total of 116 inhabited houses given by the census enumerator in 1851 seems to have come from sub-division of old houses into two or three, as well as to development along the Ely road, away from the village proper. Thus there was no great need for the multiplication of buildings in the village centre. The village kept its appearance of venerable age, alongside the ghosts of old bondage tenements in the evening shadows on the grass.

WATERBEACH

Waterbeach village is even today dominated by its green. Cut up by the remains of criss-crossing routes, it epitomises the incoherence of the whole village plan, and a stranger has the greatest difficulty in taking his bearings. This confused pattern is not new; but was already present in the generation after parliamentary enclosure. Clay wrote:

That pleasant feature of village scenery, the green, on which the booths for the May feast are erected, and where the customary smithy stands, once well deserved to be called a green. On the contrary, of late years, it has been so worn in almost every direction by traffic, that it has hardly the least title to its original name.[1]

For Cambridgeshire, Waterbeach green is on an ample scale, although certainly not the largest. But the pattern gives strong hints of encroachment, and not all of it recent. A comparison between the first edition of the OS 25″ map (1878 survey) and a modern revision indicates the extent to which such encroachment has taken place in the last hundred years. On the earlier map, the largest section of the green was not the present large triangle which remains intact, but the degraded rectangle to the south-east of it. Even then this had already been invaded by the gas works, and earlier still by a public house. The west side of the green has apparently been encroached upon to a much greater extent still, and at a much earlier date. Seventeenth-century houses still stand up against the present sidewalk on that side. Yet the road coming in from the crossing over the Old Tillage has obviously been diverted just past the almshouses, and its former line can be traced by staggered intersections at the rear property boundaries to the High Street where this latter bears faintly right at the old Denney House.[2] A similar but much smaller encroachment appears to have taken place at the opposite end. On the north-east side, the boundary before encroachment lined up smoothly with the rear property boundary which runs towards the north. Nor is the southern boundary free from suspicion of encroachment. Originally Waterbeach green must have been large

---

[1] *Waterbeach*, p. 31. See Fig. 11.
[2] I owe the understanding of staggered intersections to Dr Peter Eden, but the application to Waterbeach is my own.

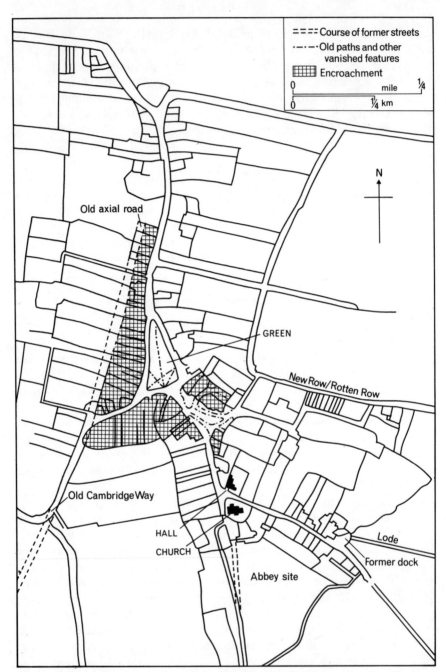

Fig. 11. Waterbeach: property boundaries. Waterbeach village green, in spite of its large size today, has suffered much encroachment through centuries (based upon the Ordnance Survey map of 1878).

138

enough to make a very considerable economic contribution to the life of the peasant community. Denson makes such claims for what was left on the eve of enclosure, and even stronger ones for it as a social centre.[1]

The evolution of the village centre here, in spite of the ragged, untidy appearance of the pattern on the ground, is the story of the functional development of the intersection of main routes, inside a varying economic setting. In studying the field-names, there were some grounds for suggesting an early two-field phase, certainly not later than the twelfth century. At this stage the most important way in the parish would have been from the centre to the two fields, the ancestors of Baneholefeld to the east and Wulfholesfeld to the west, stretching out to the north of the village. These, together with the future Winfold Common, could be served from a way running north from Denney End. This road, as a causeway, also continued to the higher, and drier, pastures of Denney, and the fens of Chittering.

Thus the main economic axis of the village is represented by the old line of the High Street traced above. Air photographs show that the old Cambridge Way, after following this straight line, exactly on the present road from the almshouses to the crossing of the Car Dyke, continued quite straight for some distance into the fields, and then followed a slightly sinuous line on to Milton and Cambridge. Somewhat later, as the fields developed, Cambridge Way would have served a more immediate purpose also in giving access, and central access at that, to the third field, which as often as not took its name from the road, Cambridge Way Field.

The two more violent bends in this road, which today inconveniently follow the one at the crossing, derive from an old field path. The first section of the path ran along the Car Dyke, and continued as two feeder tracks to the two windmills; the second linked up with the field paths of Landbeach parish. This part of the present main road was relatively minor until the construction of the Milton–Ely turnpike in the 1760s.

The encroachment, and the bending of the roads through the village centre, suggest a powerful pull which caused development to move to the south-east. As Denney Abbey developed, particularly with the coming of the Templars, and as its economic importance in the parish grew, the northwards pull would also have grown stronger, an this may account for the ribbon development out from the green to Denney End. The road that passes to the east of the triangular green after forking from the High Street, continued as straight as it could over the rest of the green to the church, which it passed at the west end, on straight into Waterbeach Abbey. A path still carries on without veering to the watergate of the abbey. From there it runs through the middle of a long field between the

[1] *A Peasant's Voice*, p. 16.

boundaries of the old Hall Field and The Hollow to the Car Dyke. Early medieval names for the Car Dyke, Rowditch and Eldelode, suggest that it was still of some navigational use in Norman times, when Waterbeach Abbey was built.

So far the forces described account for the northern triangle of the village centre, but there were still other pulls towards the south-east, the Cam with its ferries and fisheries, and perhaps even more important, its docks and wharfs. Today, Station Road still seems to connect the village to the railway station only as an afterthought, and this is exactly what it is. The purpose of this street was to connect with the dock, which is now filled in and forms the yard opposite 'The Star' public house, by an earlier vicarage. The still open lode to this from the Banks Farm was the only one kept open as a navigable channel (Fourth Public Drain and Public Wharf) at the parliamentary enclosure.[1] The original purpose was perhaps, not only as Clay suggested, to bring stone for the building of the church, but also for building the abbey. It would appear probable that the Norman period, as at Cottenham, saw one of the most striking developments of the pattern of the village, and what began with the stone church would have continued on a larger scale with the abbey for a century.

The tongue of ground between the High Street and Fen Lane appears mostly to have been taken out of field land early on, and as old enclosures on the award map the plots still bear the characteristic shape of open-field strips except at the southern end of the green.[2] This is also true of the area further east, the square south of Pieces Lane, 'an ancient lane' in the award. In this part of Cambridgeshire, furlongs taken out of the field and put down to grass, are called 'Pieces'. It is not possible to assign a date to such enclosures, but two of the charity entries in the court book may well refer to them. In 1573 Robert Banckes agreed to a rent charge to the vicar and the Town, in return for lands surrendered to him. He was to allow a footpath and common of pasture over 'Thurlebanes'. Later he bought out their common of pasture over the 'Pieces'.

But a good deal of other development in the village appears to be medieval.[3] Croft and toft boundaries appear to survive in part across the street from the old abbey site, adjacent to the dock. Further north, out towards Fen End, there is the suspiciously medieval name of 'Back Lane'. Fortunately we do not have to rely on this name alone: previously it also bore the name of Rotten Row. This name occurs from 7 Eliz. on, and is the one used in the award. It does not appear in the medieval entries: instead we find 'le Newerowe' from 36 Ed. III on. The house-plots as they survive appear to be without crofts, and are unusually cramped for medieval sites in this part of the country. The documents have ways of

---

[1] Waterbeach Enclosure Award, 1818, in CRO, Q/R Dz 8, pp. 389–475.
[2] CRO Q/RDc 31.   [3] WcD 15 Eliz. I; cf. *Waterbeach*, p. 72.

referring to them which suggest the same poverty: 36 Ed. III '...to John Belts of one Chamber in le Newerowe with a Backside adjoining...'; 36 Ed. III '...Matilda Pannell one Chamber in Newerowe...'; 2 Hen. VI Admission of Symon Brunne 'to a place in New Row' ('*ad unam placeam in Newerowe...*').[1] This was the medieval way from the village to the fens. In the period of generally falling population, that of Willingham seems to have gone on increasing rapidly, and this has been explained as due to the possibility of an easy life which its fens afforded to run-away villeins and other doubtful characters. Waterbeach has been cursed with the same reputation. Layer says of it:

'a Fenn town of large Extent...having large and spacious commons and marish grounds as most of the fen towns have, which is the cause that a multitude of poor and mean people do resort and inhabit there, to live an easy and idle life, by Fishing, Fowling and Feeding of Cattle.[2]

Denson told a similar story of the real opportunity that conditions in the common lands of Waterbeach still offered a poor man just before enclosure, but from the poor man's point of view. What we may have witnessed in the references to New Row and Rotten Row is the building of a medieval slum for fenmen. It is not likely to have been the consequence of the closure of Waterbeach Abbey, for the house only moved to Denney.

There are thus several strong economic forces influencing the development of the pattern of Waterbeach village centre. The very straight street alignment which would have been a natural result of its open-field agriculture seems to have been submerged by what may well all be later elements in the village economy. The church, the abbey, the lode and the dock are certainly much later than the foundation of the village, as far as we can investigate them. The crucial question, on which the evidence is so far silent, is whether there was a wooden church before the stone one, and if so, where it was sited. The ferries and the waterway can have had little influence on village development until the causeways and the lode were constructed. Any previous traffic which used the Eldelode, the Car Dyke, would have only reinforced the linear tendency since this canal crossed the old axial road. Fisheries and exploitation of the fen could have taken place better from small scattered settlements before the construction of the causeways, and the special development of the village for what looks like ease of access to the fen, appears to have come in the fourteenth century when the smaller riverside settlements may have been flooded out. One might plausibly put forward the hypothesis that what we can see in Waterbeach is a street village, which later developments have turned into a

---

[1] WcD under regnal years.   [2] BM Add. MS. 5823, fol. 22.

green village; in fact, the opposite direction of development from its neighbours. This would be going further than the evidence justifies. It is indeed the direction of development, but we are not justified in assuming quite so simple a point of departure, although this is far from impossible.

Some of the South Cambridgeshire villages which result from forest clearance show signs of having been compounded from what began as scattered smaller settlements. There obviously were subsidiary settlements in Waterbeach but the axe does little to dry the fen, and on very small fen islands such settlements must have remained temporary and tiny. But such there were in favoured spots. A Charter of 1352 in Corpus Christi Archives shows at least part of one:

all my messuage...in the town of Waterbeach as it lies in length and breadth next the great bank between the tenement formerly Benedict Pittock's on the one part and the tenement formerly Isabelle le maryner's on the other part...[1]

With this went all manner of common rights in the fen, but no field land. Most important of all, three paths went with the holding in order to reach it. This is almost certainly where Banks Farm, otherwise Banks Cottage, formerly stood. Appropriately enough for Isabelle, it is now the clubhouse of the Cam Sailing Club.

Clayhithe Ferry[2] also seems to have had someone living there in medieval times. In the court book we find under 49 Ed. III: 'Lawrence King takes to farm a certain parcel of land at Clayeth, together with an house thereupon lately built, and heretofore devised to John Albyn.' In Elrington's Lease, 1539, there was a house at Cleyhith called the Feyry-house, with two osier holts, etc.[3] The fishery belonging to Denney at Mere Were in Stretham also had a ferry, with a cottage and osier holt.[4] But osier holts seem normally to have been too wet to have houses. At the end of a Terrier of 1704 in the parish chest comes a note: 'N.B. There never was a house in Jesus Holt, in Common Plat, or in Townsend Close, or in the Town Holt, or in Kettles Holt.' The island of Elmeney, abandoned by the Benedictines early on, would serve as a possible base for fenland farming in drier times, as it had for the Romans. As a close of Denney it would not have needed to wait for parliamentary enclosure, and Reaney notes that it was named by Cole in 1740 already as Causeway End Farm.[5]

But the greatest of the subsidiary settlements in the parish was Denney Abbey (see Plate III(a) and (b)). Originally a separate manor, it never had a separate field system, its arable lying intermingled with that of Water-

<hr/>

[1] CCCC, XXXV, 41; Appendix B.   [2] See Fig. 4, p. 20.
[3] Bodleian MS. Gough Cambs. 69.
[4] *Waterbeach*, p. 124; cf. WPC, *Masters* vs. *Standley* bundle.
[5] Reaney, *Place-Names of Cambridgeshire*, p. 187. The farmhouse still standing there would appear, on stylistic grounds, to have been built soon after the Dissolution of the Monasteries.

beach. Surrounded by closes, it had a much larger, if much lower area outside the open fields around it than had Waterbeach. In an almost square moated enclosure, it was connected to Waterbeach by a causeway which then ran along its south-eastern side and carried on straight to Elmeney. A little over a hundred yards to the south, and butting squarely on to the causeway, is another set of earthworks. Many explanations have been offered, but the site must probably await investigation until the airfield closes.

The successive phases of its life, a Benedictine cell under Ely, a Templar infirmary, a house of Poor Clares, and after the Reformation a farmhouse, are all well preserved in the buildings still being exposed and restored by the Ministry of Works. The nuns' fourteenth-century refectory, which had been altered into a barn, lost its wall-paintings after the Ministry removed the roof to forestall collapse. Much further investigation remains to be done. One oddity in plan so far not yet explained, is that although the cloisters were moved after the nuns came, both monks and nuns had cloisters on the north/English Benedictine houses, founded as late as this seem normally to have had their cloisters on the more climatically suitable south side. There seems little reason for this, although north-side cloisters appear to have been built also at Swavesey, the nearest small religious house on this side of the Old West River. One possible explanation is that as a hospital under the Templars, the south side was required for an infirmary from which the permanent invalids could watch the Mass from their beds. One of the most interesting features of the plan so far discovered, is that the rebuilding under the countess of Pembroke seems to have been designed to provide a suitable residence for the countess as well as the nuns. Never a large house, it seems to have struggled after the countess's death. Exposed to flood and isolation, tempest regularly threatened it. For instance, in 1325–6, during its period in royal hands before going to the Poor Clares, the solar, garderobe, granary, oxstall, great stable, kitchen and other buildings, all seem to have lost much of their thatch in a westerly gale, as did all the walls.[1] It was in some ways a more suitable site for the Templars than for the Poor Clares in its dangerous isolation. In 1350 John de Lexham, clerk, and divers other malefactors and disturbers of the king's peace broke in by force and tried to seize and abduct certain nuns.[2]

The later story of the house under the Poor Clares is one of poverty and dilapidation, and has been told often enough elsewhere. As a farmhouse, it was of a much more convenient size than many old religious houses. Masters prints a good engraving of it as frontispiece of his *Short Account* (see Plate III (*b*)). Much more of the Tudor work is showing in this than is now visible.[3]

[1] PRO SC 6 766/12, Ministers' Accounts.   [2] PRO C 47 50/7/160.
[3] For the history of Denney Abbey see *VCH Cambs.*, vol. 2, pp. 259, 295ff., see also S. D. T. Spittle, 'Denney Abbey', *PCAS* LXI (1968).

By contrast, Waterbeach Abbey has only earthworks to show today, and after one brief emergency dig, most of the plan is still concealed from us. In 1765 the evidence in the *Masters* vs. *Standley* case showed that many villagers were completely ignorant of its existence, so well had stone robbing been done long before. But some of its farm-buildings were then still standing in the Hall Yard, and the main site had become the Pound Close.[1] Just enough earthworks remained at the old island of Elmeney to convince us that the Benedictines actually attempted to live there in their first attempt at founding a cell in the parish, but these have now been cleaned, and the remains can only be found as soil marks, crop marks and sherds, with medieval and Roman intermixed.

THE NUCLEATED VILLAGES AND
THEIR BUILDINGS

Neither Cottenham nor Landbeach had a religious house in its bounds, nor did their topography tempt settlers away from the village centre until recent times. We have seen that squatters were stopped from building in the fens in Cottenham by the Agreement of 1596. The earliest record that we have of detached settlement in Landbeach is from the eighteenth century, when Goose Hall was built where the new turnpike joined the Roman road. It was a place where the flocks of geese being driven south to market could graze and stay overnight. As such it was not wanted near other houses.[2]

The features common to all three are often symbols of the life of a nucleated village. The greens of all three have been discussed, and in all three the smithy seems to have stood on the green, or former green. Clay has been cited as witness for this in Waterbeach. In Landbeach the smithy, which was pulled down before the First World War, stood on the corner opposite the site of the village cross, that is, on what had been the green until it was eventually lost after the new one had been formed at the north end. Cottenham had its smithy approximately where the war memorial now stands, upon the fragment remaining of what looks like a former triangular green that appears to have been encroached upon at least as far back as the seventeenth century, to judge from the houses. All had at least one pound, and these figure regularly in all the medieval court rolls. One in Landbeach is still standing, a small overgrown brick enclosure against the street at the north-west corner of the churchyard. Each village once had its Camping Close near the church. These village recreation grounds

[1] WPC, *Masters* vs. *Standley* bundle.
[2] LPC, correspondence in tithe Book: the rector feared an establishment for geese might be set up next to his garden.

are generally thought to have medieval origins, but the references all seem to come from post-medieval sources.[1]

The patterns and development of these villages have, at least superficially, a strong resemblance to patterns found elsewhere. For example, the plan of Olney in Buckinghamshire shows two kinds of property boundaries very like the two which are found in Cottenham.[2] The chief difference is that in Olney the expansion on to old open-field land took place on one side only instead of to both north and south. In Olney the development was from 'organic' village into 'planned' market town. As was suggested earlier, part of the development in Cottenham may have been due to the granting of a market in the thirteenth century, or it may have been simply due to the expansion of population and the consequent need for more homesteads.

The development of the south-westen sector of Landbeach village was very similar except that the road formed the eastern boundary of the furlong, and so the croft and toft developed to the full depth of a selion's length, as in Olney rather than Cottenham where the new road bisected the furlong.

There seems to be a remarkable similarity in the development of two of our villages in their expansion, and many of the planned towns. No grant of a market can be traced in Landbeach, but the Ordnance Survey marks the site of the market cross near the cross-roads where there was formerly a large area of common land, and the presence of such a cross is confirmed by the field books of the fifteenth, sixteenth and eighteenth centuries. A guildhall stood in Landbeach for a century from 1528.

These hints of quasi-urbanisation appear to offer a tentative explanation of Professor Beresford's problem about this county: 'Only Cambridgeshire seems to have possessed the secret of managing without plantations.'[3] If Landbeach had a market it was probably unlicensed. It had no burgage tenements, but it did have those tenements noticed above where the field book says, 'he holds by charter' ('*tenet per cartam*'), implying an artificially-created free tenement as distinct from both bond and ancient freehold. Nearby Rampton, a small village like Landbeach, as well as its market

[1] E.g. *Waterbeach*, p. 51; in Landbeach Mickleburgh's lease to Rivers Taylor, 1727.
[2] M. W. Beresford, *New Towns of the Middle Ages* (1967), p. 107.
[3] *Ibid.*, p. 283. In fact Cambridgeshire did not quite manage this. There is convincing evidence in Swavesey to suggest that it was redeveloped and moved towards the priory as a planned market town by the de la Zouches in the mid-thirteenth century. Earthworks show the streets and tofts of an earlier village on a different axis to the present one, centred much nearer to the Huntingdon road. Remains and place-names suggest that the castle probably linked with the ditches and ramparts which enclosed the new town and dock area into a single system. The parochial aisle was added to the Saxon-styled priory church in the mid-thirteenth century, judging from the early English arcades with water-holding mouldings inserted into the earlier chancel wall. In the Hundred Rolls of 1278–9 the de la Zouches had burgage tenants there, and the entry for Longstanton shows by its villein carrying services that Swavesey and Cambridge were alternative markets for the sale of the lord's corn.

grant, had a castle commanding an important road junction, but it, too, had no burgage tenements, and does not seem to have risen to town status either in scale or as a lawful borough. We seem to have a steady gradation in North Cambridgeshire from borough, to market town, to village. The landscape patterns seem to suggest common elements, with the effective differences 'mainly in scale. The expanding village produced similar patterns of property boundaries to those of the planned towns. Organic expansion which spilled over on to old open-field land must always have required decision and regulation which elsewhere is called planned. The one shades in to the other: the distinction cannot be clear-cut.

The formal development of towns in Cambridgeshire may well have lagged because of the excellence of its communications by water, and its deep involvement with the international fairs at the very time most favourable to town development elsewhere. The enormous international demand for agricultural produce in the thirteenth century may have siphoned off bulk transactions and left local trading so relatively slight that little was required in the way of formal arrangements and privileged status to conduct it.

With the exception of Waterbeach when there was a resident lord of the manor at Denney Abbey or Denny Abbey House, in the seventeenth and eighteenth centuries, and of Cottenham during the time of Katherine Pepys, these villages seem to have been free of domination by the big house, and the parsonage has been more important than the manor. In their day, the rectories of Cottenham and Landbeach seem to have been among the finest houses in their villages, but the same does not appear to have been the case in eighteenth-century Waterbeach. Cole agreed with Masters to accept what was supposed to be a better house when he took up residence there as vicar. From his account it appears to have been what was probably the most common type of peasant house in this area: 'You observe I have a parlour, Hall and Kitchen: there is also a little brew house, which is correspondent to the rest of the House, which will have, when they are dry, 3 or 4 places to sleep in, with 2 good garretts.'[1] There have been at least two new vicarages built in Waterbeach since then, the changes reflecting the rise and decline in social status of the clergy.

The rectories of Landbeach and Cottenham are early and late examples of the great rural rebuilding in this area. Behind a nineteenth-century classical stone porch and an eighteenth-century symmetrical brick façade, that in Landbeach is mainly the work of William Sowde, rector 1528–44, and Master of Corpus Christi. He rebuilt the house as a chambered hall with two unequal cross-wings. The beam over the great fireplace in the

---

[1] F. G. Stokes (ed.), *The Bletchley Diary of the Rev. William Cole, M.A., F.S.A., 1765–67* (1931), p. 309.

hall bore his initials until it was destroyed in 1863. The chimney, of narrow brick with crow-stepping, is set on to the external wall. The main timbers of the hall ceiling carry double ogee mouldings. All this is quite consistent with Sowde's dates. In a note of Sowde's, copied by Clifford into the parish field book, he complains that he will never get back from the house the value of what he has spent upon it. The cellar is of fourteenth-century date with stone ribs and brick panels in the vaulting. The roof of its vault is above ground level, and projects outside the house awkwardly to a line which may well represent the outer wall of a former aisled hall, reduced by Sowde to the line of its arcades as a north wing of the new house. A drawing by Masters in the Collectanea of the house as he came to it (see Fig. 12 (*a*, top)), shows a covered way formed by continuing the roof of this wing down to single storied height. This enables the main front door to be in the same wall as the end of the parlour, the west wall of this wing. The passage behind the door was thus continuous with the former screens passage. This passageway again would suggest the lines of an earlier aisled hall.[1]

The north wing as rebuilt by Sowde consisted of buttery, pantry and parlour with chambers above. The quality of the stonework, substantial archways leading to each of the rooms, show that this wing had unusual importance. With one parlour in this wing and a second in the south, the plan is rather abnormal. The leases of the rectory, both before and after the rebuilding, help to show the reason for this. The sixteenth century rectory at Landbeach had a treble purpose. Since the rector was likely to be also the Master, or at least a Senior Fellow of Corpus Christi College, it had to be a substantial farmhouse for the person who would take the farm of the rectory lands. It had also to provide accommodation for a resident curate. Finally it had to provide suitable rooms for a cleric of some importance when he came to stay for the three principal Christian festivals, and perhaps more. Thus the hybrid form represented the addition of what was mainly a clergy wing on to what was a farmhouse of pseudo-hall and cross-wing type.

The rebuilding of the rectory so early, in the van of the fashion for change, meant that it was old-fashioned as soon as similar houses had followed suit with even more modern ideas. By the late eighteenth century it was not adequate aesthetically for Robert Masters. His changes were designed primarily to give symmetry to the west front (see Fig. 12 (*a*, foot)), even to the extent of a false sash window to balance. The brick façade, even before Tinkler's porch was added, gave a classical air to what was still in spirit a building in the medieval tradition.

---

[1] *Landbeach*, p. 89f. discusses Rectory House. LPC, Collectanea, contains more information, and Masters' drawings of the house as he found and left it, with alternative schemes. LPC Tithe Book has later accounts, particularly of the garden.

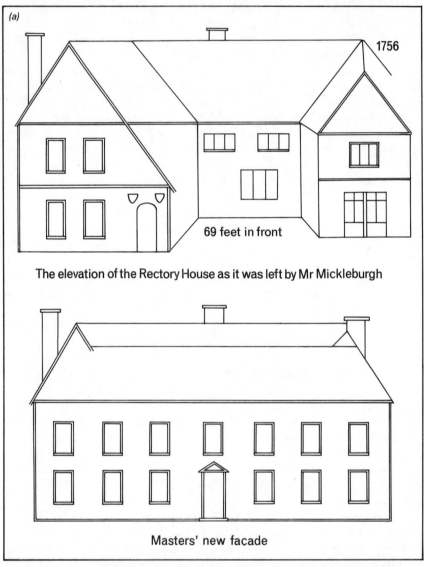

Fig. 12. Robert Masters' sketches of Landbeach Rectory illustrate (*a*, top) the house as he found it; (*b*) the changes he planned (dashed line = new exterior wall built to turn the courtyard into a grand entrance hall); and (*a*, foot) the house as he left it (source; LPC, Collectanea).

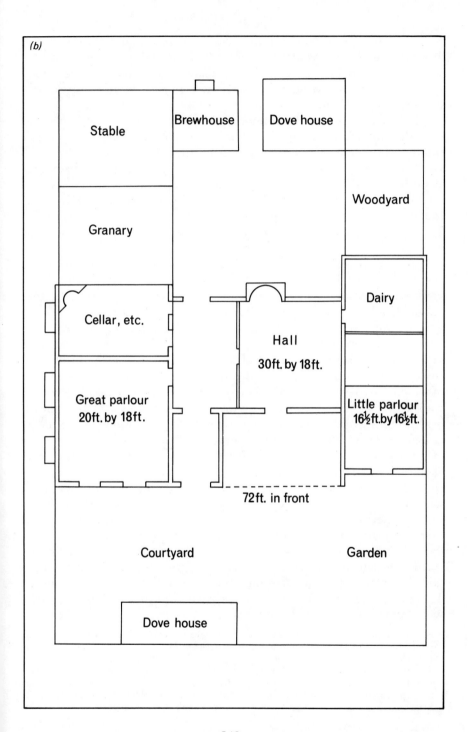

(b)

Stable

Brewhouse

Dove house

Granary

Woodyard

Cellar, etc.

Dairy

Hall
30ft. by 18ft.

Great parlour
20ft. by 18ft.

Little parlour
16½ft. by 16½ft.

72ft. in front

Courtyard

Garden

Dove house

The old rectory at Cottenham was not modernised until 1696–8.[1] Even then part only of the medieval great hall was pulled down in order to add another wing to balance that already there. The result, with its most attractive brick, is a delightful house, well able to measure up to the standards of the eighteenth century.

A full commentary on the housing of the area would alone require more space than the whole of this study, but it is possible to make a few general comments. In spite of the fires, especially the 'incendiary fires' of the nineteenth century, which were very frequent in both Cottenham and Waterbeach, all three villages show an impressive number of houses still surviving of the types identified by the Royal Commission on Historical Monuments as peasant building of the first half of the seventeenth century.[2] The probate inventories, which are on the whole unusually good and very specific as to rooms, unfortunately only begin after the Restoration, but give an even stronger impression of large-scale rebuilding up to the newer standards. There is no doubt at all that in the second half of the seventeenth century, as far as the evidence of the inventories go, the outstanding house socially in the area is Denney Abbey. Perhaps its most splendid phase was as a gentleman's farmhouse and country home.[3]

The peasant tradition of building continued long after new methods and new styles had been introduced. The first brick house that can be discovered in Landbeach, the present Beach Farm, seems long to have been one of the only two. Its plan and style would date it to the period before the Civil War, but it is still referred to in the fen book in 1665 as 'John Annis's brick house'. Modern requirements appear to have found the peasant housing of the eighteenth century on the whole less satisfactory than that of the seventeenth. Consequently there are fewer houses from the later date still standing, if indeed there ever were many. Denson gives a very clear account of cheap housing being provided by the peasants for themselves by clay bat construction as late as 1821.[4] In so far as these survive still, the thatched roofs have nearly all been replaced by slate or tile. Far more of the thatched roofs have survived on the earlier peasant houses, although a number of these, too, have changed to tile. But worst of all, corrugated iron came in as an emergency covering for dilapidated thatch when skilled thatchers could not be found, and once in place, it often remained. Traditional methods and materials achieved an effect which planners would imitate if they could, but for all their powers are impotent to create.

[1] For Cottenham Rectory: BM Ad. MS. 5847, p. 83, Bishop Patrick's licence to Thomas Jekyll, rector, to re-build 1696, and the cancellation on completion of the work in 1698. CRO Cot. C35, Cottenham Glebe Terriers for 1638 and 1645; copies in CUL, EDR.

[2] *Notebook* lists a whole series of mid-century fires. See also L'Estrange, *A Sad Relation of a Dreadful Fire.* The Great Fire of Cottenham appears to have happened ten years after that of London.

[3] CUA in year bundle for 1666, the inventory of Richard Kettle, and 1686, the inventory of Joseph Kettle. [4] *A Peasant's Voice*, pp. 28–9.

TOPOGRAPHY, ECONOMY AND SOCIETY

THE MIDDLE AGES

The villages of the fen edge seem in many ways well endowed for sustaining peasant communities. In each the arable base was well matched by ample pastures and hay for winter feed. By its return in manure, this abundance of fodder gave field systems of the Midlands type a much better chance than average to work well. The richness revealed by the lush landscape provided the peasant economy with a sound foundation of self-sufficiency. Over and above this, the products of the fen offered easy sustenance for those with little property; for those more fortunate it provided supplementary diet and a cushion against famine; in its variety lay opportunities for taking advantages of wider markets. From the earliest times of which we have detailed records the waterways opened up such markets[1] and made this a favoured area until the railways brought still wider markets with wider competition.

With these natural blessings came also the danger of both gradual and sudden risings of the waters. But this, if seasonal only or not too prolonged, like the flooding of the Nile, was rarely an unmitigated hardship. And so the farming, like the landscape, was well mixed and balanced. To the core of a typical Midland village, with its nucleus of timber-framed and thatched houses and barn, grouped in their tofts, almost surrounded by ample open fields, were added pastures for all seasons and extensive natural water-meadows. On the fringes were areas that mesolithic man, the hunter, fisher and fowler, had found a paradise. In this setting it is not surprising that change was slow and that the system continued essentially intact so late.

But its maintenance depended on keeping a balance between competing interests, and delicate adjustment of the economy to the topography of each village. The social structure of the three villages, as it appears in our first reliable comparative records, the Domesday Survey,[2] shows a remarkable reflection of the variations in the landscape. In Cottenham over half of the recorded tenantry are villeins (probably half-virgaters or virgaters), while only 41 per cent are cottars and bordars. In contrast, at Waterbeach,[3] 94 per cent are cottars and bordars and not much over 5 per cent villeins. Landbeach came between the two extremes with about a quarter

---

[1] *Rot. Hund.* vol. II, Longstanton, and CCCC, XXXV, 145. See above, p. 32.
[2] *VCH Cambs.*, vol. I, pp. 360ff.
[3] Beche as distinct from Utbeche (Landbeach).

of its tenantry villeins, and 72 per cent cottars and bordars. One could almost express the variation in social structure between the three villages at this point as a simple mathematical function of the proportions of culti-vable land above and below the twenty-foot contour.

From the Hundred Rolls one can make a similar comparison on the basis of land held. If we take holdings of less than five acres as smallholdings, it appears that in Cottenham 32 per cent of the tenantry are smallholders, compared with 45 per cent in Landbeach, and 91 per cent in Water-beach.[1]

Such a pattern is not simply a product of height above the critical flood level, important though this is. The closeness of the Cam and its flood-plain to the houses of Waterbeach compared to the much greater distance of the Old West from the houses of Cottenham, would have affected the chances of making a living with little land. Joist Fen and Chittering lay beyond the fields in Waterbeach, whereas Cottenham had relatively extensive hards in the fens at no great distance from its homesteads. The resulting specialisation in free-ranging beef and horses at Waterbeach, and in dairying at Cottenham would again have helped to differentiate their social structures in later times.

In the Middle Ages the difference in the nature of the rivers was much greater than today. The Old West seems to have been well embanked on the south side from very early times,[2] but the meanders and creeks and pools of the Cam seem to have been unconfined until much later, in the mid-eighteenth century. In the Domesday, Waterbeach is rated at 1,450 eels against Cottenham's 650. In the fen reeves' book[3] Cottenham had a Town Boat in the nineteenth century, but only Waterbeach had a boat builder.[4]

But even Waterbeach with its capacity to sustain families on minute holdings could not increase its population indefinitely, especially at a time when much more of its land surface must have been regularly disappearing under the black waters in the early fourteenth century.

The Extent of Agnes de Bray's Lands in 1316,[5] 37 years after the Hundred Rolls, makes it possible for us to examine this period, so critical for population and landscape, a little more closely on the smaller of the two Landbeach manors. The comparison of two lists of landholders, compiled at different dates and for different purposes, calls for cautious

---

[1] Cf. B. F. Harvey, 'The Population Trend in England Between 1300 and 1348', *TRHS* 5th series, XVI (1966), 29: 'The size of the peasant holding was determined by several factors, but perhaps it is most aptly considered as a function of the prevailing economy: small-holdings were dominant where abundant woodland or waste emancipated the peasant from a dependence on his arable land which could not have been other than cruel.'

[2] *Rot. Hund*, vol. II, p. 411, and Atkyns in BM Harleian, 5011.

[3] Mr Mervyn Haird's Collection.

[4] E. R. Kelly, *The Post Office Directory of Cambridge, Norfolk and Suffolk* (1869).

[5] CCCC, XXXV, 145. Cf. *Rot. Hund*, vol. II, pp. 453–4.

conclusions only. The Extent contains detail which was important for its purposes at the moment when it was taken, but similar items may not have affected the more general survey: tenements waiting to be let out at the next court might well have appeared with their old holder's name in 1278–9. Roger de Burdeleys, who was a lord of a manor in Cottenham, was listed in 1316 as holding thirty acres in Oakington of the Manor of Brays: he is clearly not a resident head of a family in Landbeach. The two Thomas Juddes in the Extent possibly were the same man, but may not have been in view of the medieval economy in Christian names.[1] In the Extent, Tebaud's cottage is in the lord's hands but has been let, for one year, to one of the villeins. Three of the freeholders are entered with their holdings, but with marginal notes to the effect that these are in the lord's hand. This could mean, in itself, recent high mortality. Five tenants of Brays at each period seem also to be landholders in the other manor.

	Free	Villein	Other lesser	Total
1278–9	6	9	5+8(−1)	27 or 28
1316	13−1	12	4(−1)+3−3?	27 or 32

In spite of the uncertainties, the comparison suggests that population in the Brays manor was at least maintained, and had quite possibly continued to increase until very nearly 1316. But this is not more than a probability, even if it fits the expected pattern.

Comparison of the same two documents, however, suggests much more convincingly marked social changes. The increase in the number of freeholders is quite remarkable, even if they are still mostly holders of fragments. Their names in 1316 hint strongly at immigration: Robert le Taylour de Over, John Frost de Waterbeach, Thomas Preist de Cotten-ham, Richard de Asshwelle, and Robert de Brandon. Only the last has a name corresponding to one in the Hundred Rolls, where we meet Richard Brandon. If the others really represent new residents (two could still live in their named villages), then a dwindling population may be being replaced by an influx of new men.

In 1278–9 the freehold land was just over 25 acres, but had risen to almost 50 by 1316 (omitting Roger de Burdeleys). Assised rent (less 20s. from Roger) had increased surprisingly little, from 18s. 6d. to 20s. 10½d. If we take the marginal notes which seem to be the rent actually collected, then it would have fallen below half the theoretical total of 1278–9, a fall per acre to less than 25 per cent.

The most startling change is the villeinage: in the Hundred Rolls nine held 5 acres each, and five 2½ acres each, but in 1316 there were twelve

---

[1] But cf. CCCC, XXXV, 124, 9 Hen. V, where out of seven tenants mentioned, two are John Judde, one being distinguished as senior.

with a uniform 10 acres each. The total area of their arable had rather more than doubled.[1] At such an early date this is unlikely to be due to a confusion of customary and measured acres: the total freehold acreage seems to have increased in step with the total bond land. Unfortunately the royal survey gives no precise figure from which the demesne might be calculated.

What information we have suggests a very rapid invasion of meadow and moor by the plough. The information on the demesne in 1316 (discussed earlier in connection with the growth of the fields) suggests that a good deal of the expansion may be compensation for old arable now subject to flooding, but the assarting of new land for the tenants would appear to be greater than that alone. Once started it may well be proceeding under its own impetus.

New freeholders, with or without other holdings, appear to be taking advantage of this to acquire fresh smallholdings. Among them is the brother of the lord of the Manor of Chamberlains, John. His interest in his brother's manor appeared to have been mainly for raising sheep. In 1316 he was acquired an additional messuage with eight acres from Brays, and is taking over a croft as well. It could be that the land which is designated '*pastura communia nisi seminata*' is for him the main attraction. The investigation of medieval sheep-rearing made earlier, shewed that at this date it was more likely to be gentlemen that were doing well rather than the more modest peasant flocks.

The changes of names between the two documents may have some significance. The Hundred Rolls gives occupational names among both freeholders and crofters, but not in the villeinage. These are Bercator, Seman, Faber (three different men are called Faber), Piscator and Cocus. None of these are listed in 1316. The Taylour that appears in this year is 'de Over'. This is one of the most common trade-names in later medieval documents of Landbeach, frequently as an alias. If the 1316 list means that craft-names are being dropped as their owners become accepted, then most of these craftsmen must be recent arrivals in the late thirteenth century. Their absence from among the villeinage is not surprising in view of the heavy burden of labour services and other feudal restraints. Their tiny holdings are suggestive of the poverty of the local craftsmen relative to the peasantry, and there is a similar picture centuries later when probate inventories can be found for these villages,[2] except where the craftsman is also a peasant.

The names derived from places within the village, Atteflod, Attefen, de la Lane, in le Herne, are those that survive long in various forms in the

---

[1] As well as new assart the 1316 totals would include flooded land being then used as common pasture and the effective arable holdings might not have changed much.

[2] CUA in year bundles for the whole county.

Landbeach records. They are all villeins. The freedom of the other villagers may have been two-edged.

In trying to fit this fragment into a wider picture of the development of the whole area under study, it is necessary to consider population growth relative to the number of families that could be supported under the open-field agricultural technique. Landbeach, in spite of being the latest of the three villages to be settled (if we have earlier interpreted the evidence aright) was nearer to its practical limits of cultivation by Domesday than either of the others, although Waterbeach does not seem far behind. There is no inconsistency here. The ratios of potential to present ploughs in the Domesday, as long as we do not attempt to turn them into absolute figures of arable area, suggest that this was the view of the men on the spot in 1086–7: Landbeach ploughs had reached a proper limit; those of Waterbeach nearly so: and Cottenham had rather more space left.

Domesday ploughs

	Potential ploughs	Actual ploughs
Landbeach	5½	5½
Cottenham	19	16
Waterbeach	5½	5

Not all the parish boundaries were defined at Domesday, and a comparison of hidage figures, and areas at the time of parliamentary enclosure sheds little more light:

	Hidage		Acreage at enclosure	
	Domesday	Hundred Rolls	Total	Arable only
Landbeach	11	2K Fees	2,207	767
Cottenham	26+	27+	7,107	1,576
Waterbeach	6	4½	4,864	600

It would be quite consistent with the examination of the social structure of the three villages at Domesday to suggest that already at that date a far higher proportion of the population of Waterbeach was deriving more of its income from other sources than the cultivation of arable, than in the other two villages. So extreme in fact was the smallholding character of the villagers, that there would be much to explain away if we made any other assumption than the Waterbeach ploughs were already operating in that marginal zone where the fen ebbed and flowed. The rise of the water-table might well have already begun. This would immediately alter the relative potential development in the villages. While the two villages had been closely connected before the Norman Conquest, it would seem highly likely that any encroachment of the fen on Waterbeach arable would be reflected in additional pressure for assarting in Landbeach. Thus the process by which the arable cultivation of Acre Field in Landbeach first began, according to our reasoning, must, from what we know of the fen, have continued to operate from time to time over a long period, while any general deterioration was going on. It would be difficult to justify the relative penetrations of the Landbeach and Waterbeach ploughs below the twenty-foot contour without this sort of pressure. Thus the vagaries of the fen in conjunction with the force of the medieval population explosion, multiplied the demand for arable on the old sheep-lands of Landbeach. Its earlier phases we can only arrive at by inferences: when we can see a little to its operation near the end of the thirteenth century, expansion is almost over and the invasion of the black waters is turning assarting into a more desperate struggle for survival.

It would be difficult for us to believe that in 1278–9, with the agricultural techniques then available, population was not pressing on its limits in this area.

Landholders

Source ...	Domesday	Hundred Rolls 1278–9
Landbeach	32	58
Cottenham	63*	128
Waterbeach	47	95(?)†

Notes
    * 3 serfs mentioned in Cottenham.
    † Hundred Rolls for Waterbeach defective, but total landholders probably correct.

The ease with which lords here as elsewhere, were able to fill vacant holdings during the Black Death have suggested that behind the landholders counted in the Hundred Rolls there was probably a great reserve of men waiting to step into dead men's shoes. If this is so, then the rate of increase between Domesday and the later survey may be still greater than the figures suggest. The density which medieval population seems to have attained at its peak here is even more astonishing if we look forward. If we estimate the population in 1278–9 by the use of a conventional multiplier for family size, 4·5, and ignore the hidden reserve of the time, we get a much larger figure than the 235 found for Landbeach in the 1811 Census. For Waterbeach we would only need a multiplier of 4·8 to surpass the corresponding figure for that village. Only Cottenham of the three was able to sustain substantially more people at the beginning of the nineteenth century than in the late thirteenth century;[1] and population may well have continued to increase for another generation until after 1300.

[1] Cf. C. T. Smith, 'Settlement and Population', in J. A. Steers (ed.), *The Cambridge Region* (1965), p. 142.

It was upon this hard-pressed society that the disasters of the fourteenth century struck, and the Malthusian checks of famine and pestilence, easing the pressures on the land, produced new strains.

Dr Palmer provided a collection of figures with suggested multipliers from which a history of population in Cambridgeshire might be constructed.[1] Unfortunately, examination of his figures for our three villages shows them to be unreliable. For Domesday, confusion between the manors of Waterbeach and Landbeach has resulted in totals of landholders which are quite wrong. From the Subsidy Rolls for 1327 he gives the number of tax-payers as 128 in Cottenham. A count of the printed lists[2] gives a total of 132 for Cottenham. The discrepancy may have been partly due to Palmer's deducting the numbers of lords of the manors, as he sometimes does for Domesday. For the Poll Tax of 1377, the figures for Cottenham are missing. For comparison between the two series Palmer suggests a multiplier of six for 1327, and four thirds for 1377, but since in no less than 29 towns and villages in Cambridgeshire this produces a higher population figure in 1377 than in 1327, it is very doubtful if we can with confidence compare the two series or use them for estimates of population.

For the Bishop's Return of Households of 1563 Palmer gives 121 for Cottenham, 36 for Landbeach and 45 for Waterbeach. The figures for Landbeach and Waterbeach seem far too low, and Dr Margaret Spufford counted the Waterbeach figure as 70. There appear to have been at least ten more inhabited homesteads in Landbeach than this in the Field Book of 1549. For the 1664 Hearth Tax, Palmer's figures again seem to be in error. He gives 167, 66 and 79 for Cottenham, Landbeach and Waterbeach respectively where Dr Spufford has 216, 66 and 107 for houses, or 230, 67 and 106 for householders.[3]

The Compton Census of 1676 contains no return for Waterbeach. Its figures for Cottenham, 560 and 14 non-conformists, and for Landbeach, 126 and 1 non-conformist, divided by C. T. Smith's[4] divisor of 2·8 give probable numbers of households of 205 and 45 in the respective villages. For figures as small as that for Landbeach, reliance on a general divisor may be unwise; the resultant in any case seems low compared with other sources in the same period,[5] although not impossible. But the Cambridgeshire historian who has studied these returns for the whole county, Dr

---

[1] W. M. Palmer and H. N. Saunders, *Documents relating to Cambridgeshire Villages* (Cambridge, 1926).

[2] J. J. Muskett and C. H. Evelyn-White, *Lay Subsidy Rolls for the Year 1327*.

[3] I am most grateful to Dr Spufford for her generosity in supplying me with this unpublished information on my villages.

[4] C. T. Smith, 'Population', *VCH Leicestershire*, ed. W. G. Hoskins and R. A. McKinley, vol. III (Oxford, 1955), pp. 129–75.

[5] E.g. LPC, 1639, 'A rate for the Clerk's Wages' gives 58.

Spufford, cast grave doubts on their usefulness; 'it is a difficult or impossible source on which to base estimates of total population'.[1]

Even when corrected, Palmer's figures give us very little reliably comparable material from which to discern population trends in the three villages between the Hundred Rolls and the Hearth Tax. Even the Returns of 1524 and 1525 show too wide a variation in the differences between the two years: the probable margin of error is greater than any plausible change (see Table 7).

TABLE 7. *Numbers of households or tax-payers*

Source ...	*DD	HR	LS	PT	LS	LS	BR	HT	C
		1278–9	1327	1377	1524	1525	1563	1664	1676
Landbeach	32	58	28	114	25	27	36	66	45
Cottenham	63†	128	132	–	82	103	121	216	205
Waterbeach	47	95(?)‡	59	207	31	55	70	107	–

Notes

 * DD=Domesday; HR=Hundred Rolls of 1278–9; LS=Lay Subsidy; PT=Poll Tax; BR=Bishop's Returns; HT=Hearth Tax; C=Compton Census.

 † Three serfs included in the Cottenham Domesday.

 ‡ The entry of Waterbeach in the Hundred Rolls is damaged, but the totals are probably complete.

What Table 7 seems to show is how much greater was Cottenham's potential for supporting increasing population than that of the other two villages. One may not feel confident enough in the 1327 figures to argue that this was already happening then, but in the sixteenth and seventeenth centuries, when Cottenham changed to the more intensive five-field system, when general economic trends probably favoured its special suitability for cattle, and when its commoners had attained more complete control than in the other two villages, the higher rate of increase which the figures suggest is at least plausible. Cottenham was to show a similar capacity to support an increasing population in the nineteenth century after enclosure even when people were drifting away fast from its neighbours.[2]

But for the period of low population in the later Middle Ages, although the tax returns give little help, there are incidental hints in the local sources, which give us glimpses of some of the changes from time to time.

It is particularly unfortunate that our records do not help us to see the effects of the Great Famine on the population in the second decade of the fourteenth century. The marginal notes of lands in the lord's hand in the Bray Extent discussed above are for small freeholders, and *suggest* that

[1] Margaret Spufford, 'The Dissenting Churches in Cambridgeshire from 1660 to 1700', *PCAS* LXI (1968), 67–95.

[2] *VCH Cambs.*, vol. II, pp. 136–40.

mortality was then striking, but nowhere do we get information to estimate its severity and general incidence.

For the great Black Death of 1348–9 we are much better served. Miss Page's study[1] of its effects on the Cambridgeshire manors of Crowland is well known, but most commentators fail to note that these are *minimum* figures. Miss Page emphasises that her very proper zeal to eliminate any possibility of double counting must make the totals an under-statement. Even so for the Cottenham manor she counts 33 deaths where there were no more than 58 holdings. The other evidence we have for this area is congruent with this pattern.

One of the few Reeve's Account Rolls[2] which survive for the Chamberlains manor is Richard Pelle's for 1348–9. Heriots from villein deaths are noted from John Fenland, Thomas Richards, William Saundre, John Saundre, Richard Pelle, Henry Gardiner, John Gardiner, William le Melner and John le Melner. In addition, the rector has died and left a legacy to the manor. Judging by the dates of the deaths on the nearby Crowlands manors, these nine deaths should cover the worst part of the outbreak but by no means all of it. The names suggest that when it struck one member of a family others were likely to succumb. There is no information at all except for this group of landholders. We do not know how the women and children stood up to it.[3]

Yet it was not universally fatal. Richard Pelle the reeve (we do not know the relationship to the Richard Pelle who died) had been sick and excused duty in the early summer. In December he was removed from office, recovered but incapable of performing his duties adequately. Yet the loss of nine men in what was only part of the epidemic represents a very high mortality: in the Hundred Rolls for this manor there were only thirty customers, nine of them crofters who may not have been heriotable. On the other Landbeach manor the number of customers had already decreased between the Hundred Rolls and the Extent of 1316.[4]

Our evidence on the incidence of the second pestilence of 1361 is less helpful, but the Court Book of Waterbeach cum Denney,[5] which only extracts records of deaths incidentally when special tenurial issues are involved, has recorded no less than fifteen deaths in three courts of this period. The second pestilence may well have struck more severely than the first. Certainly deeper changes seem to come more rapidly in its wake. If it were not as severe in itself, it struck a weakened, if reconstructed, society, and made full restoration of the old ways impossible. There is never quite the same orderliness in village affairs again.

[1] *ECA*, pp. 120–5. [2] CCCC, XXXV, 182.
[3] See, for recent summary, J. F. D. Shrewsbury, *A History of Bubonic Plague in the British Isles* (Cambridge, 1970).
[4] CCCC, XXXV, 182, the Account of Richard Pelle.
[5] WPC, WcD.

The symbols of this are the empty spaces in the village pattern as new closes break the housing area, uncultivated plots from time to time in the open fields, and the ceaseless struggle of the lord's officers against dilapidations and waste. By the end of the century, if the court roll evidence is to be believed, this is reflected in the disorderly behaviour of the peasants, which looms so much larger in our records.

As on the nearby Crowlands manors, there is much supplementary evidence in the Landbeach records for depopulation after the Black Death. Shortly after,[1] in 1350, the lord is calling for the names of all those who have appropriated and taken away doors (*hostias*) shutters (*fenestras*[2]) and other timber from divers tenements in the lord's hand. Ruinous walls and fences of empty tenements were allowing beasts to stray into both hay and corn. There were fourteen cases of default in the autumn works in 1349, and in the previous year Henry Sandre, John Sandre, John Fenlond, John Everard, and William Sandre had sent insufficient men for hay-making. In 1349 and 1350, grants were made in forms designed to meet the special needs of the moment; the 'tenacreslond' of bondage surrendered by Richard Pelle was granted for life only to John Martyn. Further grants were made conditional on repair of tenements, or for small cash rents plus a few desperately needed harvest-works. There appears to have been some months' delay in seizing some of the empty tenements, but in 1350 the lord, who had six in hand, was leasing out small parcels, and cultivating arable in hand up to the equivalent of almost a quarter of his demesne arable.[3] Leases at will seem to have been easily revocable. In 1342 in Cottenham, for instance, six leases to villeins, amounting in all to about thirty acres of arable with pasture, were cancelled and the land seized 'because the Abbot has been deceived'.[4] The deception might have been in the rent which was very low, 18d. for 4 acres of arable and $1\frac{1}{2}$ rods of pasture. In 1380 on the Chamberlains manor, three tiny pieces of demesne were seized because they had been occupied without licence by three of the chief villeins.

The second pestilence may have encouraged the leasing of the entire demesne at Landbeach Chamberlains. In 1362 Agnes Knyth is referred to as farmer of the said manor this year past, but how much she had in farm we do not know. The Court Roll of 1365 preserves a lease of the entire demesne, 206 acres, in parcels ranging from five to thirty acres, to 16 villeins. We do not know when the demesne was resumed. The rent of 18d.[5]

---

[1] CCCC, XXXV, 121.

[2] L. F. Salzman, *Building in England Down to 1540* (1st ed. repr. with corrections, Oxford, 1967), gives this meaning for '*fenestra*'. Cf. Chapter 3.

[3] CCCC, XXXV, Court Rolls 121; Account Rolls (Reeve's) 181 and 182.

[4] CUL Queens' Ad. 36.

[5] CCCC, XXXV, 146.4. Still higher rents were being paid by the villeins with holdings of over 20 acres in 1352.

per acre was so high that it not likely that it could have been maintained. Four years later the manor was purchased for the College.

According to Masters,[1] the College let it at farm for some years, but then stocked it and resumed the lands. But the College was certainly letting it again in 1429. There are three consecutive twelve-year leases recorded in the rolls from that year on. In the first, all its lands were let to a syndicate of villeins. These eight villeins had the option of paying 8*d.* an acre if they would hold it for twelve years, or 8½*d.* for nine years. Clearly it was not a landlord's market. Twelve years later all the lands were let at farm to the rector, Master Adam, to divide among the tenants. This time the rent was 9*d.* per acre. In the third lease, the rent is the same, but the lessees are three peasant partners.

Master Adam Clark appears to have held the rectory from 1429 to 1462.[2] Not a master of the College, nor yet a fellow, he appears to have been resident in the village and able to develop his personal economic interests there as few of his successors could. With the rectory, he held from the College a cluster of properties in and around the old manor-house site: an orchard, the pasture called Madecroft, Berys Acre, ten acres of meneland, the hall yard and sheepcote, garden and rickyards, the great barn and Priors Close. In 1441[3] he took 22½ acres in Milton and Landbeach from John Hood of Waterbeach. In the Waterbeach Court Book he appears both as landholder and trespasser. He is rather more than a yeoman-parson; almost a resident gentleman. He was combining the agricultural interests of the rectory with lands held by a long line of gentlemen graziers before him, John Chamberlain,[4] Sir William Castle-acre,[5] and Sir Thomas Bradfield.[6] This holding appears to be taken over later by a resident chaplain or curate, Dominus John Sweyn, after Master Adam's time, and afterwards by a succession of holders who included the lady of the Manor of Brays. Under Cosyn as rector and Master, it came back to the rectory. It was on part of this that Matthew Parker exploited the difference between the old rent and the new to make provision for his wife.

Not only gentlemen and near-gentlemen could take advantage of demesne land coming on to the market. At least six of the Chamberlains villeins in 1352 had expanded their holdings to over 20 acres.[7] Office could certainly help here in placing the interested party at the position where he could get a start on his rivals. In 1411 John Martyn appeared as the lord's 'serviens', presenting trespassers. In 1422 he was in turn presented for taking illicit fruits of office for the past ten years: non-payment of rent (8*d.*

---

[1] *History of the College of Corpus Christi.*
[2] *Ibid.*, Appendix p. 21, and CCCC, XXXV, 110, 150.
[3] CCCC, XXXV, 113. [4] CCCC, XXXV, 36.
[5] CCCC, XXXV, 101. [6] *Ibid.*
[7] CCCC, XXXV, 146.4.

per acre on four acres demesne arable); holding without title or licence a toft and a rod of meadow, late Agnes Miller's; over-digging turves; and allowing his son, Roger, to live at Chesterton without licence. In the next year he was ordered to wage six-handed justice on a claim of William Emmes' that John still owed William 6s. 8d. for wages from the time when John was bailiff. But he failed to appear, or to pay the £5 fine which was imposed for the other offences. Two years later he had still failed to produce his son, and the penalty for this was raised to six marks.

On the Brays manor in 1401–2[1] we learn that the demesnes had been let to John Bolle of Dullingham, and John Herrys of Cambridge, for the past seven years. In 1408 Thomas Letys had a demesne lease subtantial enough to include foldage rights, which he obstinately misused on lands other than the demesne, letting the right to others, as well as using it on his own land. When this offence was again being raised in 1414, it appeared that he might be only one of half a dozen farmers of the demesne. In 1420 an ordinance forbade this misuse of foldage by any farmer of the lord's lands. We do not know the date of the resumption of the Brays demesnes. The Keteryches and the Kirbys were resident lords of Brays. Elizabeth Keteryche and both the Kirbys held Chamberlains lands as well as their own. By the time of Richard Kirby, he had not only taken back the demesnes, but was engrossing copyhold and freehold land to himself.[2]

When Crowlands demesnes were leased in 1430 in both Oakington and Cottenham, the entire demesne was given to a bondman of the abbot's in each village, on a stock and land lease for a malt rent. Neither appeared ever to have been resumed by the abbey again. At the Dissolution William Pepys was both bailiff and lessee at Cottenham, with a lease dated 1509, a fine start for an old villein family in a life in higher society.

THE EARLY MODERN PERIOD: GENTLEMEN, ENGROSSERS AND COMMONERS

As in the Middle Ages, so in the early modern period, gentlemen came and went in these villages, but the community of peasants lasted on. If the villages of Cambridgeshire, both fen and upland, had any general characteristics which could account for the longevity of their open fields, it was probably the extent of their commons. Bloch quotes Retif de la Bretonne as saying, 'The little parish of Saci, since it has commons, governs itself like a large family.'[3] The commoners' meetings and officers gave the communities a strength that was long ago noted by Cunningham, who

[1] CCCC, XXXV, 124.
[2] See Ravensdale, 'Landbeach in 1549'.
[3] M. Bloch, *French Rural History* (1966), p. 180; this is the translation of *Les caracteres originaux de l'histoire rurale française* (1931).

saw in Cottenham a school of self-government which he thought was to be numbered among the ancestors of American democracy.[1]

Landlord initiative seems to have navigated these villages through the crises of the fourteenth century, but in the economic and social strains and stresses of the Tudor period the commoners seem to have been more firmly at the helm: landlords and gentlemen were then the unsuccessful disturbers of the old ways.

Cottenham offered the richest prizes in this area for acquisitive gentlemen. The first serious inroads seem to have been attempted as early as 1488.[2] Thomas Thursby of Norfolk, gentleman and encloser in Castleacre and Holt in his own county, was, according to Leadam, cited by the Enclosure Commission of 1517 for enclosing a hundred acres in Cottenham from 1488. The citation reads as follows:

And that Thomas Thursby, gentleman, of the County of Norfolk, allowed one messuage in Cottenham to fall into decay and a ruinous state when 60 acres of arable land and 40 acres of meadow used to be let at farm in the fourth year of the late king Henry VII.[3]

This appears not to refer to actual enclosure, in spite of Leadam's assertion that it does, but to what seems to have been a still worse social crime in the eyes of contemporary moralists – destruction of a dwelling for the sake of the sheepgate and land. Thursby was high sheriff of Cambridgeshire and Huntingdonshire in 1513.

The scale of Thursby's operations in Cottenham seems to have been similar to that of intrusive medieval gentlemen in this area: with Sir Francis Hinde of Madingley we meet something much more considerable. He began by engrossing manors, acquiring the lordships of Crowlands and Lyles and a moiety of Sames in Cottenham. In 1560 he was claiming 5,000 acres of 'fen and marish grounds', including two several sheepwalks in Longhill, Marehill, and Tilling.[4] He claimed also that Thomas Brigham, 'a very lewd, perverse and wrangling fellow', and John Pepys, had led rioters at midnight and laid open his closes. It is not clear when these closes were first made, nor their history before the Agreement of 1596, which is printed by Cunningham. But in spite of Agreements in 1560 and 1580, some of them were laid open again by the time of the third Agreement, only to be restored again as enclosures for the lord. As such they lasted into the nineteenth century. All the closes detailed in 1596 are identifiable, and are the only ones in Cottenham on its draft enclosure map.[5]

[1] *Common Rights*, Introduction.
[2] I. S. Leadam, 'The Inquisition of 1517', *TRHS*, new series, VI–VIII (1892–4).
[3] BM Lansdowne MS.1, fol. 186 (see Appendix B); Leadam, 'The Inquisition of 1517', VIII, 303 has a misprint of xl for lx which would have only made 80 acres.
[4] PRO, SC 4 P & M 3/18.
[5] CRO 152/P9, 1842.

Their later history is now without irony: among those challenging the Agreement was Katherine Pepys. In 1614 Sir Edward Hinde sold his interests in Cottenham to Thomas Hobson, the famous carrier of Cambridge. Marriage to his son, and a second widowhood, brought them to Katherine. It was in her time that Cottenham came closest to dominance by the big house. Both Lordship House[1] and Katherine Pepys' school have only been demolished in living memory, and the Pepys arms lie buried to cover an old well. Since her time the substantial peasant and yeoman families have eluded any squirearchical control.[2]

The creation of lords' severals in the fens of our villages, was an alternative to the enclosure of arable for pasture in much of the rest of the Midlands, but in getting his wishes, the squire withdrew from the commons and strengthened the peasant independence by leaving the villagers to set up their own machinery for the control of what was left in the way of common pasture. Before this, the multiplicity of manors was some check on the acquisitiveness of the lords. In the example just cited in Cottenham, engrossment of manors was possibly a necessary preliminary. In nearby Rampton, where manor and vill had been co-incident, many 'pieces', furlongs of arable taken out of the rotation and put down to grass, are prominent in the hands of the lord in the eighteenth-century field maps. The early enclosure out of the fens in Waterbeach might well have been impossible but for the amalgamation of the two manors of Denney and Waterbeach.

In the three villages of our study, the forces of resistance prevented the enclosure of arable before the nineteenth century except in a very few small parcels near the village centres.

In Landbeach, Kirby, lord of the Manor of Brays, was in 1549 accused of carrying out a policy similar to the one Thursby had tried in Cottenham, but on a larger scale: 'He and his predecessors have letten all his tenements fall down to the number of fourteen, which were standing within the mind of man, and some of very late days decayed.'[3] He appears to have been forming home paddocks by taking toft and croft from his tenants, and enclosing small pieces of nearby common and arable, as a basis for the management of flocks large enough to overstock the commons. It was the opposition of Matthew Parker, rector and Master of Corpus Christi College, lord of the Manor of Chamberlains, that stopped Kirby from going further. Parker's predecessor, William Sowde, had been negotiating exchanges that would have given Kirby much of what he wanted.

---

[1] See Plate IV(a).

[2] CPC, Rectory, Miscellaneous Register. The efforts of Frere, a nineteenth-century parson, to establish a proper social deference came to grief, too. His letters to his bishop in his trials with the Nonconformists show that the peasants had found a justification for their social independence in their own chapels.

[3] CCCC, XXXV, 194.

Under some of Kirby's successors, probably beginning with Sir John Barker in the mid-seventeenth century, and certainly under William Worts and his trustees, it became usual to let the Manor of Brays divided into three farms.

Waterbeach seems to have been more completely engrossed by a few big farmers. Masters wrote in 1795:

The Farmers of Denny, Waterbeach and Rectory, (the property of Henry Pointer Standly, Esq:) occupy nearly two thirds of the Parish, there are not many other capital Farmers resident there. Causeway End Farm, those of Messrs Wiles, Hall, Huckings and Watson are the principal: the rest of the lands are divided into small parcels and let to such as have a stock of milch cows.[1]

It was against such inequalities, as being economically wasteful and socially iniquitous, that Denson preached.[2]

One can see something of the growth of economic inequalities and the opening of a social gulf in Waterbeach from the probate inventories. That of Richard Kettle of Denney Abbey in 1666[3] shows little money, little stock, and little household comfort, valued at £58 4s. 4d. in all. In Joseph Kettle's, also of Denney Abbey, in 1686, the whole of the remaining building of the abbey had been taken over and converted into a very large farmhouse. The old parlour of the countess of Pembroke was made into a gallery, and there were eleven rooms altogether. His purely personal effects were worth £100, and his total assets at Denney came to £1223 15s. 0d. In addition he had the lease of a farm in Cambridge, and his property there was worth a further £817 13s. 4d. The inventory for John Robson suggests possibly even more elegance, with yellow, red, blue and green chambers, in what would seem to have been Denney House in the centre of the village. Robson's assets were valued at £1445 8s. 10d.

Waterbeach cum Denney remained in Royal hands after the Dissolution of the Monasteries until Charles I sold the reversion in 1614.[4] There were opportunities for both steward and farmer. In 1610[5] three of the copyholders were examined as to the activities of John Yaxley who combined the position of steward with that of farmer. His friend Haslop held the title of 'bailye', but was a man of straw: accounts were paid to Robert Spicer, Yaxley's son-in-law, and the money was sometimes a long while in reaching its proper destination. Yaxley had sold copyhold timber, seized the Town Land, taken its profits for a year, and released it upon

---

[1] *Short Account*, p. 2.
[2] Denson, *A Peasant's Voice*.
[3] CUA, in year bundles but with MS. index.
[4] PRO, Parliamentary Surveys, E317 No. 2.
[5] PRO, SP 14/57/43.

composition. Further he had taken thirty pounds of the church-wardens from the Town Stock. He had returned ten pounds, half the entry fine, to Edward Banks to bribe Banks not to join with the other tenants who were demanding their rights on Lammas grounds, copyhold closes held by Yaxley from which he was excluding the commoners. Yaxley later became alderman of Cambridge. He built the charity cottages later known as Robson's in 1626. It was through Yaxley's daughter and the Spicers that the property eventually came to the Robsons.

If outsiders came and went over the generations, and stewards who took no profit struck no roots in the villages, families that rose from among the peasantry seemed to remain rather longer after the Tudor period. In Parker's Tabular Terrier[1] all the old Chamberlains holdings are traceable for seventy years or more, freehold as well as copyhold. The core of the community at this time appears to have been a group of ten peasants holding twenty acres or more each. Most of this was copyhold. John Gotobed had gathered three freehold farms as well, and was farmer both of the manor and rectory in addition. His son Henry once is called 'Gent' in the parish registers. After two generations the Gotobeds disappeared from the village. By 1665[2] the Annis family had replaced them, not only economically as the most substantial farmers on the Chamberlains manor, but also socially as church-wardens. By 1727[3] they, too, had gone, replaced by the Taylors, who emerged at the parliamentary enclosure as the largest owner-occupiers in the village. The fine farmhouse, 'John Annis's brick house' of 1665, although probably built some thirty years before that date, was owned by Uriah Taylor in 1813. It remained almost the solitary splendid brick farmhouse of the village for a century and a half,[4] and then was soon to be degraded and divided for another century, superseded socially by the early Victorian farmhouses of the later, yellow, Cambridgeshire brick.

The dominance of the village landscape by this fine farmhouse in the seventeenth and eighteenth centuries reflected the social change in the village, the rise of the moderate farmer, and the beginning of the end of the peasant community. By the time of the Enclosure Award of 1813 no less than 29 out of the 47 landowners have less than five acres each. But this change had been well on the way by 1727. In that year the Speculum[5] recorded 55 households, but in the Dukman Book there were only 41 holdings of land, and these were in the hands of 28 people, plus the lord of Milton. Thirteen of these held less than 20 acres each; in fact this group

[1] CCCC, XXXV, 174.
[2] LPC, Fen Book, 'A survey of Real Property', 1665.
[3] LPC, Dukman Book; CRO Q/RDc 18, award map with schedule.
[4] The former Black Bull public house received a brick skin over its timber frame probably about 1700.
[5] CUL, EDR, B8/1.

held only a fraction over 17 acres between them. The base of family arable self-sufficiency of the older village had gone.

POPULATION IN THE MODERN PERIOD

These changes in social and economic structure appear to be associated with, and perhaps caused by changes in population. For Landbeach, at least, we can call on better local sources than those supplied by Palmer and discussed above. There are two kinds of these which can help us to estimate the part played by population pressure in changing the old village: counts of households, families or houses, and the entries of baptisms, burials and marriages in the parish registers. The first type of evidence shows a surprising stability in the village from middle Tudor times, growth being very slow until the nineteenth century:

1549	1639	1664	1727	1781	1798	1811	1851
46(?)	62(– ?)	66	55	49	55	61	116[1]

The figure for 1549 may be too low, since it is possible that some of the tenements that appear to be empty in the field book are inhabited. Four of the occupants of houses in 1639 held two each, and 58 (surprisingly the number of landholders for the village in the Hundred Rolls) may well be the proper number. The eighteenth-century figures are all of families, and although the family size may have been slightly higher at the end of the period, there can hardly have been any massive increase in population until the second decade of the nineteenth century at least. The parish registers[2] tell another side of the story (see Fig. 13). The excess of baptisms over burials was at times very considerable: in 1590–1609 35 per cent, in 1690–1709 41 per cent, and in 1800–9 49 per cent. In the fifty years after the Civil War it was the burials which on the whole exceeded baptisms. But in periods when natural increases took place on this scale there must have clearly been considerable emigration from the village in order to produce such slight changes in the number of families and the population of the village.

The registers suggest periods of population pressure due to natural increase, from about 1563 to 1625, 1632 to 1654, 1691 to 1707, 1767 to 1779. After a brief interval of high mortality the figures turn up again, and by the end of the century take on a pattern of more rapid increases which the census returns reflect thereafter. This buoyancy of the fertility rates seems to have found some relief from the 1850s in Landbeach and

---

[1] Sources: 1549 Field Book; 1639 'A rate of Houses for the Clerk's Wages'; 1664 Hearth Tax; 1727 Speculum in CUL, EDR B8/1; 1781 table in Collectanea, LPC, Masters; 1798 List in Register LPC; 1811 and 1851, Census.

[2] LPC: these start from 1538 and are one of the most complete sets in the county.

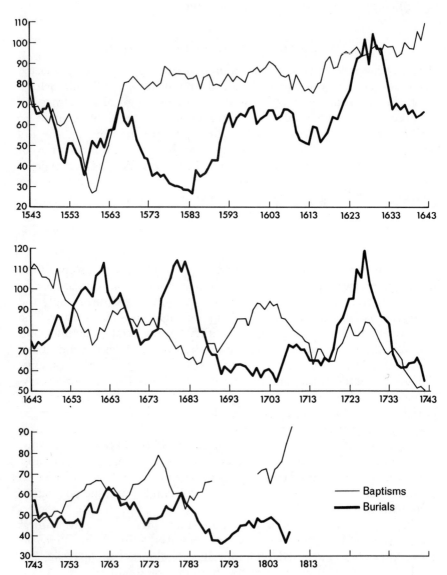

Fig. 13. Recorded baptisms or births, and burials in 9-year moving totals from parish registers at Landbeach.

Waterbeach in the drift from the countryside, and in Cottenham from the intensive exploitation of the fens after enclosure and ploughing up.[1]

It seems impossible to get any more detailed picture of emigration out of the villages until the family reconstitution now in process for Landbeach is complete. But we can see something of the opposite flow of immigration at the end of our period from the 1851 Census, in the enumerators' returns:

Total inhabited 'houses':	116
Man and wife both born in Landbeach:	18
Man only born in Landbeach:	36 (of which 4 widowers)
Woman only born in Landbeach:	10 (no widows)
Neither born in Landbeach:	52

By this time only about a third of the married people of Landbeach had been born there: nine of the men and eleven of the women came from beyond the county boundaries. The old way of life of the peasant families seemed to have gone.

About the same time as this census was taken the family tradition in the Sanderson family in Cottenham was breaking. Until his grandfather died, Jacob 'had to work as a common labourer, thrashing in the barn from Michaelmas to May Day for half a crown a week'. Before enclosure he had helped himself out by keeping his Uncle Few's pigs after harvest, and was always paid for this. At the age of fifteen he was sent out to do the ploughing, unaided and untrained. His father expected much of Jacob's work to be unpaid, as he would inherit the land. At harvest, he says, 'My place was with the men, work as they work, fare as they fare, except pay, which I had none, but food.' When he asked for 6d. a week pocket money he was instead given a hen. From this he managed to make a profit of 25s. which he banked, but after he had drawn only 5s., the bank failed and he lost all the rest. In the end he had to leave home to force his father to allow him proper wages in order to get married.[2] Jacob's father had expected him to wait before seeking his independence or marrying until he had inherited. Such a tradition must have helped to keep the population in check in peasant families.

[1] *VCH Cambs.*, vol. II, pp. 136–7.
[2] Notebook.

OCCUPATIONAL AND SOCIAL
DIFFERENTIATION

There was a touch of variety in the villages shown in the Hundred Rolls, when craft-names suggested subsidiary occupations. The probate inventories for the late seventeenth century show a considerable development of this in so far as they give any direct or indirect indication of status and occupation in Cottenham: such information is not so rich in Waterbeach, and less so in the smallest village, Landbeach. But it is comparatively rare in any of the inventories to find a craftsman, publican or shopkeeper who does not have a holding in the field as well.

Kelly's *Directory* for 1869 gives a much more comprehensive list of trades. The publicans, who are the most common occupation other than agriculture, are as common as were medieval ale-wives, and the dwindling of their numbers (to the point of extinction in Landbeach village) is a very recent story.

It is very difficult to gauge how much of this occupational variation was reflected in the landscape. In the Grant of Chantries[1] for Cottenham we get a momentary glimpse of some differences in the village street scene:

Also all those our eight messuages, tenements and cottages and all houses, buildings, shops, cellars, solars, curtilages, orchards, apple-trees and gardens.

But since most village shop-keepers and craftsmen were also peasants, with peasant houses, their shops and workshops would only have provided small variations in the common theme of the street.

From the late Middle Ages on, the materials of the buildings in these villages were predominantly timber-frames with lath and plaster and thatch, until the nineteenth century, and in spite a variety of styles, there must have been a very homogeneous and unified street scene until after the parliamentary enclosures. It is not easy to envisage what variation the shops added. The oldest clearly recognisable shop in the three villages is at number 21 High Street, Landbeach. Here there was originally an open hall house, end-on to the road. A little shop, half a bay square, was added at some time as a cross-wing running alongside the road. The shop, too, has had a ceiling inserted, not later than the early eighteenth century. There was no internal communication between house and shop. Although the whole wall along the street was subsequently given a brick skin, the shape and pattern of the let-down shutter and counter have been preserved. Agricultural, industrial and commercial buildings at this time would have merely provided variations on the same visual scene as the

---

[1] BM Add. Ch. 7060, m. 2; see also Appendix B.

houses, much as ancilliary occupations embellished, but did not remove, the peasant way of life.

Brick, from the first, was associated with social differentiation. In the fifteenth century it was used for manorial buildings, including farm-buildings.[1] Little of this remains: the cellar in Landbeach Rectory, and perhaps some of the walls now hidden by stucco in 'Crowland House' in Cottenham. Masters used it to give a fashionable façade to the rectory at Landbeach, but used the traditional materials rather meanly for his charity cottages. The rather older bricks in the rectory wall, appear to have been brought by water from Ely by Mickleburgh, rector from 1727 to 1756. He began the process which continued right up to Tinkler's time (rector 1843 to 1871), and converted the rectory from what had been primarily a farmhouse, into a fine country gentleman's residence. As Robert Masters had moved the main entrance from the yard to the street side, and made a grand entrance hall, degrading the hall, which sufficed Matthew Parker, to a kitchen, so his son-in-law, Burroughes, in 1799 converted the parsonage cowyard into a pleasure garden. He planted Cedars of Libanus, *Pyracanthus*, Red Cedars, *Arbutus*, *Arbor Vitae*, Striped Holly, Portugal Laurels, Junipers and Swedish Junipers, *Lauristinus*, Yew Trees, Poplars and other shrubs for decoration. Peaches and nectarines were planted in the same year, walks were altered and a new lawn laid.[2] Tinkler added a bay window and a Renaissance stone porch. The new farmhouses after enclosure echoed the new pretensions in their names, 'The Limes', 'The Willows', 'The Acacias'. Thus, later in time, Landbeach began to catch up with its larger more affluent neighbours in social display. Formal gardens and pleasure-grounds, like those in the Stukeley drawings of Cottenham earlier in the eighteenth century,[3] set off new features, or whole new houses built in larger style, of better materials (and altogether more expensive), for the village upper classes.

As lands were engrossed in the seventeenth and eighteenth centuries, some tofts and crofts ceased to be small farmyards. But the fens, and the common rights enabled small men like John Denson's father to build up farms of their own through dairying. The suitability of the area for horticulture provided an alternative for others, and many crofts became orchards or commercial vegetable gardens. Hemp, flax, onions, leeks and herbs appear in the early records of Chamberlains Manor as well as in Crowlands. Orchards and fruit-growing seem well-established on the medieval demesnes. Cunningham concluded from seventeenth-century tithe schedules that it had attained some importance. Parker in 1553[4]

---

[1] E.g. CUL Queens' Cd. 66, 2000 'de waltyle'.
[2] LPC, Tithe Book.
[3] Plates IV(*a*) and (*b*).
[4] LPC, Field Book, note on tithes.

specifically included tithes on pigs, wool, fruit, wood, hay, corn, hemp, flax, in addition to the previous garden tithes on leeks, honey and wax. But it is from Waterbeach towards the end of the eighteenth century that we first get clear evidence of substantial market-gardening. In Masters' tithe Estimate for 1772,[1] we find 68 owners or occupiers holding 33 orchards, 48 gardens, 28 closes and 18 holts. His *Short Account* of the parish in 1795 confirms a flourishing horticulture long before the coming of the railways:

> The soil likewise is peculiarly adapted to Gardening, insomuch that there are no better Asparagus, Cauliflowers, Cabbages, Beans and Peas, than it produces; and many persons diligently cultivating and carrying them to the Cambridge Market acquire a comfortable maintenance thereby.[2]

When parliamentary enclosure came, the crofts and tofts, which had been converted to horticulture as the core of a smallholding, still provided a visual bridge between the new brick and slate farmhouses in their ornamental grounds, and the tiny brick and slate terraces or courtyards of the new labourers' cottages. The coming of the railways, which finally established the victory of the new materials and styles, paradoxically, in opening wider markets for the horticultural and dairying smallholder, helped conserve their houses by enabling the owners to carry on successfully. The revolutionary factor which altered the appearance of the village centres was fire-raising.[3] Social discontents, in which enclosure played a part, broke out in arson, devastating to timber-frame and thatch. One of the worst such fires in Cottenham in 1850 accounts for the homogeneity of the village street scene there: many of the houses in the High Street had to be rebuilt at this time.

THE NEW LANDSCAPE

The new landscape of the fields after enclosure, when field and fen became one, must, at first, have been more bare than the old. The trees along the drifts and ways that were ploughed up, would have soon gone. In this area ditches often did the task of quicksets elsewhere. Soon small market

---

[1] WPC, various papers relating to tithe.

[2] *Short Account*, p. 2. Cf. Willingham: the obituary of Mrs Ann Gleave, born 1793, in the *Cambridge Independent Press*, 26 July 1890, tells how her father, at the beginning of the century 'took fruit, butter, etc., to London every week during the fruit season in a four horse waggon. At that time conveyances going to Cambridge had to ford running brooks on their way, and one horse can now do on those roads what it would have taken four horses to do at that time...Men and women would tramp to Cambridge on market days bearing as much as five dozen of butter on their shoulders'. I am indebted to Mr Dennis Jeeps for drawing my attention to this notice.

[3] See above, Chapter 3, p. 85; *Notebook*; *Illustrated London News*, 13 April 1850, pp. 247 and 248; *Waterbeach*, p. 23.

gardens pushed out into the arable along all the main roads, and began to variegate the scene. But in the twentieth century, with the coming of the bulldozer, men are again laying field to field, and grubbing hedges and trees to make larger units. Even old Roman farm sites, like Bullocks Haste in Cottenham, which have resisted the plough with their unevenness until now, are beginning to go down. Blossom time still lights the orchards and commercial flower gardens in a blaze the old village never knew, but only to emphasise the mathematically simple shapes of the new fields like a magnificent suburban garden. A few corners of the old landscape survive because of their awkwardness: the unkempt trees and undergrowth at the junction of the Rennels Brooks would be uneconomic to tame. The hedge of 1235 along Beach Ditch has been cut, burned and tidied, but in what is left, wild pear still flourishes near the old Peyretre Furlong of the field books. Along Alboro' Close Drove, on another Roman site, coming to the Car Dyke, if the weather is right one is startled by the change in the landscape. Here is a fragment of the improved fen of the eighteenth century. There is no wild fen nearer than Wicken. The remaining osier holt near the Landbeach–Cottenham boundary has a new untidiness, being scarcely wanted as the old crafts die. But on the banks of the Cam in Waterbeach the willows still grow splendidly with thinning and control, but where pollarded too closely revenge themselves by growing gnarled and twisted. The watercourses are becoming sharper and straighter with mechanical cleaning, but only on their banks in the remoter parts of the fen do many wild flowers survive.

In the village centres the cost of maintaining old buildings, and the profit to be taken from their sites has begun a new devestation in the late 1960s. The harsh materials and ungainly proportions of the latest building fashions, squatting awkwardly among the survivors of the past, leave them decaying and discouraged. In Landbeach alone of the three are there enough of the old houses scattered along the street to convince us that it is still a village and not a suburb. But even there, this may not last much longer.

There is good cause in the deterioration of the landscape for nostalgia like Denson's. But his idyllic view of the vanished peasant community was already turning into the Victorian ideal of Self Help. On the other hand Jacob Sanderson recollected the trials of enclosure in the tranquility of old age, half a century later, without sentimentality:

Now a great change came over Cottenham, the Enclosure. Old times were to pass away and all things to become new. No more stocking of the Commons on Old May Day, nor Dye Feast, or Officers chosen, nor Auditermakers Days. Nearly all the old landmarks were removed and a fresh order of things substituted in their place. Three old watermills taken down, Undertaker, Chare Fen and Setchell, and two steam engines in their place. Smithe Fen and Chare Fen. New drains were dug or made, and fresh roads made through the Fens and Fields, everyone knowing his own allotment. There is not one now in all the Town but what has changed hands since then, both in the Town Fields and on the Fen. In my time one generation passeth away and another cometh.[1]

When the excitement of paring and burning and breaking up the fen was over, the cultivator either stood to gain handsomely from the newly-tapped riches of the peaty soil, or, if things went wrong, to lose all in his new vulnerability to the market. Even the Ivatt family, the most substantial of the farmers at enclosure, saw their fortunes fade by the end of the century. For the small peasant the threat was immediate:

Recollect the second year after Enclosure being a very dry summer; no rain from March till Midsummer Fair Day, 24 June; the first year after the land being broke up after being skirted and burned. The oats did not come up till a week after the rain; never came to perfection. Cut them in November; icicles as we reaped them. Stack them in the Fen; stock would not eat them. They heat in the stack; carried them about the land for manure.

My Father had twelve acres; never sold a bushel. One of the most trying years he had to struggle on through life.[2]

[1] Notebook.
[2] *Ibid.*

CONCLUSIONS

Although we have a picture of the pattern and fortunes of the Roman settlement of this area, based on field archaeology, the Dark Ages are still very dark. We know virtually nothing of how Roman rule ended here, and less of how the intense late-Roman settlement by small farms was superseded by far fewer nucleated Saxon villages. The problem of what happened between the early pagan penetration (revealed by the spade in cemeteries, and in the few poor huts on the bank of the Waterbeach Car Dyke) and the formation of the villages centuries later (according to the opinions of the place-name experts) is still unsolved. Nor do we know when and how the small fields and farm boundaries of the Roman-British farms, as revealed by the air photographs of the fens, were replaced by the ridge and furrow of the open-field arable. Yet the little that we know for this area in these lost centuries probably makes it favoured compared with much of the rest of the country.

When the documents become plentiful enough for us to feel some confidence in the conclusions that they suggest, we meet with three mature villages each enjoying the advantages of the fen as well as arable, and even more, the benefits of the association of these two sources of wealth. Colonisation of the area seems to have been completed early, and there are hints that Landbeach, after a later start as a separate community, had rapidly overtaken its neighbours. The arable basis of their economies, seen from the point of view of the peasantry, was moderate in Cottenham, modest in Landbeach, and subordinate to fen exploitation in Waterbeach. The Domesday figures suggest that the period of colonisation by the plough was almost complete, but the Hundred Rolls in turn suggest that in the intervening two centuries the lands of each village had become capable of supporting twice as many families. The overspill of the housing area on to old open field, so clear in both Cottenham and Landbeach, appears to have taken place during this period.

This expansion of population may be paralleled in many parts of the Midlands. But here, unlike most Midland villages, the ultimate limit of ploughland was only in part the parish boundary; the seasonal rise and fall of the black waters of the fen would halt the plough short of the rich frontier area which in summer produced abundance of lush feed and winter keep.

In this frontier zone the differences between the three villages were most sharply reflected in the landscape. Here Cottenham, relatively rich in ploughland, seems to have kept its ploughs clear, not only of this frontier zone, but also clear of the further zone of hards, land subject not to normal winter flooding but vulnerable to the sudden and extraordinary floods of the fen edge. Only a few insignificant hemplands seem ever to have passed these bounds. But in Landbeach in the fourteenth century it was into such an intermediate zone of hards that the ploughs were forced to operate desperately in face of the worst flooding recorded in her history. In Waterbeach with its fields so much lower, and with river and fen in some places so close to the homesteads, the margins of the fields and margins of the fens must often both have taken their appearance from hastily-sown risk crops in the spring.

But if the fen held a constant menace in its waters, the abundance of its fish and fowls afforded great resources for survival. These might have been reduced and eroded by mowing and feeding which improved the primitive fen, had not the water imposed a limit. Thus a balance between the different uses of the fen, built up in the Middle Ages, was maintained. The landscape evolved, in no small measure, as a result of the interplay between changes in population and changes in the water-table.

But the population suggested by the Hundred Rolls must have been a strain for the agricultural technique of the time to support. It was this over-stretched economy that was struck by the worst famine and pestilence of European history. The crisis was common to most of Europe, but as well as common disasters, the fen-edge communities had to contend with more – the most catastrophic flooding of their local history. Struck at their most vulnerable point, their peculiar trials must have been especially severe.

If arable was reverting to fen in Landbeach in the first half of the fourteenth century, the lower-lying Waterbeach must have fared worse, and in all three parishes much of the improved fen would have deteriorated towards car. But the reversion seems to have been only temporary, as the compensatory assarting into pastureland in Landbeach seems to have been mostly temporary.

The old balance between field and fen came back, but without the strain of excess population to feed: the advances in cropping methods were no longer necessary. But improved weather conditions brought no simple restoration: as the lords, under the new circumstances were tempted to become rentiers, so the peasant community gained more *de facto* control over the actual use of the land.

The late medieval and early modern period saw more specialisation of regions in each village's fens. Greater market opportunities allowed the peasant to exploit the local natural advantages while still keeping up his general agricultural activities and remaining a peasant. Paradoxically this extra profitable use of the fen seems to have strengthened the conservatism of the arable farming.

The clashes of the Tudor period between the peasantry on the one hand, and commercially-minded lords and gentlemen on the other, led to a separation out of the lords' interests into their own severals. For the rest, the commoners were more firmly in the saddle than ever. Market forces which favoured the exploitation of Cottenham's fens by the development of its milch herd and cheese-making helped indirectly in the more intensive exploitation of its arable by the five-field system. But the commoners were able to take control of this by the agreement of 1596, and after exacting this price, were able to direct the common agriculture with no major change for two centuries.

The efforts of enclosing landlords, in the long run, left little that was different behind them; a few small grass paddocks and empty house-plots near the village centres, and a few fences and bars in the remoter parts of the fen. But the old ways of common field, pasture and fen were more firmly entrenched.

The Great Drainage schemes of the seventeenth century affected the local landscape less than local piece-meal works. The enclosures for their profit (the Adventurers Grounds and the Drainers Grounds) were out on the peripheries of Cottenham and Waterbeach. The fens were soon as wet again as ever. Nature played her cat-and-mouse game with the drainers to restore the balance, each success in draining being followed by peat shrinkage and a falling soil level.

The human side of the balance between man and his environment responded, too. Our best sources for local population history, the parish registers and counts of families or houses in Landbeach, show a surprising long-term stability.

The second half of the eighteenth century brought signs of the revolutions of that age even to the fen edge. The Cam became intensely busy as a commercial canal. The Milton–Ely turnpike cut across old boundaries, altered the relative importance of ancient field ways, and left the medieval Via Regia into the fens to become a muddy overgrown track. When the age of steam followed, effective drainage tamed the fen as the railway came to draw off its wealth. The market, which had been an auxiliary to the peasant way of life became master. The old, functionally planned peasant family houses were sub-divided and sub-divided again, as containers for the population, which now grew again in an uncontrolled fashion. The designation 'Pauper' became frequent in the burial register. By the time when enclosure and steam drainage reduced field and fen to one commodity, land, whose use was controlled by the market prices, the old community was already fast breaking up. The passing of the common fields may not have directly destroyed the common social ways of the older village life, but such customary ways did not long outlive the change.

War-time propaganda and interest in technical improvement, in the struggle for survival against Napoleon, met with little serious resistance. The peasant ideal lingered on in Denson as in Cobbett, but the capacity of the community to contain its own growth, by adjusting its ways to its environment, had gone. Arson seems to have been a more common reaction among those less literate than Denson. What is astonishing is the relative success with which adjustments had been made for so long. Much of the conservatism of the old order was born of confidence in the ability of the local constitutional machinery to respond to the fickleness of the fenland waters as well as the weather.

In the end the old way of life had to go, as the division of labour became wider and wider geographically. When parliamentary enclosure came late to this area, it found the old arable remarkably intact and little changed. The balanced landscape which had evolved to sustain local peasant communities, was replaced by one designed on the drawing-board for more efficient economic exploitation. More of this landscape blows away each March in the dust-storms.[1] Men changed with the fields, and men too, were freed from ancient custom.

[1] A. K. Astbury, *The Black Fens* (Cambridge, 1958).

APPENDIX A

In discussing historical field systems we strive to discover and express technical generalities, but almost invariably our documents derive from, and are specific to, particular sets of fields. Most of the agricultural technique behind the documents was either customary and taken for granted, or expressed orally and rarely set down. Yet in following the changing agricultural patterns of a small area it is clear that there were accepted notions of the proper way to go about the job of raising food there, and that these notions belonged in part to each particular village, and in part to a wider cultural tradition, and subject to wider economic pressures. Much of what we can learn of system in any locality is inference from marginal references, or imported assumptions from elsewhere in place and time. When, in later periods, technique becomes self-conscious and vulnerable to criticism, such importation of foreign ideas may well have been done for us by the critics. Descriptions usually come from outsiders whose views are based on their own presuppositions. The interplay between the purely local and the more general creates most serious difficulties in matters of terminology.

If we treat the problem like the completion of a jig-saw puzzle we find ourselves working with broken fragments of pieces culled from a variety of different pictures, or a variety of versions from the hands of different artists, even where the object originally depicted was the same. The result might well be expected to be ill-fitting, incomplete and with pieces left over.

The different purpose of different kinds of documents find expression in a single language, but this may conceal a very local dialect of usage, as stability forms habits which narrow and particularise terms, while elsewhere change expands their possible meanings. The context of words may not make the local connotations of a term clear: the context of purpose may sometimes help rather more. A term may carry a whole cluster of connotations, but in a particular place may be used for one only. The word 'field' itself is one of the most variable in usage in the villages studied. Its purpose may be simply to denote that the land in question was arable, and nothing more. It may mean an area within a continuous boundary or it may not, Church Field in Cottenham, for instance, having Church Hill as a detached portion – an accident of local history. It may or may not mean a cropping shift: clearly More Field in Landbeach is in two shifts. It may coincide with a cropping season as well as a shift and so be used as substitute for it, as 'in seysona de milnefeld'. Conversely it may be identified by crop rather than by proper name: 'in le peasfeld' or 'le barlifeld'. When once embodied in a proper name the name may outlast the conditions that made it appropriate as with Meadow Field in Landbeach, which could still be so called after it had ceased to be ploughed.

A more common source of confusion is the way in which proper names may change, or worse, the way in which new and old alternative names and nicknames may co-exist side by side. Acrefeld, Stratefeld and Mill Field are not three old fields of Landbeach but one. Mikelfield in Oakington was the occasional name for the Mill Field, but only when flooding of its partners had left it disproportionately large in the rotation. As with other place-names, even in early documents field-names may tell us more of the history of the land than of contemporary farming practice. The frequency with which early place-names may change is a snare that may trap the unwary reader of a series of historical documents into double and treble counting.

The purposes of the documents relating to the fields in the three villages which I have here studied may be grouped roughly into: land title or transfer, valuation, and regulation. The documents dealing with transfer or title are charters, court roll entries, rentals, indentures and leases. Any of these may include a terrier. Their main purpose in describing land is to identify a holding, and in many cases local knowledge is so certain that extent, kind and place may be omitted from the written record. On the other hand these descriptive elements may for particular reasons be much elaborated. Sometimes, but not very often, where care is being taken to produce a balanced holding with arable in each shift, identification is by quantity in each of the fields, with the implication that these are identical with shifts. This is most likely to happen where a new holding is being carved out. Where an old holding is being passed on intact the old holder's name may be sufficient identification. When precision is needed, the details of the lesser units matter more than the greater: the size of each selion, its abuttals, and its furlong may make mention of its field redundant. In such cases the word 'field' is sometimes added to the name of the furlong, merely to re-affirm that the land is arable, but incidentally introducing a new 'field-name' as a result, with scope for misinterpretation.

The written word in the early documents is almost invariably derived from oral information given by illiterate informants, and fitted by a scribe into a more or less standard pattern. The Reeve's Account Roll for Landbeach Chamberlains in the year of the great Black Death illustrates how far this could go in emergency: the roll appears to have been made out beforehand in neat black writing, leaving spaces for the amounts. These have been hastily filled in and unnecessary items crossed out in a looser hand in ink that faded brown. But nevertheless one is left with the impression in documents of the fourteenth century, that those who composed them were more familar with the agricultural operations of the villagers than were the Tudor and later lawyers. The decline of direct demesne cultivation, the disappearance of labour services, and the narrowing of the work of courts to exclude managerial functions, leave us much more dependent on conveyancing lawyers who are not worried by a mixture of old names and new or loosely-used terms, as long as title is secured. In using technical terms for conveying rights they tend to use wide-ranging terms to include all possible details that may be in future asserted (e.g. 'with all rights of sheepgate and foldcourse thereto belonging'), like the plumber who always leaves a job for next time.

Sources whose primary purpose was regulation, and which give continual side-lights on the working arrangements of village agriculture, are ordinances. In time these may become embodied in custom and their origin lost: conversely, many ordinances appear simply to be affirmations of long-practised custom now in danger of violation. The chief source of our knowledge of early custom and ordinances is the record in the court roll, usually of the breach of custom. By-laws are frequently cited, but in our villages there is no mention of any moot as their originator and guardian. The manor courts, or *ad hoc* assemblies like that in Cottenham church at Easter 1344, seem to be their progenitors until we come to the commoners' meetings of early modern times. But even when partial codification seems to be attempted from time to time, we are given nothing like a complete summary of all the regulations; only those dealing with areas particularly prone to dispute, especially boundaries, physical and legal.

The detailed practice of cultivation emerges most clearly from documents intended for purposes of valuation and accounting. A proportion of the medieval extents and surveys, including those contained in 'Inquisitiones Post Mortem' of the early fourteenth century, like a proportion of the probate inventories of the early modern period, show something of the fields under crop and fallow at particular moments. Tithe disputes may show the same with more complete coverage, and even give this detail for a sequence of years. Names and topography may have little significance until related to cropping, and our best source of information about medieval cropping is the manorial reeve (or the royal servant doing the equivalent service on a manor in royal hands). The accounting system of charge and discharge may not be a good guide to profit and loss, but it can be an excellent guide as to how the demesne has been worked. But the normal reeve's account roll is only a summary of the information he has furnished. The return of grain may often, but not invariably even in a good set of rolls like those of Crowlands, give a good idea of how the fields have been worked.

Two original full sowing schedules for Oakington were discovered stitched in with the Account Rolls for 1362–3 and 1364–5. Their form helps to explain some of the unusual features of the Extent of the Lands of Agnes de Bray of 1316 in Landbeach. Sowings are recorded, beginning with wheat and moving on in order through the other grains. The fields are distinguished in their turn. Land sown is recorded in selions and acres, and grouped in 'pieces'. This term seems to be some sort of work unit, mostly of six selions but occasionally much larger. A piece seems not to have been a block of selions, but a group which could be reached by one access way, and they are designated much more frequently by the names of access ways than by furlongs. Here then is a very general word appropriated in a special kind of document for a narrow technical meaning. In neighbouring Waterbeach and other nearby parishes the same word can be found with the different technical meaning of an enclosed furlong. In East Anglia proper it often has yet another quite different connotation.

The use of the term 'piece' in the sowing schedules is significant. Selions were visible man-made topographical features derived from one kind of work unit, a day's ploughing. But sowing required a larger unit of a group of selions that could all be reached on a day's trip into the field, or the possibility of covering the full amount due for a day would be lost. And so there existed another invisible classification of the demesne arable, known perfectly to the reeve, but which has come down to us only through the accident of the survival of what was intended as a rough preliminary to the preparation of the summarised return.

The description of fields in the Extent of the Lands of Agnes de Bray in 1316 shares some of the peculiarities of these sowing schedules in that those parts of the fields that are described in detail (and these appear to be the areas in danger from flood) are much more commonly described by access ways than by furlongs, and many of the dole-names appear to be unique to this document. Where a field was partially flooded, dry islets could be ploughed only if they had access for a plough. Many that had not, might be in that year, or part of it, suitable for pasture only. Thus both a special kind of agricultural work, and the peculiar needs caused by rising water-table, produced documentary forms and technical terms differing from the normal in their dependence on access ways, the description reflecting the practical necessity.

Figurative use of language as well as technical, can create further snares. In Cottenham the similarity of appearance in the lay-out of meadow strips to the lay-out of the open fields led to the use of the terms 'furlong' and 'Headland' in parts of the former. But far more often than not the peculiarities in local names and usage, which suggest something different from the common pattern of the Midlands, can be explained from the detailed local history, and usually behind this is the topography, the fluctuating topography of the fen edge. Historical changes brought different and active significance to features formerly neutral. But the villagers seem to have remained wedded in thought to the old ideas of what was proper, never to have noticed the difficulties that they have left us to face in understanding their meanings, and to have been in no hurry at all to accept the better ways offered them by outside experts.

APPENDIX B

p. 6 Audita Reg[inaldi] monachi et fratrum de Elmeneia frequenti queremonia, quod videlicet in eadem insula ab aquis nimis infestari et in Dei servitio impediri solent...in insula que vocatur Deneia in eminentiori videlicet loco propter aquarum inundationes et in competentiori ad ecclesiam et edificia sua construenda et ad ortos et virgulta facienda, ut ab illa insula propter aquarum ut dictum est, incommoda ad hanc insulam commodiorem mansionem suam transferant, remanente tamen ad usus illorum predicta insula, videlicit Elmeneia...

Liber Eliensis, pp. 389–40, ch. 141 (1133 × 1169)

p. 6 cum mansum Abbatissae et Sororum Minorum de Waterbeache in loco stricto, basso, et corrupto, ac alias pro mora earundem minus sufficienti situetur.

Cal. Pat. Ed. III, vol. IV, 1338–40 (1898), p. 242, quoted in *Waterbeach*, p. 102

p. 24 Congregari enim tunc preceperat rex naves usquequaque et cum nautis ad adventum ipsius in Contingelade occurrere, ut collectam illic aggerationem lignorum et lapidum ad Alrehethe transferrent.

Liber Eliensis, p. 185

p. 35 Dicunt quod calcetus et pons ALDERHETHE est regalia via et fuit fracta et dissoluta jam per sexdecim annos elapsos et debet reperari per Episcopus Eliensem et per tenentes suos et ibidem passagia per batellum fuit et homo transiens cum equo dedit pro passagia suo (sic) obolum et homo sine equo quarterium.

Rot. Hund., vol. II, p. 453

p. 44 ...mariscum de COTEHAM incipit ad CLAYBREGE et extendit usque ad magnum pontem de HALDERHETH et de dicto ponte per magnam ripam usque ad CHAR' et de le CHAR' extendit usque ad TYLLINGE.

IBID., p. 410

p. 52 Item dicunt quod idem tenuit in pisterino domini unam feminam extraneam ad expensis domini per quod tempus ignorant. Item dicunt quod idem Johanis misit unam careccettam turbarum domini p.c. vid. ad domum Johanis de Waldeseef apud Westwyk ubi Milsent, concubina sua, manebat.

CCCC, XXXV, 121

p. 112 Jurati presentant quod Willielmus Warde obstruxit quoddam fossatum in Cotenham quod fuit divisa inter Henricum Arneburgh et Willielmum le Wode et plantavit salices in medio fundo eiusdem fossati appropriandum totum fossatum sibi ipso ubi est divisa inter feodum domini Episcopi Eliensis et feodum domini Abbatis.

CUL Queens' Ad 36

p. 112 Jurati presentant quod idem Willielmus [Cosyn] fecit domino purpresturam appropriando sibi solum domini iuxta manerium videlicet in longitudine viij perticas et in latitudine iij pedes. Ideo ipse in misericordia. Et preceptum est Juratis quod ipse in presencia dicti Willielmi si interesse voluerit metas ibidem ponant prout iure fuerit etc. et dictam purpresturam omnino adnichilent etc.

ECA, p. 358

p. 116 de dominicis in War' et aliis seysonis dismissis hoc anno diversis hominibus pro veschis fabis et pisis seminandis ut patet per parcellis.

Denney Account Rolls, 1324–5

p. 133 Item pro quodam antiquo bondagio cum crofta, olim vocatus Willielmi Osbernys, modo vacuum viretum dicti collegii et in manibus collegii iacente iuxta dominium Chambreleyns modo in tenura collegii ex parte orientali, et communem aque cursum ex parte occidentali, cuius caput australe abbuttat super illam viam regiam que vadit ex transverso inter bondagium communiter vocatum Denys modo dominium Willielmi Keterych et predictum viretum modo in dominio collegii. Et caput boriale abbuttat super aque cursum antiquum qui discurrebat inter dominium Chamberleyns et Madecrofte alias tenementum Thome Bradfelds perquisitum ad collegium...

...viretum collegii quod olim fuit Willielmi Osberns avi patrui Johanis Sweyn qui Johanis colebat totum viretum predictum pluribus vicibus teste Magistro Adam et Domino Thoma parochiali presbytero ibidem.

CCCC, XXXV, 150

p. 142 ...totum messuagium meum...in villa de Waterbeche prout iacet in longitudine et latitudine iuxta magnam ripam inter tenementum quondam Benediti Pittocks ex una parte et tenementum quondam Isabelle le maryner ex parte alia...

CCCC, XXXV, 41

p. 163 Et quod Thomas Thursby de comitatu Norfolciense armiger unum messuagium in Cottenham in decasum et ruinosam permisit cum lx acre terre arabilis xl acre prati ad firmam dimitti solebant anno quarto nuper Regis henrici vijmi.

BM Lansdowne MS. 1, fol. 186

p. 170 ...Necnon omnia illa octo messuagia tenementa et cotagia nostra et omnia domos edificia shopas cellaria curtilagia ortos pomeria et gardina nostra...

BM Add. Ch. 7060, m. 2

APPENDIX C

TABLE OF EQUIVALENTS

LENGTH

1 foot≃30 centimetres or 0·3 metres

1 yard≃0·9 metres

1 perch≃5 metres

1 chain≃20 metres

1 furlong≃0·2 kilometres

1 mile≃1·61 kilometres

1 metre≃3·3 feet

1 metre≃1·1 yard

1 metre≃0·2 perches

1 metre≃0·05 chains

1 kilometre≃5 furlongs

1 kilometre≃0·62 miles

CORN MEASURE

1 quarter≃217 kilogrammes

1 bushel≃27 kilogrammes

1 pound≃0·4 kilogrammes

1 kilogramme≃0·0046 quarters

1 kilogramme≃0·037 bushels

1 kilogramme≃2·2 pounds

AREA

1 acre≃0·4 hectares

1 rod≃0·1 hectares

1 square pole≃0·0025 hectares or 25 square metres

100 hectares = 1 square kilometre

1 hectare≃2·5 acres

1 hectare≃10 rods

1 hectare≃400 square poles

1 square metre≃0·04 square poles

FURTHER READING

PRIMARY SOURCES
MANUSCRIPT SOURCES
NATIONAL COLLECTIONS
The Public Record Office

'Inquisitiones Post Mortem'

C 132/27	35 Hen. III,	Robert le Boteler de Beche.
C 133/25	8 Ed. I,	Christiana de Furnival and William de Eylesford.
C 133/26	10 Ed. I,	Peter de Sabandia.
E 152/4	21 Ed. I,	Walter son of William Pelham.
C 133/74	24 Ed. I,	Maud Brom.
C 133/82	25 Ed. I,	Waren de Insula.
C 134/58	11 Ed. II,	Robert de Bron.
C 134/103	20 Ed. II,	Michael de Cheney.
C 135/49	10 Ed. III,	Simon de Brune.
C 135/50	11 Ed. III,	John Fraunceys.
C 135/51	11 Ed. III,	Roger de Huntingdon.
C 135/66	16 Ed. III,	Robert de Lisle.
C 135/82	20 Ed. III,	Alan la Zouch.
C 135/84	21 Ed. III,	John de Burdeleys.
C 135/131	29 Ed. III,	John de Lisle.
C 135/149	34 Ed. III,	John Pollard.
C 135/156	35 Ed. III,	Elizabeth Burdeleys.
C 135/203	42 Ed. III,	Hugo la Zouch.

Ministers' Accounts, general series
SC6/766/12, 13, and 14 Keeper of Denney 18–20 Ed. II and 1 Ed. III.

Star Chamber Proceedings
St. Ch. 2/27/49, Forcible entry at Cottenham and assault at Waterbeach.
St. Ch. 3/6/17, Kirby's complaint, 1549.
St. Ch. 2/24/250, Reply to above. (Filed under Hen. VIII but clearly belonging to 1549.)
St. Ch. 3/156/22, *William Roffe* vs. *William and Joan Hasell.*
St. Ch. 4/3/17, Sir Francis Hinde; enclosure in Cottenham Fen.

Court of Requests
Req. 2/21/17, Pasture in Cottenham Fen.
Req. 2/112/49, House in Cottenham
Req. 2/29/45, Disputed will in Waterbeach.
Req. 2/55/3, Case of idiocy in Waterbeach.
Req. 2/153/44, Robert Hasell, town clerk of Milton.

Early Chancery Proceedings

C1/1333/31, *Betts* vs. *Kirby*.
C1/1356/17, *Hall* vs. *Kirby*.
C1/1356/18, Kirby's reply to Hall.
C1/1356/19, Kirby's reply to Betts.

Chancery Proceedings

C3/88/17, *Hall* vs. *Kirby*.
C3/105/67, Award of *Arbitrators* vs. *Kirby*.
C3/106/9, Fresh arbitration, Kirby 'very aged, sick and impotent'.
C3/107/46, *Kirby* vs. *Hall*.
C3/108/11, *Kirby* vs. *Hasell*.
C3/413/96, Waterbeach Rectory and parcel of manor.
C3/424/67, Copyhold of Crowlands.
C3/466/49, Waterbeach, copyhold of Denney.

Exchequer: Special Commissions

E178/488, 44 Eliz. Survey of the Manor of Cottenham.

Exchequer: Depositions

E134, 18 Chas. I, Trin. 4. Parsonage, town and parish of Cottenham and hamlet of Westwick. Particulars touching Smithy Fen. Meets and bounds. Tithes.
E134, 1655–6, Hil. 20. Manors of Over, Willingham and Waterbeach, and marsh or fen lands heretofore common but now enclosed. Agistment, etc. Survey.
E134, 16 Chas. II, Mich 22. Re levying of £180 on the goods of Dr Manby, parson of Cottenham.

State Papers

SP 14/57/43, 1610, Depositions in the enquiry into the conduct of John Yaxley, steward at Waterbeach.
SP 14/99/52, 1618, View of sewers.
SP 14/18/102, 1620, Petition of towns bordering the Ouse.
SP 16/230, 1632, Resistance to drainers.

Parliamentary Surveys

E 317 No. 2, Denney.

The British Museum

MS. Harleian 5011, Documents relating to the Fens.
MS. Cotton Claudius, CXI, The Ely Old Coucher Book.
MS. Cotton Tiberius, A VI, and B II, Surveys of the lands of the abbot of Ely in the thirteenth century.
MS. Lansdowne 1, Inquest of Enclosures in Cambridgeshire in 1517.
Add. MS. 33466, Book of Sewers.
Add. Ch. 33105, 33107, 33111, 33112, 33086, Charters concerned with fen drainage.
Add. Ch. 7060, Grant of Chantry Lands in Cottenham.
Cole MSS., Add. MS. 5802, 5807, 5808, 5809, 5823, 5837, 5838, 5847, 5849 and 5887; collections and topographical information.
Map room, surveyors' preliminary drawings for the Ordinance Survey, 1811.

THE UNIVERSITIES OF OXFORD AND CAMBRIDGE

The Bodleian Library, Oxford

MS. Top. eccles, d. 6, 'Thurketils Mannor at Cottenham', Stukeley drawing of 28 August 1731.

MS. Top. gen. d. 14, f. 30v., 'Cotenham 19 May 1731', Stukeley drawing.

MS. Rawlinson B. 319 (11658, f. 118), Extracts from the Court Rolls of the Manor of Landbeach from 27 Hen. III to 1598.

MS. Gough Cambs. 69 (17819 ff. 5, 1, and 87), The Alington Rental of 1542, and documents concerning High and Low Elmham in 1553, and 1663.

The University Library, Cambridge

The Crowland Abbey documents in the muniments of Queens' College are now lodged in the University Library. Miss F. M. Page gives a detailed description of these in her *Estates of Crowland Abbey*, p. 3. In addition there is a drawer unnoticed by her, which contains Collectors' Accounts that cover most of the largest gap in her series, and a very detailed Reeve's Account for Oakington.

The Ely Diocesan Registry (now also in the University Library)
Liber R., another copy of the Ely Old Coucher Book.
A/6, a volume of transcripts.
A/8, documents relating to drainage.
B/8, The State of the Diocese, 1728.
H/1, Glebe terriers.

The local collection of the University Library

Cottenham
Add. 6032, 6033, 6034, Enclosure Act, Minutes, Accounts and Claims.
Doc. 630, Enclosure papers.
Doc. 1097, Manorial documents, 1557.
Doc. 479 and 471, Compotus 1516–18, and 1527–8.
Doc. 1382, Sale of lands, 1605.

Landbeach
Doc. 642, Enclosure papers.
Doc. 1577, Claim to manor, 1637.
Maps, ff. 53(1). 94. 22–3, Enclosure award map photostat.

Waterbeach
Doc. 1605–23, Manor rolls (copies) 1665–1830.
Views an 53.91.4/52, 'N.E. View of Denney Abbey', S. & N. Buck, 1730.
MS. plans 16/a, Plan of Waterbeach Fen.
MS. plans 318, Plan of Waterbeach Level.
Maps 53.82.4, Map of Denney Lodge Farm, 1829.

Baker MSS.
Documents relating to Cambridgeshire.

Cambridge University Archives

Probate inventories from the Episcopal Consistory Court of Ely and the Archdeaconry Court of Ely, from 1660, in year bundles for the whole county. MS. index; printed index in preparation.
Books of Sewers; L77–L81.

Cambridge Colleges

Corpus Christi College, Cambridge

The College archives, drawer XXXV

Nos. 1–120, Charters beginning in mid-twelfth century.
121–124, Court rolls, estreats and memoranda. These include material from the Manor of Brays as well as the Manor of Chamberlains, and run from 1327 to 1679 with gaps.
145, Extent of the Lands of Agnes de Bray, 1316.
146, a. The Lands of Alice Bere, 1356.
    b. Custumal of Walter Chamberlain.
    c. Bestial.
    d. Farm roll of Thomas Chamberlain, knight.
148, List of customary tenants, fourteenth century.
147, 149, 150–160, Rentals, fifteenth century.
162, Terrier, n.d., fifteenth century?
163, Field book, fifteenth century (Simon Green's of 1477?).
164, Field book.
165, Rental, 1496.
166, Demesne Survey, fifteenth century.
170, Field Book, 1549; in Matthew Parker's hand with his marginal notes.
171, Rental, 1558.
172, Collection of papers relating tenants' holdings.
173, Part of survey, endorsed with list of tenements new-built on the lord's waste.
174, Matthew Parker's Tabular Terrier, signed and dated, 1549.
175, Survey, temp. D. Copcott (1587–90).
176, Statement of the four Sheepwalks, and counsel's opinion on them.
177, Terrier, n.d., fifteenth century?
179, Terrier of arable and pasture in Lordship Farm, 1786.
180, Miscellaneous documents for claims under the Enclosure Act.
181, Bailiffs' Accounts, 19, 20 and 30 Ed. III.
182 and 183, Reeves' Accounts, 21–23 Ed. III, and 10 Rich. II.
184, Receipts of farm rents, 33 Hen. VI.
186, Memorandum of expenses and payments at Beche, 7 Ed. IV.
187 and 188, Bailiffs' Accounts, 9–13, 16–18 and 22–23 Ed. IV, and 1 & 2 Hen. VII.
189–191, Bailiffs' Accounts, Richard III to Henry VIII.
192, Transcripts of early title deeds.
194, Papers in the Kirby case.
195, Lease to John Gotobed of Moorleys, 4 Eliz.
196, Lease of Rose Close, 1588.
197, File of copies of Court Rolls, 1616–1710.
198, Counterpart lease of cottage.
199, Copy of lease of houses, outbuildings and lands, 1631.
200, Will of Thomas Spicer of Cambridge, 1634.

201, Orders of Petty Sessions for the admission of eight poor people to cottages in Landbeach, 1666.
202, Sale of Crown rents, 1788.
205, Papers of the case, *College* vs. *Kypps*.

R59/31/40/1, An exact copy of a plan of the Fens as it was taken Anno 1604 by William Hayward, carefully copied from the original by Mr Taylor Smyth, Anno. Dom. 1727.

Cottenham

L1/198, Terrier of chantry Lands, 1549–50.
R/59/14/9, 10, and 11, Crowlands Minute Book 1826–8, with terriers and quit rental.
R60/2/1, Common, n.d.
R51/2/22, Pasture, 1797, 1803.
306T1, 2, 3, 5, nine lands arable adjoining Cottenham–Westwick Holme Brook, 1630.
152/P9, Draft Enclosure Map, 1842.
124/P42, Pre-1842 map of parish.
124/P43, Pre-1842 map of Smithy Fen.
Cot C 1–9, R50/9, Rectory Manor Rolls, 1428–1510.
Cot C 16.a., Extracts 1559–1617.
Cot C 17, Rentals, 1560–9.
Cot C 35.1.2, Terrier of parsonage, 1638.
Cot C 35.3, Closes in Smithy Fen, 1671.
Cot C 39.1, Stint etc. of common, 1596.
R61/5/1, Map of Pratt estate in Cottenham, 1802.
Cot 28.3, Cottage.
Cot C/27/29, Six acres to the poor.
R 60/22/5, Freehold property in North Fen, 1713.
Q/RDc66, Original Enclosure Award and Map, 1847.

The Francis Papers (uncatalogued), containing
Court Rolls for the Manor of Sames, 1554–8, 1580–1624, and 1627–36.
Court Rolls for the Manors of Sames, Lyles and Crowlands held jointly 1638–41.
Court Rolls, Sames, 1643–68 and 1717–27.
Court Rolls, Crowlands, 1509–27 with gaps.
Court Rolls, Lyles, 1601–95 with gaps.
Minute Book of Crowlands, Lyles and Sames, 1625–42.
Contemporary copy of Agreement on turf-cutting, 1344.
Agreement of 1596 (copy dated 1615).
Surrenders and admissions.

Landbeach

R51/17/54, Churchwardens' Accounts, Vestry, Commoners' Meetings, 1741–1805.
R51/17/65.a, b, and c, Lawsuits in Chancery, 1717–70.
R55/31/3/27, Lands, 1570.
R55/31/5/5d, Lands, 1620–21.
R56,5/81, Rectory, 1797.
P24/28/1, Pontage accounts, 1712–31.
Q/Rdz7, pp. 26–83, Q/RDc18, Original Enclosure Award and Map.

Waterbeach

C54/13, Fen lands, 1668.
L75/46, Charter to Denney Abbey, 1415.
R55/26/3, Parsonage with appurtenances.
R55/31/2/2, Lands, etc., 1548.
Q/RD28, Enclosure Award (pp. 389–470), 1818.
Q/RDc31, Original Award Map.

PARISH CHESTS

Cottenham – Deposited in the County Record Office except for:

Registers.
Book of general information from the eighteenth and nineteenth centuries, kept in the rectory.

Waterbeach – rich collection of which the following proved especially useful:

Court Rolls of Waterbeach cum Denney; this is in fact a book of extracts covering the period 1347–1631 in two series with gaps.
Bundle of papers relating to tithe.
Bundle of papers relating to the action between Masters and Standley.
Charity documents.
Leases and terriers of the parsonage.

Landbeach

Collectanea de Landbeach, compiled by Robert Masters.
Field Book, 1549.
Landbeach Fen.
Dukman Book.
Tithe book.
School accounts, 1883–1910.
Churchwardens' book, 1806–79, with Church Rates from 1866.
Churchwardens' book, 1880–98.
Landbeach memoranda, Bryan Walker.
Registers from 1538, and remarkably complete. The second and fifth registers contain much other material besides registration.

PRIVATE COLLECTIONS

Mr Francis Garrett of Cambridge; a collection of documents and copies relating to the history of Cottenham.
Mrs Leslie Norman of Cottenham; the Notebook of Jacob Sanderson in which he wrote his memories in 1905. These stretched back before the Parliamentary Enclosure of 1847.
A scholar's Collectanea of Cottenham, in part by a correspondent of Rev. William Cole the antiquary.
Mr Mervyn Haird of Cottenham: a collection of Cottenham parish documents which includes the last two fen reeves' books; terriers of charity lands in adjacent parishes; minute book of meetings of Town officers in mid-nineteenth century; pre-enclosure map of The Holme. Mr Haird is also custodian of the Smith Memorial Collection of photographs of old Cottenham.

THE MUSEUM OF 'THE GENTLEMEN'S SOCIETY, SPALDING, LINCOLNSHIRE

The Wrest Park Chartulary.

PRINTED SOURCES
(Place of publication London unless otherwise specified.)

Aikin, G. 'Culture of the Cambridgeshire Fens'. *Transactions of the Royal Society of Arts*, vol. 52. 1838–9.

Bendlowes, W. *Les Reports de G.B., des divers pleadings et cases en le Court del Common-banc, &c.* 1689.

Blake, E. O. (ed.). *Liber Eliensis*. Camden Society 3rd series, XCII. 1962.

Clay, W. K. *A History of the Parish of Waterbeach in the County of Cambridge*. CAS Quarto Publications, no. 4. Cambridge, 1859.

A History of the Parish of Landbeach in the County of Cambridge. CAS Quarto Publications, no. 6. Cambridge, 1861.

Cooper, C. H. *Annals of Cambridge*. Cambridge, 1842–1908.

Cunningham, W. *The Common Rights of Cottenham, Stretham and Lode*. Camden Miscellany XII. Camden 3rd series, XVIII. 1910.

Denson, J. *A Peasant's Voice to Landowners*. Cambridge, 1830.

Dugdale, Sir W. *A History of Imbanking and Draining of Divers Fens and Marshes Both in Foreign Parts and in this Kingdom.* 1662.

Farrer, W. *Feudal Cambridgeshire*. Cambridge, 1920.

Gibbons, A. *Ely Episcopal Records*. Lincoln, 1891.

Gooch, W. *A General View of the Agriculture of the County of Cambridge*. 1813. (Preface dated 1807.)

Goodwin, C. W. *The Anglo-Saxon Life of St. Guthlac*. 1848.

Lees, B. A. (ed.). *Records of the Templars in England in the Twelfth Century: the Inquest of 1185 with Illustrative Charters and Documents*. The British Academy Records of the Social and Economic History of England and Wales. LX. 1935.

L'Estrange, R. *A Sad Relation of a General Fire at Cottenham, Four Miles Distant from Cambridge*. 1676.

Lysons, D. and S. *Magna Britannia*. 6 vols., 1806–22. Vol. II, pt I, *Cambridgeshire*, 1808.

Mackay, T. (ed.). *The Reminiscences of Albert Pell Sometime M.P. for South Leicestershire*. 1908.

Masters, R. *A Short Account of the Parish of Waterbeach in the County of Cambridge and the Diocese of Ely, by a Late Vicar*. Cambridge, 1795.

Nonarum Inquisitiones in Curia Scaccarii. Records Commision. 1807.

Page, F. M. *The Estates of Crowland Abbey*. Cambridge, 1934.

Palmer, W. M. *The Cambridgeshire Subsidy Rolls, 1250–1695*. Norwich, 1912.

Palmer, W. M. and Parsons, C. E. 'Swavesey Priory'. *TCHAS* I. 1904.

Palmer, W. M. and Saunders, H. W. *Documents Relating to Cambridgeshire Villages*. No. 6, December, 1926.

Rotuli Hundredorum. Records Commission. 1812 and 1818.

Rye, W. (ed.). *Pedes Finium, or Fines Relating to the County of Cambridge*. CAS Octavo Publications, no. 26. Cambridge, 1891.

Stokes, F. G. (ed.). *The Bletchley Diary of the Rev. William Cole, M.A., F.S.A., 1765–67*. 1931.

Stukeley, W. *Itinerarium Curiosum*. 1776.

Vancouver, C. *A General View of Agriculture in the County of Cambridgeshire*. 1794.

Wells, S. *The History of the Drainage of the Great Level of the Fens, called the Bedford Level; with the Constitution and Laws of the Bedford Level Corporation*. 1828–30.

SECONDARY SOURCES

Allison, K. J. 'The Sheep-Corn Husbandry of Norfolk in the Sixteenth and Seventeenth Centuries'. *AgHR* v, 1957.
  'Flock Management in the Sixteenth and Seventeenth Centuries'. *EconHR* 2nd series, XI. 1958.
Astbury, A. K. *The Black Fens*. Cambridge, 1958.
Aston, T. H. 'The Origins of the Manor in Britain'. *TRHS* 5th series, VIII. 1958.
Ault, W. O. 'Manor Court and Parish Church in Fifteenth Century England: a Study of Village By-Laws'. *Speculum* XXIX. 1954.
Baker, A. H. R. 'Open Fields and Partible Inheritance on a Kent Manor'. *EconHR* 2nd series, XVII. 1964.
  'Evidence in the "Nonarum Inquisitiones" of Contracting Arable Lands in England during the Early Fourteenth Century'. *EconHR* 2nd series, XIX. 1966.
Barley, M. W. *The English Farmhouse and Cottage*. 1961.
Bautier, R. H. *The Economic Development of Medieval Europe*. 1971.
Beckwith, I. 'The Re-Modelling of a Common Field System'. *AgHR* XV. 1967.
Beecham, H. A. 'A Review of Balks as Strip Boundaries in the Open Fields'. *AgHR* IV. 1956.
Beresford, M.W. *History on the Ground: Six Studies in Maps and Landscapes*. 1957.
Beresford, M.W. and St Joseph, J. K. *Medieval England: an Aerial Survey*. Cambridge, 1957.
Beresford, M. W. *New Towns of the Middle Ages*. 1967.
  'Commissioners of Enclosures'. *EconHR* XVI. 1946.
  'Ridge and Furrow in the Open Fields', *EconHR* 2nd series, I. 1948.
  'The Poll Tax and Census of Sheep, 1549'. *AgHR* I, 1953.
Bishop, T. A. M. 'Assarting and the Growth of the Open Fields'. *EconHR* VI. 1935.
  'The Rotation of Crops at Westerham, 1297–1350'. *EconHR* 2nd series, IX. 1958.
Bloch, M. *French Rural History* (1931). English translation, 1966.
Bowen, H. C. *Ancient Fields*. British Association for the Advancement of Science. 1962.
Butlin, R. A. 'Some Terms Used in Agrarian History: a Glossary'. *AgHR* IX. 1961.
Cam, H. M. *The Hundred and the Hundred Rolls*. Cambridge, 1930.
  Liberties and Communities. Cambridge, 1944.
Chibnall, A. C. *Sherington: Fiefs and Fields of a Buckinghamshire Village*. Cambridge, 1965.
Clark, H. M. (Margaret Spufford). 'Selion Size and Soil Type'. *AgHR* VIII. 1960.
Clark, J. G. D. 'Report on the Excavation on the Cambridge Car Dyke, 1947', *Antiquaries Journal* XXIX. 1949.
Cra'ster, M. D. 'Waterbeach Abbey'. *PCAS* LIX. 1966.
Curwen, E. C. *Air Photography and the Evolution of the Corn-Field*. 1938.
Darby, H. C. *The Medieval Fenland*. Cambridge, 1940.
  The Draining of the Fens. Cambridge, 1940. 2nd ed., 1956. Reprinted 1968.
  The Domesday Geography of Eastern England. Cambridge, 1952.
  (ed.) *The Cambridge Region*. Cambridge, 1938.
  'The Fenland Frontier in Anglo-Saxon England'. *Antiquity* VIII. 1934.
Davenport, F. E. *The Economic Development of a Norfolk Manor*. Cambridge, 1906.
Dodwell, B. 'Holdings and Inheritance in Medieval East Anglia'. *EconHR* 2nd series XX. 1967.
Douglas, D. C. *The Social Structure of Medieval East Anglia*. Oxford, 1927.
Duby, G. *Rural Economy and Country Life in the Medieval West* (1962). English translation C. Postan. 1968.

Eden, P. 'Smaller Post-medieval Houses in Eastern England'. In L. M. Munby (ed.), *East Anglian Studies*. Cambridge, 1968.

Ekwall, E. (B. O. E. Ekwall). *A Concise Dictionary of English Place-Names*. 4th ed. Oxford, 1960.

Evelyn-White, Rev. C. H. 'A Book of Church Accounts relating to certain "Balks" in, the Common Fields of Rampton, Cambs.' *TCHAS* I, 1904.

'The Story of Cottenham, Co. Cambridge'. *TCHAS* II, 1906.

Finberg, H. P. R. (ed.). *The Agrarian History of England and Wales*. Vol. IV, 1500–1600 (ed. Joan Thirsk). Cambridge, 1967, Vol. I.ii, A.D. 43–1042 (ed. H. P. R. Finberg). Cambridge, 1972.

Fowler, G. 'Fenland Waterways Past and Present'. Pt I, *PCAS* XXXIII, 1933, pt II, *PCAS* XXXIV. 1934.

Fox, Sir C. P. *The Archaeology of the Cambridge Region*. Cambridge, 1923.

Godwin, H. 'Post-Glacial Changes of Relative Land and Sea-Levels in the English Fenland'. *Philosophical Transactions of the Royal Society*, 1940.

Gonner, E. C. K. *Common Land and Enclosure*. 1912.

Gras, N. S. B. *The Evolution of the English Corn-Market*. Cambridge, Massachusetts, 1915.

Gray, H. L. *English Field Systems*. 1915.

Green, C, 'East Anglian Coast-line Levels since Roman Times'. *Antiquity* XXXIII. 1961.

Hall, S. A. 'The Great Cattle Plague of 1865'. *Agriculture* LXXII. 1965.

Hallam, H. E. *The New Lands of Elloe*. Department of English Local History, University of Leicester, Occasional Papers, no. 6. 1954.

Settlement and Society. Cambridge, 1965.

'Population Density in the Medieval Fenland'. *EconHR* 2nd series, XIV. 1961.

Harris, L. E. *Vermuyden and the Fens: a Study of Sir Cornelius Vermuyden and the Great Level*. 1953.

Harvey, B. F. 'The Population Trend in England Between 1300 and 1348', *TRHS* 5th series, XVI. 1966.

Harvey, P. D. A. *A Medieval Oxfordshire Village, Cuxham, 1240–1400*. Oxford, 1965.

Havinden, M. A. 'Agricultural Progress in Open-Field Oxfordshire'. *AgHR* IX. 1961.

Hills, R. L. *Machines, Mills and Uncountable Costly Necessities*. Norwich, 1967.

'Drainage by Windmills in the Waterbeach Level'. *PCAS* LVI–LVII. 1963–4.

Hilton, R. H. *A Medieval Society: the West Midlands at the End of the Thirteenth Century*, 1967.

Homans, G. C. *English Villagers of the Thirteenth Century*. Cambridge, Massachusetts, 1942.

'Partible Inheritance of Villagers' Holdings'. *EconHR* VIII. 1938.

'The Rural Sociology of Medieval England'. *P & P* IV. 1953.

'The Explanation of English Regional Differences'. *P & P* XVII, 1969.

Hoskins, W. G. *The Making of the English Landscape*. 1955.

The Midland Peasant. 1957.

Local History in England. 1959.

'Harvest Fluctuations and English Economic History, 1480–1619'. *AgHR* XII. 1964.

Jackson, J. C. 'The Ridge and Furrow Controversy'. *Amateur Historian* V. 1961.

John, E. *Land Tenure in Early England*. 1960.

Jones, J. *A Human Geography of Cambridgeshire*. Cambridge, 1924.

Kelly, E. R. *The Post Office Directory of Cambridge, Norfolk and Suffolk*. 1869.

Kerridge, E. *The Agricultural Revolution*. 1967.

'Ridge and Furrow in Agrarian History'. *EconHR* 2nd series, IV. 1951.

Kosminsky, E. *Studies in the Agrarian History of England in the Thirteenth Century*. Oxford, 1956.

Lamb, H. H. *The Changing Climate*. 1966.

Leadam, I. S. 'The Inquisition of 1517'. *TRHS* new series, VI–VIII. 1892–4.

Lennard, R. *Rural England*. Oxford, 1959.

'Statistics of Sheep in Medieval England'. *AgHR* VII. 1959.

Lethbridge, T. C. 'Anglo-Saxon Huts at Waterbeach'. *PCAS* XXXIII. 1931–2.

Levett, A. E. (ed. Cam, H. M., and Sutherland, L.). *Studies in Manorial History*. 1938.

Lucas, H. S. 'The Great European Famine of 1315, 1316 and 1317'. *Speculum* V. 1930.

Maitland, F. W. *Domesday Book and Beyond*. Cambridge, 1897.

Marshall, S. *A Fenland Chronicle*. Cambridge, 1967.

Masters, R. *The History of the College of Corpus Christi and the Blessed Virgin Mary, commonly called Bene't in the University of Cambridge*. 1753.

Miller, E. *The Abbey and Bishopric of Ely*. Cambridge, 1951.

'The English Economy in the Thirteenth Century'. *P & P* XXVIII. 1964.

Minchinton, W. E. (ed.). *Essays in Agrarian History*. 2 vols., Newton Abbot, 1968.

Muskett, J. J. and Evelyn-White, the Rev. C. H. *Lay Subsidy Rolls for the Year 1327*. n.d.

National Trust, The. *A Guide to Wicken Fen*. Cambridge, 1950.

Neilson, N. *Economic Conditions on the Estates of Ramsey Abbey*. Philadelphia, 1898.

A Terrier of Fleet, Lincolnshire, from a Manuscript in the British Museum. British Academy Records of Social and Economic History of England and Wales, 1920.

Orwin, C. S. and C. S. *The Open Fields*. 3rd ed., ed. Joan Thirsk. Oxford, 1967.

Page, F. M. 'Bidentes Hoylandie'. *Economic History* I, Supplement to the *Economic Journal*. 1929.

Payne, F. G. 'The British Plough: Some Stages in its Development'. *AgHR* V. 1957.

Pevsner, N. *The Buildings of England: Cambridgeshire*. Harmondsworth, 1954.

Phillips, C. W. (ed.). Royal Geographical Society Research Series no. 5, *The Fenland in Roman Times*. 1970.

Pocock, B. A. 'The First Fields in an Oxfordshire Parish'. *AgHR* XVI. 1968.

Postan, M. M. *The Famulus: the Estate Labourer in the Twelfth and Thirteenth Centuries*. Supplement no. 2 to *EconHR*. 1954.

The Medieval Economy and Society. 1972.

(ed.) *The Cambridge Economic History of Europe*. I. *The Agrarian Life of the Middle Ages*. 2nd ed., Cambridge, 1966.

'The Chronology of Labour Services'. *TRHS* 4th series, XX. 1937.

'The Fifteenth Century'. *EconHR* IX. 1939.

'Village Livestock in the Thirteenth Century'. *EconHR* 2nd series, XV. 1962.

Postan, M. M. and Titow, J. Z. 'Heriots and Prices on the Winchester Manors'. *EconHR* 2nd series, XI. 1959.

Postgate, M. 'The Open Fields of Cambridgeshire'. Unpublished Ph.D. dissertation, 1964. CUL.

Power, E. *The Wool Trade in English Medieval History*. Oxford, 1941.

Raftis, J. A. *The Estates of Ramsey Abbey*. Toronto, 1957.

'The Social Structure of Five East Midland Villages.' *EconHR* 2nd series, XVIII. 1965.

Ravensdale, J. R. 'Landbeach in 1549'. In L. M. Munby (ed.), *East Anglian Studies*. Cambridge, 1968.

Reaney, P. H. *The Place-Names of Cambridgeshire and the Isle of Ely*. Cambridge, 1943.

Riley, H. T. (ed.). *Ingulph's Chronicle of the Abbey of Croyland*. 1854.

Royal Commission on Historical Monuments. *An Inventory of Historical Monuments in the County of Cambridge. Volume One, West Cambridgeshire*. 1968.

Russell, J. C. *British Medieval Population*. Albuquerque, 1948.

Salzman, L. D. *Building in England Down to 1540: a Documentary History*. 1st ed., reprinted with corrections, Oxford, 1967.

Schofield, R. A. 'The Geographical Distribution of Wealth in England, 1334–1649'. *EconHR* 2nd series, XVIII. 1965.

Shrewsbury, J. F. D. *A History of Bubonic Plague in the British Isles.* Cambridge, 1970.

Simpson, Alan 'The East Anglian Foldcourse: Some Queries'. *AgHR* VI. 1958.

Smith, A. H. (ed.). *English Place-Name Elements.* 2 vols., Cambridge, 1956.

Spittle, S. D. T. 'Denney Abbey'. *PCAS* LXI. 1968.

Spufford, Margaret. *A Cambridgeshire Community: Chippenham from Settlement to Enclosure.* Department of English Local History, University of Leicester, Occasional Papers, XX. 1965.

'The Dissenting Churches in Cambridgeshire from 1660 to 1700'. *PCAS* LXI. 1968.

'Longstanton'. Unpublished essay. 1959. CRO.

'Rural Cambridgeshire 1520–1680'. Unpublished M.A. dissertation, 1962. University of Leicester.

Steers, J. A. (ed.). *The Cambridge Region.* 1965.

Tawney, R. H. *The Agrarian Problem in the Sixteenth Century.* 1912.

'The Rise of the Gentry'. *EconHR* XI. 1941. Also 'Postscript'. *Ibid.*, 2nd series, VII. 1954.

Thirsk, Joan. *English Peasant Farming.* 1957.

Tudor Enclosures. Historical Association Pamphlet, G. 41, 1959.

Fenland Farming in the Sixteenth Century. Department of English Local History, University of Leicester, Occasional Papers no. 3. 1953.

(ed.). *The Agrarian History of England and Wales*, vol. IV. *1500–1640.* Cambridge, 1967.

'The Common Fields'. *P & P* XXIX. 1964.

'The Origins of the Common Fields'. *Ibid.*, XXXIII. 1966.

Titow, J. Z. 'Evidence of Weather in the Account Rolls of the Bishopric of Winchester, 1229–1350'. *EconHR* 2nd series, XII. 1960.

'Some evidence of the Thirteenth Century Population Increase'. *EconHR* 2nd series. XIV. 1961.

'Some Differences Between Manors and Their Effects on the Condition of the Peasant in the Thirteenth Century'. *AgHR* X. 1962.

'Medieval England and the Open Field System'. *P & P* XXXII. 1965.

Trow-Smith, R. *A History of British Livestock Husbandry to 1700.* 1957.

Wretts-Smith, M. 'The Organisation of Farming at Croyland Abbey, 1267–1331'. *Journal of Economic and Business History* IV. 1931–2.

Wrigley, E. A. 'Family Limitation in Pre-Industrial England'. *EconHR* 2nd series, XIX. 1966.

GLOSSARY OF SOME TERMS IN
LOCAL USAGE

ABUTTAL: an indication of the position of a strip in the field by identification of the land at its end.

AGISTMENT: the taking in and pasturing of beasts of another owner.

ASSARTING: breaking in new land with the plough.

BALK or BAULK: a field path. In this area major field paths are called 'doles' or 'drifts', usually between furlongs.

BAR(R)S: a gate.

BLACK WATERS: the flood waters standing in the fens as distinct from the white waters brought down by the upland rivers.

BROAD or BROADEL: two selions lying side by side in the same tenure and ploughed as one.

BUTT(S): small selions fitted in between a normal furlong and a boundary. In Landbeach three butts made an acre whereas the average selion was a little over half an acre.

CLOSE: a piece of land separated by a fence or ditch which excluded common rights. Also called a 'several'. Under grass it could be termed a 'croft'.

CROFT: an enclosed piece of ground, sometimes attached to a toft.

DEMESNE: land of the home farm of a manor: alternatively used of a whole manor not in the hands of a subsidiary holder.

DOLE: a field path, usually a larger one, which can, by figurative use of the language, be used as the name of a furlong adjacent to the path. The name suggests that it was allotted when the grass was shared out annually for hay, but no survival of such a custom has been found in our three villages.

DOWELL: Stake to mark a division in field or meadow, or, as a verb, to divide by placing such stakes. Cf. 'stulp'.

DREDGE: the mixed corn of the spring sowing, oats and barley.

DRIFT: a way for driving beasts (among other uses). The driving of beasts on the common to an enclosure to count them and discover strays and other foreign beasts: the written list produced from such a drift.

ENCROACHMENT: taking in land not in one's holding by ploughing too far or moving the boundary.

ENGROSSMENT: the amalgamation of holdings of land formerly separate.

EXTENT: a written description of a manor or other estate.

FIELD: before parliamentary enclosure, arable land. In these three parishes an area normally enclosed by a single boundary. The exception, Church Field at Cottenham which had a detached portion on Church Hill, had originally conformed to this definition before the expansion of the housing area had divided it. It can also be used for a cropping shift, or if the user so wishes it may be used for areas which do not coincide with the cropping shift; rarely it overlaps two shifts.

FIELD BOOK: a description of arable land by strips, furlongs and fields, bound in book form. A terrier or survey in a binding suitable for regular use over a long period.

FOREND: similar to a headland in that ploughs working on the adjacent furlong can turn on it, but which remains unsown.

FORINSEC: of tenants who reside outside the parish.

FURLONG: a bundle of parallel selions, so forming a unit within a field. The alternative word, 'wong', occurs in this area, but only very rarely and as part of a place-name.

GORE: an odd triangular-shaped piece of ploughland, usually in a corner against a boundary.

GRAVEL: a path of small stones in a river bed to form a ford or a tow-path.

GRIPE: a small ditch or large water-furrow.

GROUNDCILLING: the ground-plates of a building.

HALING-WAY: a tow-path.

HARD: part of a fen which is not subject to any but severe floods, or, in a river bed, the same meaning as gravel.

HAVEDEN or HAVEDEY: an access-way to a field or meadow. A headland.

HEADLAND: where the ploughs working on the adjacent furlong turn; normally the first selion of a furlong and, unlike a forend, usually cropped.

HEDGEBOTE: the right to lop sufficient timber for fencing.

HIDE: a fiscal unit of land, normally 120 acres, although there is early evidence which suggests 100-acre hide in Cottenham, 100-acre hide in Landbeach, and again a hide of 110 acres in Landbeach.

HITHE: an unloading place for barges on a canal or river.

HOLT (osier): a small enclosure for growing willows for wicker-work.

INTER-COMMONING: where two or more parishes have the right to pasture their beasts in the same area.

INQUISITION: the legal method of determining fact by questions to a sworn jury.

LAMMAS LAND: Land open to common as pasture from Lammas, 1 August, otherwise the Gules of August.

LEY: pasture, and frequently in this area used for permanent pasture sometimes arable laid down to pasture, but most commonly pasture that had been temporarily ploughed and then laid down again.

LODE: a ditch navigable to the narrow barges of the fenland.

MARE, MERE and MORE: wet ground of three degrees of wetness. The wettest is mere, a stagnant pool; mare is marsh, and more is rough pasture, usually wet moor.

MASLIN or MESSELDINE: the winter-sown mixed corn, wheat and rye.

MERE: (2) a boundary, as in mere-stone or mereway.

MOLE FURROW: a narrow deep furrow for drainage purposes.

PIECE: several meanings in this area: (1) an enclosure of a furlong from the open fields; (2) the selions forming a unit of work in sowing; (3) the normal vague use as 'a piece of land'.

PIGHTEL: an odd piece of land. In Landbeach the selions which had been converted into crofts centuries before are called pightels in the enclosure award.

QUARENTELA or QUARENTINA: the Latin for 'furlong' in the medieval and sixteenth-century documents.

RENTAL: a list of rents owed, often giving topographical details of some of the properties.

RODDON: a raised silty bed of a vanished watercourse, left above the level of the surrounding land by the double process of silting and peat shrinkage.

SELION: the normal small unit of ploughland. In this area usually averaging just over half an acre. Also known locally as a 'high-back', 'ridge' or a 'stetch'. In the Norman French charters 'une rige de terre'.

SEVERAL; HALF-SEVERAL: enclosed land in private hands from which common rights are excluded. Called half-several where the above only applies for half the year as in meadow.

SEWER: a drainage ditch or river that needs scouring from time to time.

SLUICE or SASSE: a door across a river for stopping or releasing the flow. Usually combined with a primitive lock in ealier times. The sasse was a simple flash-lock. The small sluice in a drainage ditch was usually called a staunch.

SOWING SCHEDULE: the detailed account of the work of sowing, giving place, kind and amount of all the seed sown on the demesne by the reeve. The summary of this is entered in the reeve's account under the return of grain, 'from which in seed...' ('*unde in semine...*'). The originals are very rare.

STETCH or STITCH: alternative for selion, but not very common in this area.

STRIP: a unit of ploughland in one tenure, within a continuous boundary. Usually one or more selions, rarely a fraction. The term is not used by contemporaries in this area.

STULP: noun or verb; stake or boundary marker, or as a verb to place these in position.

SUMMER GROUNDS: fen, flooded in winter, but dry enough for pasture in summer.

TATHE: Benefit that feeding sheep give to the ground by manure.

TENACRESLAND: the standard bondage holding in medieval Landbeach.

TENEMENT: a house and the land with it.

TERRIER: the written description of the lands of a tenure, also called a SURVEY.

THACK: thatching, thatching material, or rough grass feed.

TOFT: the enclosure in which a house stands.

TOWN or TOWNSHIP: the built-up area of a village, or alternatively the inhabitants. A vill as opposed to manor.

TURBARY: turf-cutting; the customary area for cutting turf; or the right to cut it.

WASTE: open land not ploughed, enclosed nor kept for meadow, but usually of great economic importance. Legally the lords' property (at least from the Statute of Merton) but usually employed for common grazing unless 'approved' (enclosed in part) by the lord, who was then, in law, bound to leave sufficient for the villagers.

INDEX